ARISTOCRATS

ARISTOCRATS

ROBERT LACEY

HUTCHINSON
LONDON MELBOURNE SYDNEY AUCKLAND
JOHANNESBURG

BRITISH BROADCASTING CORPORATION

PHOTOGRAPHS BY RIC GEMMELL

BOOK DESIGN BY CHRISTOS KONDEATIS

DESIGN CONSULTANT SANDI LACEY

First published 1983 by Hutchinson & Co. (Publishers) Ltd
and the British Broadcasting Corporation

Hutchinson & Co. (Publishers) Ltd

An imprint of the Hutchinson Publishing Group
17–21 Conway Street, London WIP 6JD

Hutchinson Group (Australia) Pty Ltd
30–32 Cremorne Street, Richmond South, Victoria 3121
PO Box 151, Broadway, New South Wales 2007

Hutchinson Group (NZ) Ltd
32–34 View Road, PO Box 40-086, Glenfield, Auckland 10

Hutchinson Group (SA) Pty Ltd
PO Box 337, Bergvlei 2012, South Africa

The British Broadcasting Corporation
35 Marylebone High Street
London W1

© Robert Lacey 1983

Photographs © *Radio Times* Ric Gemmell 1983

Set in Linotype Bembo by
Input Typesetting Ltd, London

Colour printing by Jolly & Barber Ltd, Rugby

Printed in Great Britain by The Anchor Press Ltd
and bound by Wm Brendon & Son Ltd,
both of Tiptree, Essex

British Library Cataloguing in Publication Data

Lacey, Robert
Aristocrats.
1. Europe–Nobility
I. Title
305.5′2   HT653.E85

ISBN 0 09 154290 1

ISBN 0 563 20032 4 British Broadcasting Corporation

For Michael Shaw

CONTENTS

ILLUSTRATIONS

MAPS

MAPS BY CHRISTOS KONDEATIS

'You should study the peerage, Gerald. . . . It is the best thing in fiction the English have ever done.'

OSCAR WILDE,
A Woman of No Importance, 1893

In any city whatsoever, in whatsoever manner organized, never do more than forty or fifty persons attain positions of command.

NICCOLO MACHIAVELLI,
Discourses, 1513

I · SIX OF
'THE BEST'

THE clouds gather. The rain falls. It could be an English summer's morning like any other. But it is not, for today is 12 August – the 'Glorious Twelfth' – and to those who love the twelfth there is no other date quite like it in the calendar, for it is the day that marks the appearance on Britain's grouse moors of an increasingly endangered species – the hereditary British aristocrat.

Gerald Cavendish Grosvenor, 15th Baronet of Eaton, 9th Baron Grosvenor, 9th Viscount Belgrave, 9th Earl Grosvenor, 8th Marquess of Westminster and 6th Duke of Westminster is just a little over thirty years old. Tall and broad, he is wearing a flat cap and plus fours, and he is carrying a double-barrelled shotgun.

The Duke's quarry this morning is *Lagopus scoticus*, a speckled bird with feathered feet whose habitat is the heather moors of Scotland and northern England. Normally known as the red, or common grouse, *Lagopus scoticus* looks considerably larger when wearing its feathers than after it has been plucked, and it breeds and grows largely undisturbed until 4.30 in the morning of every 12 August. But with that dawning the little creature's hitherto tranquil life is transformed, for under the terms of the Game Act of 1831, the common grouse becomes fair game at sunrise on 12 August, and from that moment onwards the hills are alive to the sound of gunfire.

Gerald Grosvenor is accompanied by a dozen other 'guns' sharing his day's sport, half of them friends, the other half his gamekeepers, all of whom are kitted out in identical Lovat green tweed jackets, knickerbockers and deerstalker hats. They are strung out across the heather on either side of the Duke, ten yards or so distant from each other, dogs at their heels, and at a ducal signal they begin to move forward in a broad sweep across the moor. This is called 'walking up' the grouse, for as the line advances it disturbs *Lagopus scoticus* from its nibbling at the heather shoots, and the bird, lacking the wit to bob low and keep quiet among the mottled roots where it would be virtually invisible, then flutters upwards with a cackle.

Once the drive has started, two or three feathered bundles pop up noisily like this every minute or so, and if the gun in front of them is alert, he brings down at least one bird. His Grace, say the gamekeepers, is one of the best shots in the country, and today that boast is being put to the test, for on this 12 August, Gerald Grosvenor, 6th Duke of Westminster, has entered himself in the great annual grouse race.

Time was when gentlemen walked to their London clubs every 13 August with jaunty step. It was some consolation for being kept working in town that you could sample the first cull of the Glorious Twelfth in Pall Mall next day, courtesy of the night train.

But then communications got quicker, and it became possible to have grouse for dinner in London on the day itself or sometimes, even, at lunchtime on the twelfth. Those who like their game hung would have nothing to do with it, of course. But devotees insisted that the only way to eat the bird was fresh roast, with just a slice of bacon across the breast – and besides, the contest to get the first grouse on the table was really quite fun.

By 1979 the Cafe Royal was offering grouse at a latish lunch, around 2 p.m., and two years later friendly competition had formalized into a race that brought the serving time nearer breakfast – 9.58 a.m. at the Cumberland Hotel in 1981, 9.31 a.m. at the Hilton. Rival grouse races developed in Surrey and in Glasgow.

This particular 12 August 1982, the Duke of Westminster has decided to enter the lists himself, so he is up before five. His first drive across the moors does not last very long, for as soon as he has shot a couple of dozen birds they are taken back through the woods to a waiting helicopter to be flown seventy miles straight to the Grosvenor Hotel in Chester. There they are pulled, plucked, roasted and set on the table for breakfast well before 8 o'clock, and as the times achieved by other hotels around Britain come in through the day, it becomes clear that no one has bettered this time. In the great grouse race of August 1982 Gerald Grosvenor, Duke of Westminster, has come out the winner.

It is Natalia, Duchess of Westminster, who brings news of the victory to the guns out on the moor. Her Grace, née Miss Natalia Phillips, twenty-three, is tall with streaked blonde hair like her friend the Princess of Wales (to whose son William she is godmother). Dressed in blue jeans and a bomber jacket in antiqued brown leather, she jumps into her Range Rover (registration 1 GRO). The car has been loaded with champagne to celebrate, and the Duchess also brings a substantial picnic, which is taken by the party in a little wooden chalet whose walls have been quilted with freshly cut heather.

The keepers eat separately, a huddle of green tweed figures, blending in with the open hillside. The Duke of Westminster employs eight of them full time at Abbeystead. At his principal home, Eaton Hall on the River Dee outside Chester, he has a somewhat smaller team to look after his pheasants.

You can see the Duke of Westminster's grouse moor as you drive up the M6 north of Preston. Just before you reach Lancaster, the hills on the right turn purple, and that is Abbeystead, the estate which the Duke purchased as a holiday retreat shortly before his thirtieth birthday.

Most people would be happy enough to retreat into the

several hundred acres of woodland and meadow which the Grosvenors have owned for centuries at Eaton. But there are no grouse at Eaton, and the Duke did want a place where he could get away from it all. So in 1980 he purchased Abbeystead for well over a million pounds, and at that price it would be disappointing if you could not win the odd grouse race, especially if you have your own helicopter – and you can use your own hotel as the finishing post.

By the commonly accepted laws of history, politics and logic, people like Gerald Grosvenor, 6th Duke of Westminster, should not still exist in the 1980s. In classical Greek 'aristos' meant 'the best', and 'aristokratia' meant 'rule by the best', as opposed to 'demokratia' – government by the 'demos' or 'people' – and since 1945 Britain's democratically elected governments have laboured more or less consistently to abolish, or at least to reduce, the wealth enjoyed by the aristocracy.

They have, evidently, met with less than total success. When the photographer Patrick Lichfield, himself an Earl and husband of Gerald Grosvenor's elder sister Leonora, was wondering one Christmas what to give his young brother-in-law, he hit on the idea of a Monopoly Board marked out with the properties from which the Duke of Westminster collects rents in real life. It naturally included Grosvenor Square, as well as Park Lane, Mayfair and Belgravia, and though the Earl could not discover any Grosvenor-owned railway stations, he was able to fill those spaces with the foreign airports the Duke lands at to inspect his properties.

One recent analysis of the Grosvenor assets set their value in the region of £400 million, 300 of London's most select and expensive acres, the family properties in and around Chester, several large rural estates like Abbeystead, a couple of jewellery companies, a company developing provincial shopping precincts, and an expanding network of international investments which extend as far as Australia, San Francisco, Vancouver and Hawaii. Technically the ownership of this massive business empire is tied up in a complexity of Grosvenor family trusts, yet the businesses themselves have no doubt about the identity of their ultimate boss. In the penultimate decade of the twentieth century, Britain's richest man is still a duke.

Gerald Grosvenor, 6th Duke of Westminster. 'I could never join the jet set.' Behind him, George Stubbs's painting, 'The Grosvenor Hunt'

Two styles of duke. ABOVE LEFT: *Hugh Lupus, 1st Duke of Westminster, Eminent Victorian.* RIGHT: *Bend Or, 2nd Duke of Westminster. Emeralds in the vegetables, diamonds in the bed*

Mary Davies of Pimlico, Mayfair and Belgravia; married at twelve

Grosvenor Estates, London: white stucco, Chester Street and the embassies of Belgrave Square

LEFT: *Grosvenor Estates, Cheshire; Eaton Halls, ancient and modern, with Hugh Lupus, early gros veneur*

PREVIOUS PAGE: *Eaton Hall (completed 1973) seen through the Golden Gates (c. 1740)*

*Grosvenors today. The Duke and Duchess of
Westminster with their daughters the Lady Tamara,
aged two, and the Lady Edwina Grosvenor, seated*

It is one of the paradoxes of twentieth-century history that while many kings, princes and emperors have been swept away, most aristocracies have managed to survive – and sometimes even to flourish. In modern Britain there are still some 800 men entitled to a full vote in one of the Houses of Parliament by virtue of no more than that accident of birth which made them a lord, while in the republics of France, Germany and Italy there are several thousand dukes, counts and marquises who retain all their titles and lands – and a great deal of the status that goes with them. Such is the continuing glamour of aristocracy, indeed, that there are now more titled people in these republics than when they were monarchies, since there is no longer a royal fount of honour to stop people bestowing titles on themselves. No Mediterranean boarding house is complete without its threadbare 'contessa' in an upper room.

Until less than a hundred years ago most of western Europe was ruled by aristocrats. When Herbert Asquith became Prime Minister of Britain in 1908, he was the first holder of that position not to be the owner of a substantial country estate – though he was married to a baronet's daughter. European history from the ninth to the nineteenth century is the history of noblemen – and, just occasionally, of noblewomen as well – and the rolls, chronicles and record books which are virtually our only evidence for hundreds of years of life tell us next to nothing about anyone else. Even on the eve of the First World War it was taken for granted that the nobleman had a God-given right to direct the destinies of some of the world's most powerful industrial democracies, so it is scarcely surprising that some noble families should survive today.

What is surprising, however, is the manner of their survival. The public imagination is caught by characters like Vere Hobart-Hampden, 9th Earl of Buckinghamshire, who died in April 1983 after a varied career that culminated in employment as a corporation gardener at Southend-on-Sea. But most British peers really are quite comfortably off, and while the aristocrat forced to collect pennies from day-trippers at the gate may be a cherished modern stereotype, less than 8 per cent of Britain's hereditary peers have, in fact, been reduced to opening their homes to the public. The

Duke of Westminster may be the richest, but he is by no means Britain's only millionaire aristocrat – and the same goes for many noble families in Europe.

How have these dinosaurs survived in the age of the common man? What are the origins of their power and wealth? And what are their chances in the future? This book tries to answer these questions through the history of the six families who formed the subject of the BBC television series 'Aristocrats' in the autumn of 1983. It draws partly on what they said to the camera, and partly on what they said when they were not being filmed. But it draws most heavily on their own individual family histories which could not be covered by television but which are, in many ways, microcosms of the history of Europe itself.

The six families, chosen one per country, are Grosvenor (England), Frescobaldi (Italy), Thurn und Taxis (Germany), Medinaceli (Spain), Ganay (France) and Liechtenstein (Liechtenstein). No single group, of course, can possibly represent the full complexity of a social class that has been responsible for the best – and for the worst – of one continent's civilization, and there were many criteria determining the selection of these six, not least that they should all be able to speak reasonably fluent English. But if there was one overriding consideration in choosing which families to examine in film and book, it was that their present-day activities and beliefs should conjure up something of aristocracy's classic traditions – and this particular six of 'the best' certainly lead lives today that remain more than distant echoes of vanished splendour.

It is said there was quite a crowd at Ciampino Airport outside Rome on the summer's day in 1946 when King Umberto II left Italy forever. A national referendum had just voted against the monarchy and in favour of establishing a new post-war republic, so, without ceremony, Umberto went to Ciampino to take a plane to Portugal.

The ex-king had already said goodbye to all his well-wishers, and was striding across the tarmac towards the plane, when suddenly he remembered something.

'Yes, Your Majesty?' asked one of his aides running forward.

'The accounts,' said the King. 'Don't forget the accounts. Give them to the people over there,' gesturing towards the spectators.

But the aide did not realize that the King was pointing at the half dozen staff of the Privy Purse who were standing in front of the crowd, and in the roar of the plane's engines starting up, he misunderstood what his master said, for the Italian for 'accounts', *conti*, is the same as 'counts'. And that was how everyone who went to wave goodbye to King Umberto in June 1946 became ennobled. They are known to this day as the Counts of Ciampino.

Dino Frescobaldi likes telling the story of the Counts of Ciampino Airport because it seems to him to put modern aristocracy into perspective. Titles survive in the late twentieth century, he believes, principally for the benefit of doormen in smart hotels and to give head waiters the pleasure of shouting across the bar, 'A dry martini for the Count!'

But then Dino Frescobaldi can afford to laugh at titles, since he has got one. He is a marquis, head of an ancient Tuscan dynasty which can trace its pedigree back to the twelfth century and which has lived at the same address in Florence for nearly 800 years – off the Piazza Frescobaldi, naturally.

In their time the Frescobaldi family have been knights in armour, merchants, bankers and counsellors to the Kings of England, tax collectors for the Pope, musicians, scholars, poets and explorers; they have plotted murder, been sent into exile, been publicly executed and they have gone spectacularly bankrupt at least twice. So it is only proper that they should be represented in the 1980s by a man who is less interested in the form of nobility than in its substance.

Dino Frescobaldi does not really look like an aristocrat. He is a short, friendly, rumpled man who wears thick horn-rimmed spectacles and he does not, at first acquaintance, project any of the haughtiness and disdain which the word aristocratic might imply.

But then disdain and haughtiness are the mannerisms of the aristocrat as imagined by Noël Coward and Oscar Wilde. Real life duchesses are seldom as grand as Lady Bracknell – and never as amusing. Henry James got closer to the truth in his short story 'The Real Thing' in which an artist commissioned to depict aristocrats for an illustrated magazine decides to hire two real live aristocrats as models. Somehow they never come out on the canvas looking truly aristocratic; they appear dowdy, over-modest, altogether too frayed at the edges, and not until the artist replaces them with working-class models who know how to strike a pose does he produce an illustration of which his editor can say, 'Ah, yes, *those* are aristocrats.'

Dino Frescobaldi decided to give up being an aristocrat at an early age. He was interested in politics and writing. So today it is his younger brothers who run the family wine business in Tuscany and who preside over the Frescobaldi palace in Florence, while Dino himself works as a journalist in Rome, senior diplomatic correspondent of the leading Italian daily, *Corriere della Sera*. He acknowledges that the family title probably helps to sell the family wine, but his interest in aristocracy does not extend much beyond that for, in his opinion, the noble titles and trappings which mesmerize the outside world are sleights of hand. In the centuries when the Frescobaldi really counted for something they were known by nothing more than their surname, like the other great families of Florence.

'It was only when we started losing power that we gained our title.'

The Frescobaldi were made marquises quite late in their history, in 1741, when the Dukes of Lorraine, who inherited Florence from the Medici, started handing out dignities to win the support of the town's patrician establishment. But the Frescobaldi scarcely used the honour, and nor did any of the other old Florentine families who had real pedigree.

The same went for the nobles of Venice. When the Austrians took over the city in the early nineteenth century and tried to curry local favour by handing out marquisates, the city's most ancient dynasties scorned to use them. They needed no other mark of honour than the plain surname they had always borne, the token of the history and lineage which they had created for themselves.

Being titled and being aristocratic is not necessarily the same thing. The eighteenth edition of *Burke's Landed Gentry*, published

1965/72, lists more than 1700 historic British families – among them the Phillips, from whose ranks the Grosvenors recruited Natalia, the present young Duchess of Westminster. None of this squirearchy have titles, but most live in some style on their family acres – the Phillips's home at Luton Hoo is one of Britain's stateliest residences – and quite a few have pedigrees going back to the Middle Ages, which makes them centuries more distinguished than many a parvenu peer. Of England's most titled families, the Howards – one duke, three earls, a lord and a lady – can trace their descent back to the thirteenth century, but the banking dynasty of Baring – Baron Ashburton, the Earl of Cromer, Baron Howick of Glendale, Baron Northbrook and Baron Revelstoke – only go back to 1717 when Johann Baring, a German immigrant, set up his wool trading stalls in Exeter.

'What matters about aristocracy,' says Dino Frescobaldi, 'is influence, power and money. Culture, pedigree and tradition are also important, of course, but without power and money, titles are meaningless.'

That is why he took a job with a newspaper. Being a journalist gets him closer to the centres of power in modern Italy than being an aristocrat.

Still, no morning is complete for Dino Frescobaldi without an hour riding his horse along the banks of the Tiber, and for lunch he does like to go to La Caccia, Rome's aristocratic club which is proud to have blackballed J. Paul Getty when he was at the height of his fame as the world's richest man. In the eyes of La Caccia's largely noble membership, evidently, Mr Getty's money and power alone were not quite enough.

It is the special knack of the aristocrat to persuade the world to accept him not for what he does, but for what he is; his ancestors did the doing. He is an inheritor, by definition, and though there are aristocrats, like Bertrand Lord Russell, who achieve things in their own right, the world is rather surprised by them – and the aristocracy as a whole is definitely disconcerted.

The true aristocrat, love him or hate him, is he who inherits and who passes on. His most cherished values lie in the past which has bestowed so many privileges upon him, and his ultimate priorities are concerned with the future to which he must pass on at least as much as he has inherited. He is one link in a chain of generations, and his weight is assessed in the scales of aristocracy by how strong a link he proves: did the 6th Duke do as much for the family as the preceding five, not to mention the marquesses, earls and barons of earlier generations? Or will he go down in family tradition as the one who wasted his substance, that portrait in the gallery which descendants hurry past with a disapproving snort?

This concern with past and future can give the aristocrat an indifference to the present which varies from the disdainful to the downright eccentric. When the present Duchess of Devonshire first met her future father-in-law, the 10th Duke Eddie, he was wearing a grocer's apron and was making up salmon lures with feathers plucked from the best hats of his lady friends, muttering 'Ettie Desborough, Ascot 1926' or 'Nancy Astor, Buckingham Palace 1930'. Then he tested out his handiwork by floating the lures in his bath, and putting his head under the water to see which he, as a salmon, would prefer.

In ordinary families such behaviour might be a source of embarrassment, but in aristocrats it is cherished as amiable dottiness – just as antics that would be classed as hooliganism in the hoi polloi get redefined as 'high spirits' among the upper orders. Sir Oswald Mosley's father once rode a hansom cab the length of Piccadilly, leaning out of the window and shooting out all the lights with a pistol as he went. Then he returned to the scene of his triumph to play a game of golf all the way down the street and the world admired his spirit even more.

There are psychological explanations of such behaviour. Lord Curzon's partiality for ravishing lady novelists on tiger-skin rugs and for carrying baskets of old bread round his houses to rub fingermarks off the doors has been explained by the fact that whenever he was naughty as a little boy his nanny would put his head down the lavatory and pull the chain. But it is just as likely that his lordship was demonstrating the aristocrat's frequent indifference to the existence or feelings of anything outside his own charmed world which was noted one evening by Evelyn Waugh while staying with the Sitwell family. He was standing on the terrace of Renishaw Hall, the family seat just south of Sheffield, admiring the sunset with Sir George Sitwell, the 4th Baronet. In the valley at their feet lay all the splendours and squalor of industrial Yorkshire – 'farms, cottages, villas, the railway, the colliery and the densely teeming streets of the men who worked there'.

'You see,' said Sir George, looking out distantly towards the hills beyond, 'there is *no one* between us and the Locker-Lampsons.'

Providing a link between past and future is one of the components of aristocratic magic. It makes the same appeal to human uncertainty that organized religion does, and handled worthily, it can give the nobleman something of the aura generated by representative monarchs – those social emblems of tradition and hope who, when they do their job well, persuade us to forget that royal people are just ordinary people elevated to their special position by no other qualification than the accident of birth.

The sheer caprice of the lottery which makes one baby Duke of Westminster and another his gardener's son does stick in the gullet, of course. The injustice of it is patent. But how appealing would the world be, deprived of distinction and caprice? A thousand years of aristocracy have left western Europe a legacy of elegance and achievement that no other corner of the earth can match – and the present-day nobleman remains a living monument to that.

Any father would open a few bottles and invite friends round to celebrate the birth of a new baby daughter. But Prince Johannes von Thurn und Taxis must be the only man in the world to have his bottles opened and served by his own liveried footmen in powdered wigs.

Most German princes are not royal in the British sense. In the international pecking order of aristocracy, a German *fürst* pecks in the same patch of courtyard as an English duke. But scarcely more than a hundred years ago German aristocrats were often sovereigns in their own little countries, complete with miniature courts, local governments and even their own opera houses, and under the Kaiser they were allowed to maintain their provincial magnificence until the First World War.

In the Thurn und Taxis palace of Schloss St Emmeram at Regensburg in Bavaria the magnificence has survived even longer than that. There is a throne room – the throne squats red and gold beneath a towering canopy – there is a ballroom, mirrored and enamelled white, like icing sugar, with a row of glittering chandeliers; there are several dining rooms, a succession of reception rooms and several dozen bedrooms and guest suites. In fact, there are over 500 rooms in the entire palace, and almost every one of them contains at least one clock: the palace clockmaker does nothing else but service them and wind them up.

On this dark April afternoon in 1982 Prince Johannes von Thurn und Taxis is celebrating the christening of his newly arrived daughter, the Princess Elisabeth von Thurn und Taxis. His guests include a fair sprinkling of margraves, dukes and princes, and the liveried servants bow as they present the guests with their drinks. Prince Johannes himself is a tall, healthy-looking man whose balding skull glows with the nut-brown sheen you can only achieve if your yacht commutes regularly between the Caribbean and the Med., and he is wearing a dark red carnation in his buttonhole.

He seems just a little ill at ease with his role as a proud new father, but then he has not had much practice at it: now fifty-seven, the Prince has packed his life with so many varied pleasures that he did not develop the appetite for marriage until his mid-fifties.

Princess Gloria von Thurn und Taxis, twenty-two, is a short, solidly constructed blonde with bright eyes and a loud laugh. She laughs quite a lot at the fact that her husband is older than her father – 'It's energy that matters. I'm the one always saying "Let's go home" when it gets to three' – and she finds his extraordinary wealth even more amusing: she has nicknamed him 'Goldie' – 'because he's got too much money and because it sounds so *Jewish*!'

Princess Gloria talks a lot about her Jewish friends. Their name is Rothschild. If Princess Gloria had to liken aristocrats to any other social group it would be to the Jews – and also to the

Mafia because, she says, 'they only marry their own kind, and they always stick together.' You can only be born an aristocrat in her opinion, you cannot become one.

'You can wear aristocratic clothes, you can put on an aristocratic accent and you can mix with aristocratic friends, if they are willing to mix with you. But you will always be a fake and *they* – the real aristocrats – will always know it.'

Princess Gloria is no fake. She was born Countess Mariae Gloria Ferdinanda Joachima Josephine Wilhelmine Huberta von Schönburg-Glauchau, a family whose senior line are princes of the Holy Roman Empire – which proved truly fortunate when she met up with her elder cousin Johannes in a German student cafe a few years back, since his family traditions only allowed him to marry ladies of a certain rank. Their meeting occurred in the Universitätsreitschule, a bohemian coffee house in Munich where the young and fashionable listen to rock music while gazing through windows giving on to the neighbouring riding school, and it was love at first sight. 'We have not been separated since.'

She is disarmingly frank that her principal function in life is to produce a male heir for the Thurn und Taxis family, and she is philosophical about this christening, the second occasion on which she has had to celebrate the birth of a girl.

'If God wants,' she says, 'He will grant this family a son.'

God may have a hard time not granting the Princess Gloria a son, since it is her declared intention to have about seven children – 'if not ten'. Should the Princess accomplish the larger ambition* there will be exactly one castle available for each of her offspring, with one still to spare, for the Thurn und Taxis own eleven castles and palaces in and around Bavaria, and they are the largest landowners in West Germany.

They also own a brewery, an advertising agency, a bank, a substantial chunk of the Matto Grosso in Brazil, two high technology factories producing electronic components outside Stuttgart, a factory in Spain, a factory in New Jersey, and a fair-sized farm in Georgia, USA, where they are on calling terms

---

* As this book went to press in June 1983, the Princess was delivered of a son, Inheritor-Prince Albert Maria Lamoral Miguel Johannes Gabriel von Thurn und Taxis.

with ex-President Carter. This modern business empire was built up personally by Prince Johannes, who was given charge of the family finances soon after the Second World War, and one wing of Schloss St Emmeram houses the sophisticated management team with which he supervises his world-wide interests. The Prince is the latest in a long line of Thurn und Taxis to be sniffed at by more traditional noble families who look down on 'trade', but he is unrepentant. He is rather proud, indeed, to be thought of as a businessman. When Prince Philip, Duke of Edinburgh, was invited to a boar hunt in Regensburg in 1968 (and shot five boars), HRH could not believe it was still possible for a private family to live in such a grandiose fashion, since, as he said, the house of Windsor could not possibly maintain its lifestyle without financial assistance from the state.

'What do you expect?' responded Prince Johannes von Thurn und Taxis unsurprised. 'No workey, no money.'

Prince Johannes's invitation to shoot at Sandringham has yet to be received.

Jokes at the expense of the British royal family are quite common among the aristocracy of Europe. Perhaps it is envy – after all, the Saxe-Coburg-Gothas were just dukes and princes a generation or so ago, and the German branch of the family still are. One English earl of ancient lineage likes to recount how he asked his butler, after Prince Philip had been to stay for a shooting weekend, whether he thought the royal visit had gone off well.

'Very well indeed, milord,' replied the servant gravely. 'But he is a bit *nouveau*, don't you think?'

Such a charge could never be levelled at the princely house of Liechtenstein. They like to trace their pedigree as far back as the year 955 when an early Liechtenstein helped the Emperor Otto repel the Tartars and other undesirable east folk at the battle of Lechfeld, and today they are princes of the Holy Roman Empire, ranking, in strict terms of precedence, just a little above the princes of Thurn und Taxis, since they acquired the lands which established their princely status a few decades before the Thurn und Taxis in the eighteenth century.

But in terms of practical achievement the Liechtensteins stand a clear head above every other aristocrat in Europe, for they are very nearly royal: they have managed to parlay their estates squeezed between Switzerland and Austria on the banks of the Rhine into a virtually independent sovereign state. Their principality is small (its area is sixty-four square miles), and it depends on a service agreement with Switzerland for some of its essential facilities (while petty criminals do their time in Liechtenstein's 'prison', a cell in the police station where food is brought in from a local restaurant, major malefactors have to be boarded out in one of Switzerland's jails). Yet Liechtenstein sits as a fully fledged member of the Council of Europe, and it has one full vote in every decision, the equal of Britain, France or Germany.

Prince Franz Josef II of Liechtenstein has a disconcertingly strong handshake for a man of seventy-six. He stands up straight to his full six foot three, and his rude health and solid frame are testimony to the bracing alpine air of the little country he has helped to create. His features, however, scarcely display his thousand years of selective Teutonic ancestry, for his complexion is somehow oriental, and ignorant visitors to his principality have been heard to wonder why there are so many postcards on sale which appear to depict the Emperor of Japan.

The Emperor of Japan is, in fact, the world's only head of state to have held his position longer than the Prince of Liechtenstein. Franz Josef took over his romantic statelet in 1938 – though that was partly for unromantic reasons of tax. The majority of the family possessions at that date lay outside the principality in eastern Austria, Czechoslovakia and Hungary – until the Second World War the Liechtensteins owned two dozen castles in those countries, with over a million people living on their estates – and to avoid one round of the inheritance taxes on these vast possessions Franz Josef's father had renounced the succession to allow the family properties to pass directly from grandfather to grandson.

It was an early example of the adjustments which aristocrats have had to make to sidestep the inconvenience of life in the age of the common man. But the Liechtensteins need not have bothered, since in 1945 they suffered a still greater inconvenience.

The Red Army marched into Vienna, and the peoples' republics established in its wake confiscated all the estates of the nobility.

The Liechtensteins lost twenty-two castles and the several hundred thousand acres of land that went with them but they were luckier than most of eastern Europe's aristocracy, who were effectively liquidated as a caste overnight. At least the Liechtensteins still had their homes in Vienna – along with their little principality on the banks of the Rhine, which they had, until then, rather regarded as the scrag end of their landholdings. Originally acquired for the title that went with it rather than for any economic motive, the principality of Liechtenstein had been inattentively administered by bailiffs throughout the nineteenth century, and few of the family ever bothered to go there.

Still, if one single quality distinguishes aristocracy from the rest of mankind, it is the ability to survive. It is the basic condition necessary to create a lineage maintaining its sense of identity across the centuries, and left with less than 10 per cent of the land they had owned at the height of their glory, the Liechtensteins buckled down in 1945 to the new realities of their world. Working with the 20,000 inhabitants of their principality, they managed in little more than twenty years to turn the largely rural, undeveloped society of Europe's poorest country into the richest – the only country that can afford to import the Germans, Swiss and Austrians as foreign labour. Today, over 25 per cent of Liechtenstein's income is derived from the tax advantages it offers foreign companies, 11 per cent comes from the sale of postage stamps – and it is the world's second largest exporter of false teeth. On such varied and inventive economic bases Prince Franz Josef's subjects today enjoy a per capita annual income ($16,200) third only in the world to that of Kuwait ($17,000) and the United Arab Emirates ($19,000).*

Inside his castle Prince Franz Josef has a Rembrandt hanging over his television. He has got several more Rembrandts, a sprinkling of Van Dycks and nearly a dozen Rubenses – not to mention

---

* The list continues: 4, Switzerland (annual per capita income $13,987); 5, Monaco ($12,000); 6, Luxembourg ($11,900); 7, Denmark ($11, 587); 8, Federal German Republic ($11,080); 9, Sweden ($10,749); 10, Jersey ($10,350); 11, Belgium ($10,271); 12, Qatar ($10,100); 13, USA ($9,637). Great Britain on this scale, from *The World in Figures, 1981* by *The Economist*, comes 41st ($6,372).

a hundred other classic paintings which add up to one of the most valuable private art collections in the world. The Prince used to own the only Leonardo left in private hands – until he sold it to the National Gallery of Art in Washington for a price rumoured to be around $6 million.

After the sale his daughter Princess Nora, who happened to be working in Washington for the World Bank, decided to go and look at the painting again. She was amazed to discover it hanging in solitary splendour, lit by spotlights, with a guard to watch over it in its own little room. In Liechtenstein it had just been one of the paintings round the house; she remembers it propped against the wall while she played round it with the friends she had brought home from school.

The quiet and happy life of the Liechtenstein family in their castle above the Rhine was somewhat disrupted in January 1983 when Prince Charles, who had learned to ski in Liechtenstein, returned there for a holiday with his new wife – and the uninvited entourage of long-lensmen and journalists who dog her everywhere. The Liechtensteins were horrified at the daily charade of decoy cars and pursuit, and they could not help noticing how the strain of it all was beginning to tell on the Princess.

'But then,' said one of them, 'her family background hasn't really prepared her for this sort of thing.'

The Spencers, after all, have only been earls for about 300 years.

Taking the long-term view is what helps aristocrats to survive. Prince Franz Josef might have thrown in the towel at the nadir of his fortunes in 1945, but he nourished the firm intention of regaining the eastern castles and estates of his forefathers and he retains his ambition to this day, Iron Curtain notwithstanding. He has no doubt that his family will one day regain what they lost in 1945, and while such a dream might be expected of a seventy-six-year-old gentleman whose godfather was the last great Emperor of Austria, it is shared with equal conviction by his thirty-seven-year-old son, the Crown Prince Hans-Adam.*

---

* On 3 July 1983, Franz Josef II announced his intention of stepping down as ruling prince of Liechtenstein in favour of his son Hans-Adam in the spring of 1984.

Even taller than his father, and prematurely grey, Hans-Adam has earned the respect of Swiss bankers for the skill with which he has reorganized the family's own private Bank in Liechtenstein AG into a streamlined and aggressive operator on the international money market, and he is not famous for wishful thinking or fantasy.

'The Communist system is breaking down. Hungary, Czechoslovakia, Poland, they are all signs that it cannot carry on. Our lands in what is now Czechoslovakia used to be one of the most prosperous parts of Europe. Today they are under-developed, and one day soon they will ask for help – capital investment and expertise. We have got that, and we will offer it.'

What does the Liechtenstein family want with twenty-two castles?

'I'm not sure about the castles. They are not much of an economic proposition nowadays, and they are probably better off being used as they are – as museums and children's homes. But I am sure that some deal will be struck. We are bound to go back. Aristocracy has been thriving in Europe for more than a thousand years. Communism still has to prove that it can work for one hundred.'

Every spring Doña Victoria Eugenia, Duchess of Medinaceli, likes to visit her castle at Oca in northwest Spain to look at the camellias. They grow to their full height as trees in this moist, green, strangely un-Spanish province squeezed over the top of Portugal, and they fill their corner of the garden with special coolness and calm. After a couple of days contemplating their beauty, the Duchess goes away again, not to return for another year until they bloom once more.

Anyone but a camellia lover might consider Doña Victoria Eugenia's treatment of her Oca castle cavalier to say the least. But then she does have between 90 and 100 others to look after (she is not sure precisely how many, and is currently having an inventory taken to arrive at an exact figure) and she only started coming to Oca by accident in any case. She happened one day to be flicking through the pages of an illustrated magazine when pictures of camellias in the gardens of a beautiful castle caught her eye –

and on reading the caption she discovered that the castle, and the camellias, belonged to her.

Doña Victoria Eugenia, Duchess of Medinaceli, Grandee of Spain, and 'Mimi' to her friends, must be a strong contender for the title of World Champion Aristocrat, for she is currently the holder of forty noble titles. Aristocracy is, conventionally, a male-dominated institution. A family which can only produce females is usually held to have forfeited its 'nobility'. But Spanish women have held rights to succession since the Middle Ages: in the absence of any direct male heir a title can be passed on to a daughter. So noble titles tend to last longer in Spain than they do in most other countries, and this has meant that Doña Victoria Eugenia not only inherited the Dukedom of Medinaceli on the death of her father in 1956: she also acquired nine further ducal titles, seventeen marquisates, twenty-one titles as count (or rather countess), and three viscountcies.

This stupendous total of fifty-one titles, enhanced by the fact that twelve of them carried the additional dignity 'Grandee of Spain', qualified the Duchess of Medinaceli for the distinction of being the most titled human being on earth, the inheritor of more marks of nobility than anyone else, male or female. Yet since appearing in the *Guinness Book of Records* is scarcely an aristocratic thing to do, the Duchess has given away some of her titles to her children, and with a mere forty titles to her own name she now ranks a gracious second to her neighbour in Seville, the Duchess of Alba, who has forty-one and who rather likes publicity in any case.

The Spanish phenomenon of titles by the lorryload is a matter of arithmetical progression. Girl with title marries boy with title, and the resulting offspring is doubly titled: after several genera-tions a family's pedigree can be read off in the list of dignities trailing after its name. But it makes titles in Spain about as valuable as Monopoly money, for what really counts in a noble inheritance is the land – and in this respect the Duchess of Medinaceli has been less than nobly endowed.

By the early decades of the twentieth century the Medinaceli inheritance was a complicated amalgam of assets built up from the dowries of successive generations, but a hard-headed estate agent would have had little difficulty in dividing it effectively into two parts – a vast collection of castles, most of them no more than piles of rubble on once strategic hilltops, and, much more valuable, a collection of revenue-producing farms and estates which enabled the dukes of Medinaceli to maintain such of their residences as they wished to live in. But the Duchess's father, the 17th Duke, chose to divide the inheritance for, having married twice, he left the bulk of the revenue-producing estates to the offspring of his second marriage.

So though Doña Victoria Eugenia inherited the family titles and castles in 1956, she found herself faced with the task of struggling to maintain her ancestral dignity without the bulk of the ancestral land and income that first made it possible – and it was fortunate that she had married for love, not title. Her husband, Rafael Medina, was an enterprising engineer who was just developing workshops which today form a full-scale plastics factory in the town of Pilas, south of Seville and that factory is now run by Rafael, the Duchess's second son. Its principal produce is Cuerotex, a form of imitation leather, so the Duchess of Medinaceli is still able to maintain her aristocratic way of life in just a few of her residences – thanks to the profits from plastic snakeskin, lizard and crocodile.

Her favourite residence is the Casa de Pilatos in Seville, a grey and sand-coloured mishmash of Moorish curlicues and classical statuary brought home by ancestors in the days when Spain was mistress of the Mediterranean. Every niche and loggia of the Casa de Pilatos is littered with these trophies, but the trophies dearest to the Duchess's heart are the shelves of electroplated pots and plates that she has won in a lifetime playing bridge.

Bridge is her favourite activity. She gets up towards noon most mornings, and floats through the greater part of the day in an amiable, but somewhat distant haze, as though she were one stage removed from ordinary existence – which, indeed, she is: somehow her eyes are always drifting off you towards the horizon.

But when the Duchess of Medinaceli sits down at her green baize table, her eyes become very sharp indeed. She calls her bids and puts down her cards with rare authority. Now in her sixties, and a grandmother, she has fine soft hands, and the complexion of a woman twenty years her junior. But perhaps that is only to be expected if you have filled your life with little more than playing bridge and being a duchess.

She must be the last of a species. It does not seem possible that any future generation of her family could amble through life with such insouciance. Her son Rafael works a full day, five days a week, overseeing the fortunes of Cuerotex.

'Everybody nowadays has to work,' he says. 'In an earlier age things were easier for the class of people I come from. It was easy to make money. It was easy to live. But not any more.'

Rafael bears some of the titles that his mother has discarded. He is Duke of Feria and Marquis of Villalba, and it is his skilful management of the huge slab-sided ovens toasting vinyl into 'leather' which enables his family to survive today in some approximation of its former grandeur. But is the remedy for aristocratic decay that Rafael represents any more effective than an existence playing bridge and enjoying camellias? At least his mother's lifestyle pays a certain homage to the cult of leisure which is one component of aristocracy. If a five-day week in a plastics factory is the price of surviving as an aristocrat these days, what makes the noble different from the bourgeois?

Jean Louis, Marquis de Ganay, is inspecting his lavatory. It is a new lavatory, brand new – so new, in fact, that it is still being installed. The air is sharp with fresh paint and drying cement, and a little plaque is being affixed to the lavatory door. It reads 'Messieurs'.

Jean Louis de Ganay and his wife Philippine have decided to open their chateau to the public. It lies beside the village of Courances, near Fontainebleau, one hour south of Paris, and they have been taking their instructions from the Duke of Bedford. In 1971 the Duke wrote a book passing on the fruit of his experiences commercializing Woburn Abbey – *How to Run a Stately Home* – and his principal advice to aristocrats ambitious to follow in his footsteps is to provide ample relief facilities for visitors: 'The first thing you need is good loos and plenty of them.'

The Duke of Bedford's analysis, after more than twenty

successful years in the stately home business, is that the extraordinary spectacle of the lower orders paying hard-earned money to gaze at the treasures accumulated by the mighty and privileged can be explained by nothing more complicated than the motorcar. In the car-owning democracy people would feel silly if they were not driving their car somewhere, and a stately home represents a destination. Twenty miles or so outside town and usually set in beautiful countryside, a country house and park provide the ideal objective for a Sunday afternoon's outing, and after an hour in the car, people get out with only one thing on their minds. To look at the Rembrandts is not a biological necessity – 'to visit the loo is'. This priority dealt with, the visitors' mind naturally turns to thoughts of tea.

So His Grace's conclusion is that stately loos, pleasant tearooms and car parks that offer ample elbow room for Sunday afternoon drivers are what matter most. If these attractions have been provided, he says, then the house itself is almost irrelevant.

The Chateau de Courances is considerably more beautiful, if somewhat smaller than Woburn Abbey, and the Marquis and the Marquise de Ganay have decided to forego a tearoom, for this year at least: they will see what sort of revenues the gate produces this summer before investing in a conversion of the old watermill.

But there is no arguing with the ducal advice on loos, so now the village plumber is hard at work beneath the grand double staircase that leads up to the front doors of the chateau. Gentlemen's facilities are below the north staircase, ladies' below the south.

Jean Louis, Marquis de Ganay, is yet another tall, well-built, handsome aristocrat. His style lies partly in his looks, and partly in his dress, but mainly in his manner, for he is at ease with himself. The upper classes have nothing to prove. Like the lower classes, they know their place and they have grown accustomed to it. It is the folk in between, social nomads shuffling from lower middle to middle middle, one eye looking upwards, one eye back, who worry about making an 'impression'. The Marquis de Ganay is not ashamed to be caught in the drawing room securing the silver candlesticks by tying them to table legs with invisible nylon thread. 'People pinch so much these days,' he explains.

In the library his wife the Marquise is engaged in similar precautions. She is unrolling thick sheets of polythene to screen the leatherbound volumes in the bookcase, and she is trying to work out the logistical problems of charging five francs to view the gardens and ten francs to view the house.

'Perhaps, after people have seen the house,' she worries, 'they will cheat and sneak out into the park, without paying.'

The Ganays' well-rounded English comes from childhoods spent in the care of English nannies, and the signatures in the Courances visitors' book bear witness to the family's Anglophilia: the first autograph reads 'Elizabeth R'.

The name Courances means running water, and the fame of the chateau stems from the lakes and cascades that surround it. The water gardens gush and bubble ceaselessly, surrounding the house with freshness and calm even in the heat of summer, and from their windows the Ganays can look out in every direction over streams and mirror pools reflecting vistas of green. Worried at the damage that visitors may wreak, the Marquis has arranged for the guides to the chateau to be printed on sheets of green paper that will blend with their surroundings if they are thrown away.

It is the advent of socialism in France which has persuaded Jean Louis de Ganay and his wife to open up their home. Courances will become liable for President Mitterand's new wealth tax unless it is opened to visitors at least fifty-one days per year, and the Ganays have decided they will find weekends rubbing shoulders with the public less painful than having to sell off some family heirlooms every June when the tax assessment falls due.

Painful enough, however, for like so many French chateaux – magnificent façades only one room thick – Courances is less spacious than it looks. There is no separate wing which can be fenced off as a museum. So every Saturday and Sunday in the tourist season the Marquis and the Marquise will have to eat their lunch quickly, clear the table, and then put up the ropes for the visitors due at half-past two. For ten francs you can view chateaux in France that are more stately, but none could be more of a genuine, lived-in home.

Can any home be worth it? Most people, if told that they

can only retain their house on condition that they let total strangers tramp through their drawing room every summer weekend, would probably sell that house and find another one.

But aristocrats are not like most people. The master of Courances is happier being bound as museum curator to the family bricks and mortar than becoming the unfettered owner of bricks and mortar elsewhere, and he is slowly adjusting to Courances becoming the master of him. Concerned to make quite clear to his paying guests the areas where they might, and might not walk, the Marquis had signs prepared reading sternly, 'Défense de marcher sur la pelouse', until his wife intervened. She suggested some gentler form of wording – 'Prière de ne pas marcher ici, s'il vous plaît' – might be more diplomatic, considering the circumstances.

'We cannot talk to people like that any more,' she said.

And – considering the circumstances – the Marquise got her way.

It seems a basic rule of human organization that in any society – monarchy, dictatorship, oligarchy or democracy – there is always a small ruling class and a larger class of those who are ruled. It is usual to protest to the contrary but, in reality, power is never exercised totally by one man alone, nor, at the other extreme, by all the members of society equally.

This is obviously true today in totalitarian countries, but it is equally true in democracies, for though the ballot box allows us to exercise some periodic control over which particular elite should govern our lives, our choice is always confined to that general subgroup of ambitious and thrusting individuals whose gratification stems from the public attention and self-esteem that they derive from being members of the ruling class.

The eternal challenge to the ruling class is to provide some rationale for the special power that they exercise. Brute force alone is not enough. Violence on its own cannot sustain authority for very long. To stay on top the elite has to propose some sort of explanation to society, comforting the majority and reassuring them that they are wise to entrust their destinies to the care of this particular minority – and for more than a thousand years in western Europe both the ruling power group, and the rationale, went together under the same name – aristocracy.

The word itself goes back to ancient Greece, and classical Rome made some modifications to the concept of 'rule by the best'. But in its modern form the institution started taking shape in the obscure and troubled centuries that followed the fall of Rome – the years that historians used to call the Dark Ages.

We call no man master. Nominally we hold our lands and dignities from the King, because there must be a keystone to the arch of human society; but we hold our lands in our own hands, and defend them with our own swords.

The Nobleman in *Saint Joan*
by GEORGE BERNARD SHAW, Scene iv

The Aga Khan is held by followers to be a direct descendant of God. An English Duke takes precedence.

Letter from the College of Arms
quoted in *Housewife*

II · NOBLE
MEN

IF a farmer living today, say, on the Cheshire border with Wales, were to discover that his neighbours were stealing his livestock, he would find it quite expensive to teach them a lesson with the ultimate available in military technology. A Harrier jump jet currently retails at around £5 million – over 12,000 cows at 1983 market prices.

A thousand years ago, however, total armed response was not nearly so pricey. In ninth-century England a horse cost the equivalent of six cows, with a suit of mail and metal weapons costing roughly the same again – and an armoured knight on horseback represented the ultimate weapon. There was no known instrument of war that could better it, except two armoured knights on horseback.

The horseborne warrior had not always been supreme. The strength of the Roman armies had been based on their infantry legions, the disciplined bodies of foot soldiers who subjugated Europe, shrugging off challenges by the bareback horsemen of the Germanic tribes who had nuisance value, but lacked battering power. Riding on a loose cloth without a saddle, the best the mounted warrior could manage was to steer close to the enemy, throw his lance and then retire. If he tried to charge while holding onto his lance, the chances were he would be unhorsed on impact.

But one reason for the victories that the barbarian armies started to win over the foot soldiers of Rome in the fourth century AD was a device which transformed light cavalry into shock troops of real power. The Chinese had noticed how much more securely a man sat on a horse with the aid of two iron rings on leather thongs, and horsemen are depicted riding with stirrup loops in Buddhist sculptures of the second century BC. The stirrup seems to have come to Europe with tribes migrating out of Asia in the first century AD, and the Goths adopted the gadget to lethal effect. In AD 378 their cavalry caught the Romans on the flank at the battle of Adrianople and massacred them.

The face of warfare was transformed. Man and horse had been combined into a heavy and aggressive military weapon. With better balance and a surer seat the horseman could wear armour. He could carry a more substantial shield and, above all, his lance could be used as a battering ram. It no longer needed to be thrown. The impact of the heavy horseman was to become the key factor on the field of battle, and the man who could afford a horse and the equipment that went with it became a key figure in the community.

Europe was a friendless, frightening place in the centuries following the collapse of Rome. Most people spent their entire lives in small settlements cut off from the nearest habitation by miles of still uncleared woodland. Their horizon was the forest, in which lurked ferocious beasts like the boar, and from which might emerge without warning raiders from a hostile tribe. Goths, Visigoths, Huns and Magyars – successive waves of predatory peoples jostled for living space in the vacuum created by the breakdown of the Roman Imperial structure, and in this dark and obscure confusion the man who could give protection became an almost magical figure to his fellow human beings.

His horse subdued enemies, and it also subdued distance. He could travel, see things, meet people and have experiences about which the earthbound villager could only fantasize. The forest held no fear for the horseman. In times of peace he could demonstrate his power over it by hunting down and killing the wild boar, and in time of war he held in his hand the power of life or death.

So the origins of European aristocracy are military. In the Dark Ages the leader of any tribe or community was he who exercised military power, and the aristocrats of the tribe were those henchmen who could match him in toughness. It was a matter of survival. Membership of the social elite was not a matter of refinement but of brute force, and the titles borne by modern aristocrats bear witness to their rough and ready origins on the field of battle.

Duces were the Roman high commanders who held territorial responsibilities, and as the barbarian tribes took over the empire, their leaders called themselves *duces* as well (*herzog*, the German for duke, means 'leader of an army').

Earls or *eorls* were Anglo-Saxon institutions. When the Danes invaded England they bestowed that title, from the Danish *jarl*, on the military viceroys entrusted with the governorship of the English shires, later to be known as 'counties'. After the Norman Conquest an earl's wife was, and is, a countess, and on the mainland of Europe count (*conde*, *conte* or *comte*) was the equivalent rank deriving from the Latin *comes*, 'companion', the term appropriated by the Franks for the friends and outriders who made up the escorts of their rulers. The deputies of counts were vice-counts – viscounts.

In Germany the equivalent of a count was a *graf*, and a rank above the grafs were the *markgrafs* (margraves), marquises and marquesses. They derived their superior status from the particularly difficult lands which they captured or were given to protect – frontier areas known as marks or marches – and today the order of precedence recognized by aristocrats in every country of Europe derives from the hierarchy of power hacked out by broadswords in misty forests a thousand or more years ago. At the top are the dukes and at the bottom are the barons and knights, the individual mounted warriors who originally made up the basic military units in the pyramid: the German for knight is *ritter*, a rider; the French is *chevalier*, a man on a horse.

Yet a General and his High Command do not, of course, automatically qualify for classification as aristocrats. All aristocracies are elites, but not all elites are aristocracies, and the mere fact of being a dominant social grouping does not turn military men into 'noble' men.

Nobilitas, the Latin root of the French *noblesse* and hence, via the Normans, of the English word, originally referred to a specific subgroup who held office in the Roman republic. It was a technical term implying no value judgement. But *nobilitas* was appropriated by the tribes who inherited western Europe from the Romans along with *comes* and *dux* (the singular of *duces*), and the word expanded and extended towards its modern sense of bravery, dignity and highmindedness – the ideal moral basis of power.

'You see before you the wrath of the Lord breaking forth. There is naught but towns emptied of their folk, monasteries razed to the ground or given to the flames, fields desolated . . . Everywhere the strong oppresseth the weak and men are like fish of the sea that blindly devour each other.'

The lamentation of the bishops of the province of Rheims in AD 909 is typical of the misery voiced in the surviving literature of the ninth and tenth centuries. Anyone who could bring some order out of this chaos was good by definition, no matter how harsh his order might be, and power was bound to seem almost divine to those who benefited from it; it is no coincidence that the words 'Lord' and 'Seigneur' can be applied interchangeably to God in His Heaven, or to the local occupant of the manor house.

Kings were special recipients of this reverence. The long-haired rulers of the Franks were priest-kings who made particularly explicit the role that monarchs can still play, mediating for their societies with the intangible and eternal. In times of war God smiled on their victories; in times of peace Heaven resided in their justice – and their lieutenants, the noble men, were wreathed in the same magic. Frankish counts shared in the king's charisma and also embodied it at a local level, administering justice on his behalf. They were go–betweens, the vehicles by which royal authority was communicated to the provinces – together with ideas, gossip, fads and fashions. Many centuries later the foreign habit of eating with a fork was to spread across England in this way, aristocrats picking up the habit at court, then bringing it home where their neighbours and servants observed how usefully this novel implement could be deployed in conjunction with a knife.

But being a go-between was a two-way process, for the local count or earl had a charisma based on his own regional status. He needed his contact with the royal aura, while he also needed the local powerbase which prevented him becoming a royal dependent – and as European society slowly groped towards some form of structure at the end of the Dark Ages, this ambivalence worked itself out in terms of land.

Land was a primary necessity in the world of the mounted warrior. An infantry army could be based in an urban environment, but a knight needed at least enough land to sustain one horse, and it was this basic military requirement which shaped European landholding between the eighth and fourteenth centuries into the pattern subsequently known as the feudal system. The King allowed his mightiest subjects to hold their lands in return for their support in times of war; they, in turn, sublet sections of their territories to lesser lords, and the lesser lords sublet further to create links of personal allegiance which stretched from the monarch to the humblest peasant tilling the soil.

This chain of mutual protection proved to be the mechanism that imposed some order upon the chaos of previous centuries, turning the 'Dark' Ages into the 'Middle' Ages, and the essence of the system was the exchange of land for arms – not 'money, which scarcely existed. Yet since the value of any particular piece of real estate was represented by the number of knights it could support, it followed that whenever a warrior died, his lands must revert to the lord above him in the chain. Widows and infant children were no use on the field of battle, and an able-bodied, arms-bearing son of the dead knight might not necessarily be loyal.

So in its purest, theoretical form, the feudal system allowed land to be held for one lifetime only, and on death, estates reverted to the liege lord. Titles like margrave, earl and count were not hereditary; they were strictly military ranks and were no more family property to be handed onto the children than ranks like brigadier or field marshal are today.

But feudal theory could not long remain proof against the hereditary principle, for if the kings who granted lands were endowed with charisma, the land itself had a magic that was to prove even stronger.

When Gerald Grosvenor arrives home from a hard day at the office his helicopter sets him down between three very different symbols of his family history. In front of him sits the latest Eaton Hall, Britain's most modern and unlikely stately home, a low, flat, white-tiled building, unkindly compared by some to the county ambulance headquarters.

To the left of the Duke soars a prickly Gothic clocktower, easily confused at a quick glance with Big Ben whose architectural epoch it shares – a remnant of the Victorian Eaton Hall built by Gerald Grosvenor's great-grandfather – and right in the middle of the lawn, its base lapped by the waters of a goldfish pond, rises the bronze statue of a heavy-set, not to say paunchy Norman warrior in chain mail.

This warrior, who is seated astride a bronze horse of equally stalwart proportions, is one of the heroes who first made Grosvenor a name to conjure with. Indeed, he is said to be the origin of the Grosvenor name itself, for family legend has it that Duke William of Normandy's closest companion when he took possession of England in 1066 was a huntsman, a *veneur* in Norman French, whose generous bulk earned him the nickname of the 'Gros Veneur'.

Generations of Grosvenors have been raised on the tale. When the Conqueror heard that the wild raiders of the Welsh hills were creeping across the River Dee to steal the cows belonging to the good farmers of Cheshire, he gave his friend the Gros Veneur the rank of Earl of Chester with responsibility for keeping the Welsh on the right side of the river. The fat huntsman, whose first name was Hugh, carried out his mission with such enthusiasm, wreaking rapine and violence amongst the local population, that he became generally known as Hugh Lupus, 'Hugh the Wolf'. When a later Hugh Lupus, the great and good Victorian Grosvenor who was raised to the rank of duke, conceived the notion of commissioning some memorial to his namesake in the 1860s, he almost abandoned the project on discovering the unsavoury character that his predecessor had possessed.

'I found so bad an account of our hero,' he wrote to the sculptor G. F. Watts, 'that he dissipated his goods, was much given to his belly, had so many bastard children and so on – that I am rather shaken in my intention of erecting a statue to *his* honour!'

But this, of course, is the sort of thing you must expect to find if you go burrowing too diligently into the character of your forebears – for how else could a Grosvenor hope to rise in the age of the bold bad barons except by being a bolder, badder baron than all the others?

So the statue was erected, and it stands in front of Eaton Hall to this day, indifferent to the complaints of spoilsport historians who point out that the present-day Grosvenors are not linked to the first Earl of Chester but to his great-great nephew, Hugh of Kevelioc (see source notes). Hugh Lupus has his hand raised to catch a hunting falcon which is just settling down onto his fingers, and his horse is headed down along the mile and a quarter drive that stretches from the gates of Eaton Hall, rearing up proudly, eternally poised ready to go a-raiding towards the hills of Wales.

The Liechtenstein family have no statue to their Gros Veneur who is also a Hugh, Hugo of Liechtenstein, a knight who traced his descent from the heroes who fought alongside the Saxon Emperor Otto at the battle of Lechfeld in AD 955. But he plays the same role in the family history – he was the founding father.

At Lechfeld, near Munich, Otto checked the advance of the Magyars, one of the tribes who, like the Slavs and Huns, had been moving into Europe from Russia. To consolidate his victory he planted the eastern approaches to Bavaria with fighting men, and, in classic feudal fashion, these territories, today occupied by Austria, Hungary and Czechoslovakia, were placed in the care of military governors, each of them maintaining knights on the land around the strongpoint he was allocated.

One of these strongpoints was a crag of light stone – the 'Lichten Stein' – set among the hills south of Vienna, and this became the name assumed by Hugo's warlike forebears who parlayed their military ability into status and power. In feudal Europe no business could better the dividends yielded by a successful war, and the skill shown in battle by the Liechtensteins secured further eastern territories for themselves – and for their sons. Hugo, who flourished early in the twelfth century, and who is the first Liechtenstein of whom reliable historical evidence exists, had inherited his eastern estates from his family – so by that date the transformation of temporary military rank into hereditary social status was already established.

In theory the Emperor Otto and his successors had retained the right to reallocate the tenancy of the Liechtensteins' land, for the feudal principle of ultimate overlordship was not lightly given up. Spiritually it was enshrined in a solemn ceremony of oath swearing, and materially it required payment of a 'fine' by each successive warrior tenant, as if they were taking over their estate for the first time, solely by virtue of their overlord's gift.

But, in practice, the sons of a man who had fought to maintain a particular piece of land naturally came to regard that land as their own. Long before western man was taught to love his country, he learnt to love the land on which his father had raised him. Aristocracy predates patriotism. As early as AD 877 the Emperor Charles the Bald, Charlemagne's grandson, had had to promise that the feudal estates of any followers who died on his expedition to Italy in that year would automatically be handed on to their sons. It seems probable that the Emperor Otto operated on a similar basis a century later – and once the hereditary principle became established, then aristocracy followed, for it is the sense of 'family' which turns a ruling class into a noble class.

Land lies very close to the heart of European aristocracy, but family is the heart itself. Ancestors are venerated, lineage is defined, concepts of the 'dynasty' or 'house' are cherished, and they are marked by social signals ranging from heraldic emblems to special manners, dress and accent. To preserve family identity into the future, rules of inheritance are elaborated, and concepts like 'blood' come to matter greatly – together with all manner of lofty and exclusive fancies to do with 'pedigree'.

This was the process that started to transform the character of Europe's military magnates from the tenth century onwards. Families identified themselves with their own particular estate, which they came to see as their inalienable patrimony, along with the home that they built upon it. Passing on this patrimony from generation to generation – with token homage to the liege-lord – required the consolidation of family rules and organization, usually in favour of the eldest male child, with younger sons entering the church or going off in search of other lands. Women-folk were married off to neighbours of similar status whose friend-ship might provide an additional source of local fortification, and as generations passed away to be buried side by side in the family chapel, the pedigree developed.

It is, obviously, impossible to put precise dates to social changes which advanced at different paces and displayed different shapes depending on their local context, but aristocracy in its modern form took its time a-coming. In the ninth and tenth centuries thousands of Germans had their names written down in the *Libri Memoriales* of the Bavarian monasteries. These were books in which rich and poor had their names recorded in order to enjoy the benefits of the monks' prayers, and the same family names recur, often accompanied by a limited set of Christian names which were obviously traditional in that family and which could, therefore, be taken as signs of an established sense of family identity.

But there is no evidence that the titles which are recorded in these early monastery lists were handed on inside families as their Christian names were. Indeed, there is no great sense of social distinction of any sort – no awareness yet of a separate and elevated caste of 'nobility'. Counts, margraves and dukes are listed indiscri-minately alongside names that carry no title.

Not until the late eleventh and twelfth centuries do monastic records show evidence of self-consciously noble dynasties, with titles and dignities handed on from one generation to the next, together with the trappings that indicate belief in an inherent social superiority – the idea that a man enjoys status not so much for what he does, but for what he is. Heraldry, a very obvious proclamation of inherited status, did not come into existence until the twelfth century. There is only evidence of Europe's greater lords using seals after AD 1125, and the earliest coloured example of heraldry known to Sir Anthony Wagner, former Garter King of Arms, is an enamel plate of around AD 1150, commemorating Geoffrey of Anjou, founder of the Plantagenet dynasty.*

Castle building was another token of aristocratic development, since the castle was the only effective defence against the mounted knight. But until the end of the tenth century only dukes or counts who were ruling large territories could afford the capital investment involved – and it was to this small group of castellans that contemporary chroniclers restricted titles like 'dominus' or 'messire' as an indication of special homage and deference.

But by the year 1200 almost every knight, however limited his means, had scraped up the resources to dig his moat and create a stronghold, usually a wooden stockade. Apart from its military value, this fortified base provided a powerful focus for family identity – hence the profusion of German noble dynasties whose names end with -burg (castle) – and this was the period when chroniclers also started according an elevated social status to smaller castellans. The rank of knight became the low water mark below which *nobilitas* ceased, and above it rose a soaring hierarchy of distinction in which titles like count, marquis and duke were no longer military ranks but rather reflected the extent of their holders' lands. They were titles inherited by the lottery of birth.

Yet once social distinction came to reflect the possession of hereditary land rather than military ability, the identity of the aristocrat had assumed its modern form, since a man who inherited a great estate did not have to fight personally to preserve it. His inheritance gave him the wherewithal to maintain other men who could do his fighting for him, and this brought about a fundamental change in the noble ethos.

The word 'noble' itself remained a value judgement in ordi-

* The name Plantagenet itself is said to have originated when Geoffrey, the husband of Henry I's daughter Matilda and father of Henry II (1133–89), seized a flowering branch of broom, *planta genista*, and wore it in his helmet as an emblem.

nary speech – but whenever people referred to 'the nobility' they were no longer necessarily specifying the bravest, most dignified and high-minded members of society. They were referring primarily to those who owned the land.

The purpose of the aristocrat is most emphatically not to work for money.

NANCY MITFORD,
Noblesse Oblige, 1956

'I been rich. I been poor. Rich is better.'

SOPHIE TUCKER, 1884–1966

III · MONEY
COUNTS

WHEN Diana Frescobaldi, aged twelve, celebrates her birthday, the drink is by Coca Cola, the cake is a confection of her grandmother's pastry chef, and as for the villa, that was designed by Michelangelo. Table football is set up in the loggia under the watchful eye of a huge marble lion, and as the heat goes off the sun the children dive into the pool beside the cypress-fringed lawn. Mothers wrap up their offspring in huge white fluffy towels, while fathers sip the family wine and gossip about their business. Then the gates of the drive are thrown open, and the cavalcade of cars heads back into town.

Diana Frescobaldi has a choice of villas in which to hold her birthday parties, since her family own eight large country estates in the hills around Florence, as well as the family palace off the Piazza Frescobaldi in town: one house holds the archives, another produces the red wine; there is one estate where Lamberto, Diana's big brother, does his motorcycle rough riding, and another where her sister Fiammetta tends maize for a college project; there is a castle for entertaining foreign business clients, and another for relaxing privately at weekends.

It is about half an hour's drive from any one Frescobaldi estate to another, or back into Florence again, and, shuffling from one outpost to the next, the family often seems to be in perpetual motion. In winter they spend more time in Florence, in summer you will often find them out in the hills. Their existence is a continually changing mixture of town and country and, give or take the odd Fiat or Honda, it is very much the system of peregrination which the family's founding fathers pursued over eight centuries ago.

Like the princely house of Liechtenstein, the Frescobaldi family claims a descent going back to the times of the Emperor Otto. After this formidable warrior had pushed the east folk out of Germany he headed south across the Alps into Italy and in AD 962 he had Charlemagne's crown as Holy Roman Emperor bestowed upon him by the Pope. Otto took control of northern Italy in the process, and as in eastern Europe, he planted his new territories with warriors who owed him feudal allegiance. Today Florence's most ancient families trace their pedigrees back to the hundred or so feudal knights whose castles controlled the Tuscan hills.

The Frescobaldi claim descent from two of the warrior clans who came to Tuscany as tenants of the Emperor and ended up owner-occupiers – the Frescos and the Baldos. Fresco means fresh, and Baldo means bold, and today a graphic, if over-imaginative genealogical tree in one of the family's country houses (see back cover) demonstrates how the fresh and the bold came together to create a vibrant new dynasty that extended its power down from the hills into the city of Florence.

It was the comparatively peaceful conditions created by Otto and his successors in the tenth and eleventh centuries that made possible the early development of Florence. Italy was one of the few places in Europe where something of Rome's old city culture had been preserved after the barbarian invasions, and Florence sheltered inside its original Roman fortifications at the point where the Via Flaminia crossed the River Arno – the site of the present Ponte Vecchio. It was an ideal position as international commerce revived after the Dark Ages to take advantage of the trade routes opening up between the Mediterranean and northern Europe.

The city's speciality was cloth – spinning, weaving, fulling, dyeing. Banking and financial facilities developed to service the production and distribution of this early medieval fashion industry, and Florence's increasingly prosperous population provided a healthy marketplace for the agricultural estates of the neighbouring hills. Noblemen came into town to supervise the sale of their produce. Their womenfolk came to order clothes. They built themselves town houses, and so began the half-town, half-country style of existence that the Frescobaldi and other Florentine dynasties pursue to this day.

Florence's urbanized feudal noblemen were known as *grandi* or *magnati*, and they soon came to dominate the life of the town. From springtime onwards they would spend much of their time in the cool of the hills, hunting, hawking and supervising the harvest. But with autumn it was time to go down to market again, and winters would be spent inside Florence socializing, and, to an increasing degree, reinvesting their agricultural profits in commercial enterprises in the town.

The dominance of the *magnati* sprang from the military protection they could afford the city in times of trouble. They were indubitably the upper crust. But successful businessmen from the town bought estates in the country alongside those of the traditional feudal nobility, and the offspring of both military and mercantile stock were allowed to mingle and marry, so that, by the middle of the twelfth century, Florence and its surrounding countryside were unified under the control of an elite which was a mixture of the old military families and the rising urban bourgeoisie.

This relatively harmonious interaction of warriors with merchants was unusual in the early Middle Ages. In northern Europe the developing cities often came into conflict with the landed noblemen who controlled the countryside around them. Robber barons pillaged the packhorse trains of traders, and towns retaliated by giving support to kings and emperors in their battles against overmighty feudal subjects. Merchant and aristocrat were competing for scarce resources.

But the wealth generated by Florence, Venice and other northern Italian cities created an identity of interest between the town and its *contado* – the neighbouring locality. The combination of small industrialized settlement with fertile surrounding countryside made up a balanced little economic mechanism in which all components prospered: in terms of comfort, culture and general enjoyment of life, Florence with its *contado* was a self-contained social unit two centuries or more in advance of anything north of the Alps.

So from an early date the noblemen of the Tuscan hills found they had more in common with their local town than they did with their military superior, the regional margrave. When Pope and Emperor disputed the overlordship of Tuscany following a gap in the margravial succession in 1115, Florence took the opportunity to establish its own authority over its *contado*, and thanks to the hill warriors, the city had a strong army to enforce its claim. The Frescobaldi name figured on the Florentine rolls of honour for the battles for Arezzo in 1288 and Pistoia in 1313.

Yet by this date fighting was only a family sideline. The Frescobaldi held onto their country estates. Land gave them status, a leisurely summer lifestyle and security. But the mercantile development of Florence was offering all manner of other investment opportunities. Claiming the patronage of St Matthew, the financiers of the city were displacing the Lombards and the Jews as Europe's bankers: their accounting was streamlined by the use of Arabic numerals and double entry book-keeping and they showed how trade could be speeded up and simplified by using paper credits instead of cash. In 1262 they issued the first letters of exchange – and their credit was so good that their own coin, the florin, became acceptable as currency all over Europe.

The sheer volume of wealth generated inside twelfth- and thirteenth-century Florence proved irresistible to the *magnati* of the country hill forts, and the Frescobaldi put up no more resistance than their fellow nobles. They came down into town to make their own profits in the marketplace, and by the end of the

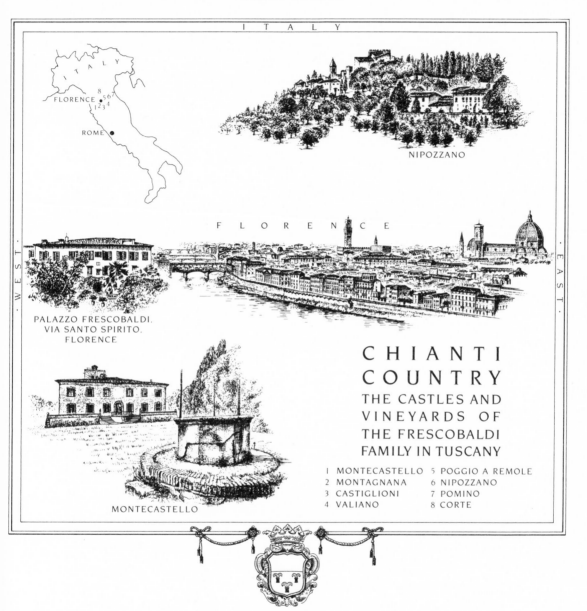

ITALY

FLORENCE

WEST · EAST ·

NIPOZZANO

PALAZZO FRESCOBALDI,
VIA SANTO SPIRITO,
FLORENCE

MONTECASTELLO

CHIANTI COUNTRY
THE CASTLES AND VINEYARDS OF THE FRESCOBALDI FAMILY IN TUSCANY

1 MONTECASTELLO	5 POGGIO A REMOLE
2 MONTAGNANA	6 NIPOZZANO
3 CASTIGLIONI	7 POMINO
4 VALIANO	8 CORTE

thirteenth century they were proving to be as fresh and bold at business as they were upon the battlefield.

The centre of Florence lay on the north side of the River Arno, and land there was at a premium. So the Frescobaldi set themselves up on the south bank, where land was cheaper because it lay on the wrong side of the river. Then, in 1252, the family built a bridge connecting their land to the town, so they were not on the wrong side any more. Today that bridge is the Ponte Santa Trinità (the modern structure, the fourth on the site, is a copy of a design by Ammannati) and the land where they set up their trading base is the Piazza Frescobaldi.

Traffic hurtles through the Piazza Frescobaldi nowadays, and up the nearby Via Santo Spirito where the Frescobaldi's palace stands. The family inhabit the upper floors in a maze of high-ceilinged silk- and brocade-hung chambers where Renaissance masterworks jigsaw together like snapshots in a crowded album. Life is communal. Each of the four brothers who head the clan has his own family apartment there, but wives and children, sisters and cousins with their own cooks, cleaners and butlers intermingle in the warren of staircases and corridors, gathering together in one or other of the salons or dining rooms for a meal or drinks, then dispersing again to their own corner of the building. The lower floors are let off to expensive-smelling leather shops and interior decorators who sell white marble and gold knicknacks to Saudi sheikhs. Spare space should earn money.

Money was the family business from the start – taking a percentage on almost anything – and the Frescobaldi's knightly traditions soon took on a financial tinge. When Charles of Anjou came to Italy to conquer Naples and Sicily with the blessing of the Pope in the middle of the thirteenth century, the aid the Frescobaldi gave him was not military in the conventional feudal sense. They formed a syndicate with other Florentine entre-preneurs to lend Charles 3000 livres, and this financial backing proved crucial to his success. Members of the family went south in the wake of Charles's army – he repaid his debts by granting the Frescobaldi trading concessions in his new domains – and when he came north to Florence in 1273 to thank his backers, the new King of Naples and Sicily set up his tents in the gardens of the Frescobaldi.

To medieval rulers the Frescobaldi represented a new sort of nobleman, much more useful and flexible than the conventional knight on horseback, for the technology of war was changing. Around the turn of the twelfth century a new and frightening weapon had come into use, the crossbow, with a firepower so lethal that in 1139 a church council denounced it as an inhuman instrument of destruction. A crossbow dart could pierce chain-mail, and in northern Europe the longbow had a similarly devastating – and democratizing – effect upon the mounted warrior.

The knightly response to this, sheet metal beaten into an articulated 'suit' of armour, increased the shock power, but greatly decreased the flexibility of cavalry on the battlefield: unhorsed and flat on his back, the heavily armoured knight was a ludicrous and pathetic figure – and the advent of gunpowder completed his obsolescence. Brass cannon were being cast in Florence in 1324, and in 1346 the English army used them for the first time at the battle of Crécy.

Firearms, like the crossbow, required full-time trained operatives, and this had already led to the emergence of the mercenary fighter. At the time of Magna Carta one of the barons' complaints against King John had been his hiring of Flemish soldiers; the Popes raised mercenary armies as a matter of course from early in the thirteenth century. Oaths of feudal loyalty and obligation remained the theoretical framework of society, but, in practice, warfare was no longer a matter of fields to pasture knights' horses – it was a matter of purchasing power.

Raising cash, however, was difficult in an economy where many transactions were still a matter of simple barter. The alchemy which turned goods into money was understood by few, and the precocious development of northern Italian cities like Florence put their financiers in demand all over Europe, for the Frescobaldi and families like the Bardi and Peruzzi were part merchant, part banker, and they had discovered how those two trades could be combined to dramatic effect.

The Roman Catholic church had particular need of their services. Until the Reformation the church was Europe's largest landowner – the estates controlled by some religious orders far outstripped those of any single prince or ruler – but it was not always easy to convert the produce of these lands into useful revenue. So, along with other Florentine entrepreneurs, the Frescobaldi offered the church their services as merchant bankers – and they became collectors of taxes for the Pope.

By the year 1280 members of the family were in England

touring the monasteries on the Pope's behalf, and since the monks had little ready cash to offer, the Frescobaldi took wool instead, to the local value of the tax due from that particular establishment. Then they would transport the wool back to Florence, where the booming textile factories needed all the raw material they could get and were paying some of the highest prices in Europe.

The system suited everybody. The monks had no need to pay out cash. The Pope received the full value of his assessment without any collection expenses – and the Frescobaldi took their profit.

The English were greatly impressed by these clever Italians. England's Plantagenet kings were facing the same problem as the Pope, trying to squeeze money for their wars out of the primitive economy of a country still emerging from the Dark Ages, so they recruited the Frescobaldi to give them help. Edward I was trying to finance his massive castle-building programme in Wales and war with France, and in 1277 the family made him the first of many loans to be recorded in the archives of the exchequer.

It was a small and cautious transaction, with the risk spread prudently between three other merchant banking families, the Bardi, Cerchi and Falconieri. But one loan led to another – Edward I lived in an almost perpetual state of conflict – and by the end of the thirteenth century the Frescobaldi were acting as chief bankers to the English throne. Between 1294 (when the previous Italians to lend money to the English crown, the Riccardi of Lucca, were bankrupted) and 1311 the Frescobaldi loans to the crown totalled £155,531 8s 2d – in an age when one could live in state on £20 a year. The Frescobaldi were the Bank of England.

The Frescobaldi have been credited with establishing the Royal Mint in London, but furnaces for minting coin had, in fact, been established in England before the family arrived. All the English Mints had exchanges attached to them, however, which supervised international coinage transactions, and in 1300 one Amerigo Frescobaldi was made Warden of the exchanges of London, Canterbury, Newcastle-on-Tyne, Kingston-upon-Hull, Bristol, Exeter and Dublin.

For an Italian merchant banker to forsake the comfort and sophistication of Florence in order to teach the thirteenth-century

English how to do their sums must have been rather like a graduate of the Harvard Business School being sent on secondment to the Third World today. Early medieval England had few stone buildings and for most of the year life was a damp and draughty battle to keep warm. Coming to terms with its barbarities called for major adjustments, and one member of the Frescobaldi, Giovanni, sent home advice to those members of the family planning to follow him. When dealing with the natives, he said, you must be cautious:

Do not wear bright colours. Be humble. Look as though you are stupid, but make sure you stay on your toes. Give the appearance of being generous. Pay your way as you go. When you collect your debts, do it courteously, suggesting that *you* are the poor one. Do not get too nosy. Buy whenever you see a bargain, but be wary of deals that involve men of the Court. Do as you are told by those who hold the power, and make sure you stay on good terms with your fellow Italians. Lock and bolt your door early at night.

By 1306 there was a whole colony of Frescobaldi living in England. The family were making loans and acting as bankers to individual members of the local nobility, as well as to the City of London, and two of them had picked up well-paid appointments in the church.

But it was still the crown that was the chief source of their business, for as the Plantagenet kings overspent and found difficulty in paying their debts, so the Frescobaldi took over royal offices and commercial monopolies in lieu of payment. When Edward II found he lacked the cash to meet one particular set of obligations, he granted Amerigo Frescobaldi the right to gather the royal taxes due from Gascony and Bordeaux, so the Italian could collect repayment of his loan from source, and by 1306 royal debts to the family had grown to such an extent that the Frescobaldi were granted supervision of the customs houses in practically every major English port. Henceforward all customs duties would go not to the King but straight to the Frescobaldi.

For a few years at the beginning of the fourteenth century the Frescobaldi family were effectively running the finances of England and its possessions in France, and their importance was acknowledged in 1310 when Berto Frescobaldi was appointed a member of the royal privy council. The knights from the Tuscan hills had come to share in the magic of kingship – but through their feats with the account book, not with the sword.

One of the many stops that the Lord Odysseus made on his journey home from Troy to Ithaca was among the Phaeacians. They were holding games – racing, wrestling, jumping and discus throwing – the traditional pastimes of the ancient Greek aristocracy. But Odysseus himself was too tired to take part. He was feeling homesick and depressed, and he sat by himself in a corner, moping.

One of the princes of the Phaeacians misunderstood his noble melancholy. He suspected that this visitor who looked like a well-born fighter with his muscular thighs, legs and firmset neck, might in fact be an imposter, scared to take part in the games lest it be discovered he was not truly noble.

So the prince taunted Odysseus that he was not what he seemed.

'More like, I think, you are a sea captain, one who plies here and there, a master of trading sailors; anxious over the cargo out, watchful over the cargo home and your commercial profit.'

It was an insult Odysseus could not possibly accept, and without even troubling to remove his cloak, he jumped up and seized a discus from the pile – the biggest and thickest, far more massive than any the Phaeacians had used themselves. Whirling it, Odysseus sent the great stone whizzing through the air so that the crowd at the far end of the field had to throw themselves to the ground to avoid being hit, and his mark far outdistanced any other – conclusive proof that he was not a merchant.

This story from *The Odyssey* is the earliest known example in Western literature of the aristocrat's contempt for 'trade'. It echoes through succeeding centuries – commerce ranked far below war and public service in the Roman hierarchy of esteem – but it does not seem to have been a social issue in Europe in the early Middle Ages. It was not until mercantile families like the Frescobaldi began challenging the supremacy of the established military nobility that aristocrats started concerning themselves about how it was proper, and not proper, to behave. 'U and non-U' date from the day when the 'U's' started worrying that they might not be so superior as they had once thought they were.

The military caste was brought under threat by the attention that kings and princes started paying to merchants who could catch their ears with talk of loans and letters of credit. Prowess on the battlefield was no longer enough, and as the very titles once restricted to the mounted horsemen were handed out to clerks, lawyers and financiers, so the traditional military aristocracy sought to bolster its status with something that money could not buy, a class-based code of conduct whose name made explicit the importance that its practitioners attached to the horse and horse rider – chivalry.

Traditional feudal warriors like Hugh Lupus, the scourge of the Welsh marches, do not appear to have concerned themselves greatly with the morality of what they were doing. Their job was often a nasty one, and they usually executed it in a nasty fashion – as the Victorian Hugh Lupus discovered. But towards the end of the eleventh century, a novel notion started taking hold among Europe's aristocrats: the idea that an officer should also be a gentleman.

Traditional songs and tales of ancient heroes had provided entertainment around camp fires and in baronial halls for generations. But in the twelfth century these traditions started to become formalized into the *chansons de geste* whose purpose went beyond entertainment to articulate and glorify a code of especially knightly behaviour. *The Song of Roland*, *The Song of the Cid*, *The Song of the Niebelungs* and, most polished and elaborate of all, the thirteenth-century *Morte Arthure*, all harked back to a simple world, uncorrupted by money. They paid little heed to historical authenticity, clothing their Dark Age heroes in medieval doublet and hose, but their objectives were not historical: in an era when the knight was becoming militarily obsolete, they were a structured and self-conscious defensive reflex – like the ceremonies of knightly initiation, which also developed during the twelfth century.

The *chansons de geste*, knightly ordeals, knightly dress and even a special knightly way of talking all attempted to formalize the intangible components of aristocracy into a sort of priesthood with rules of admission which could give it a monopoly of nobility

– rather as the Catholic church's preservation of a dead language gave the religious a monopoly of contemporary knowledge. In the eleventh century the word 'knight' had meant simply a well-equipped soldier on horseback. It was essentially a technical term carrying little social significance. But by the end of the thirteenth century, being a knight had become synonymous with being a member of an elite whose separate identity was jealously guarded.

'No one shall acquire the standing of a knight,' declared the Emperor Frederick II in 1231, 'who is not of knightly family unless by grace of our special licence.' In 1235 the Cortes of Catalonia in session near Barcelona decreed that 'no one shall be knighted unless he is a knight's son' – and in Provence there were rules for the noblewoman as well: she was defined as one who goes 'neither to the oven, nor to the wash-house, nor to the mill'. In a famous case of 1393, Charles VI of France forbade a nobleman from selling the products of his vineyards with the words, 'It is not proper for a noble to be an innkeeper.'

It is difficult to imagine William the Conqueror or the Emperor Otto making any such distinction. The surviving plans of traditional feudal manor houses reveal little segregation between master and men, the whole household living together communally. Not until the twelfth and thirteenth centuries do the private dining room and the servants' quarters make an appearance.

These were the years when, in England, the House of Lords started its evolution away from the Commons and when a hierarchy inside the nobility itself started to take shape: the first English duke was created in 1337, the first marquess in 1385. In France strict sumptuary laws sought to regulate who could and who could not dress as a nobleman, and the distinction developed between the *noblesse d'épée*, the traditional military aristocracy, and the *noblesse de robe*, the lawyers, administrators and financiers on whose services kings were coming more and more to rely.

Tournaments of arms were another way in which aristocrats sought to identify military prowess with social cachet. In theory jousting and combat were good practice for the battlefield, but there is no solid evidence of tournaments being held before the twelfth century. The first records of organized tournaments date from the 1120s and 1130s – the same church council which denounced the crossbow in 1139 also denounced the new fashion of jousting – and tournament rule books made clear the essentially social purpose of the exercise: under one German set of rules the principal grounds for exclusion from the tournament – apart from murder, theft or plain dishonesty – were money lending and marrying below your social station.

The development of coats of arms and heraldry was the most graphic way in which the military aristocrats, under threat, endeavoured to protect their separate status. Theoretically, coats of arms helped distinguish friend from foe on the field of battle. But battles had been fought happily for centuries without them until the advent of the tournament. Ornamented shields started life as the equivalent of modern racing colours – which exist for the benefit of the spectator, not the participant – sporting emblems, worn for one afternoon only, to simplify the job of the tournament heralds.

The genealogical usefulness of the device became apparent when quarterings developed, with a father handing on his jousting colours, and sons being anxious to display their connections on their mother's side. The quartered coat of arms came to symbolize the social exclusiveness which the tournament of arms was intended to foster, and by the beginning of the fourteenth century it was a normal tournament rule that only warriors whose armorial pedigree could show four noble grandparents were entitled to participate.

It was a dispute over heraldry which provided the first documentary evidence of the Grosvenor family's medieval activities – in 1385, when the English army was gathering to invade Scotland. It was nearly forty years since the battle of Crécy, when cannon had first made their appearance as an English weapon of war, and Richard II was confident of repeating that famous victory.

But as the warlords gathered, a dispute broke out in the camp, for Sir Richard Scrope, first Lord Scrope of Bolton, Royal Treasurer, Steward of the King's Household and twice Chancellor of England, was indignant to discover his coat of arms being sported by an unknown Cheshire gentleman, Sir Robert Grosvenor. It was as if a Coldstream colonel had spotted a Guards tie round the neck of an off-duty Pay Corps clerk, for Scrope was one of the great of the land, and since the country squire would not yield, the dispute went to court.

The arms in question were simple enough to look at, a plain gold diagonal stripe across a shield – a 'Bend Or' in the language of heraldry. But the two claimants argued over it as if their mothers' honour were at stake. Grosvenor produced endless Cheshire dignitaries to prove that the Bend Or had been a Grosvenor symbol from time immemorial, and Scrope drummed up similar claims among his own friends, John of Gaunt, with his son Henry Bolingbroke, the Earl of Northumberland with his son, Harry Percy – and a scribe called Geoffrey Chaucer.

Against such testimony, Grosvenor really did quite well, coming away with the right to bear the Bend Or provided he would modify it with the addition of a new border round his shield. But the Cheshire gentleman was not satisfied and, in wanting all, he ended up with less than nothing, for he appealed his case to Richard II, who declared that the Grosvenors had no right at all to the golden stripe, with or without a modifying border. The Bend Or, said the King, should be borne by the Scropes alone. The Grosvenors would have to make do with golden wheatsheaves on their shield – and they would also have to pay all the costs of the case, on both sides.

The Bend Or case almost bankrupted the Grosvenors, but it did teach them a valuable lesson. Their family mythology insists that the Scropes only won because they had special access to the King, and today this leads Gerald Grosvenor to draw one simple conclusion from the fate of his ancestors: 'Only go to battle when you know that you can win.'

Such pragmatism may be less than chivalrous. If Roland had operated on that basis he would never have bothered to try to hold the pass at Roncesvalles – but he would have lived to fight another day and that, in the long term, is what aristocracy is all about. In the high Middle Ages the average noble dynasty in England lasted no more than three generations, largely falling prey to battlefield mortality, for the cult of chivalry was also the cult of death.

But while the development of the cash economy in Europe

*Head of the family, the Marquis Dino Frescobaldi,
with his wife Lisa at Poggio a Remole, one of the
family estates near Florence*

Bona, Marchesa de' Frescobaldi, entertaining in style

*From left to right, her daughters, Angelica,
Fiammetta and Diana Frescobaldi*

Knight in plastic armour. Lamberto Frescobaldi

RIGHT: *Lamberto's wine. Bottles are laid down at the birth of every Frescobaldi: 200 per girl, 500 per boy*

Monte Castello della Pineta, outside Florence,
the oldest Frescobaldi home

RIGHT: *Poggio a Remole, Tuscan home of Dino*
Frescobaldi. The great hall

*Ferdinando Frescobaldi, Marquis in charge of wine
sales, Italy*

in the eleventh and twelfth centuries ended the dominance of the mounted warrior, it did not mean the end of the social signals by which his pre-eminence had been characterized. Land retained military and economic significance, and the new rich who had profited from trade or royal service hastened to buy country estates. Riding a horse remained a token of aristocracy, and the modern character of the institution was set – not so much a fixed group of people as an identifiable set of values and conventions shared by the elite and those recruited to its ranks.

Aristocracy has been compared to a five-star hotel which passes on its cachet to each successive group of guests. Yet guests have no stake in a hotel. It was control of the land that had been the original expression of western Europe's military aristocrat, and that continued to be the distinguishing characteristic of nobility when country estates were taken over by merchants as well as soldiers. Ownership changed but the soil remained, for in a mercantile world, as in a military one, land is the enduring reality. It is sometimes possible to trace the boundaries of Europe's great estates back to Roman times, the line of river or hill stamping its ultimate authority upon transitory occupiers.

In 1311, at the height of their power and prosperity in England, the Frescobaldi were suddenly brought down when the native feudal aristocracy struck back at the power that foreigners had come to exercise over Edward II. The Italians' assets were confiscated, and every single Frescobaldi was chased out of the country. Back in Florence the family discovered that their ancient status as *magnati* had come under threat from an anti-aristocratic movement of textile guildsmen organized by a clan of demagogues whose name was Medici, and after a couple of decades seeking to re-establish their traditional pre-eminence, the Frescobaldi gave up the struggle and retired from the city.

In later centuries the family were to revive their activities as businessmen, but for the time being they withdrew to their estates and went back to being country gentlemen again. That was the great advantage of owning land.

BLUE BLOOD: that which flows in the veins of old and aristocratic families, a trans. of the Spanish *sangre azul* attributed to some of the oldest and proudest families of Castile, who claimed never to have been contaminated by Moorish, Jewish or other foreign admixture: the expression probably originated in the blueness of the veins of people of fair complexion as compared with those of dark skin.

Oxford English Dictionary, 1971

IV · BLUE
BLOOD

I T was the Spaniards who gave the world the curious notion that an aristocrat's blood is not red but blue. The Spanish nobility started taking shape around the ninth century in classic military fashion, occupying land as warriors on horseback. They were to continue the process for more than five hundred years, clawing back sections of the peninsula from its Moorish occupiers, and a nobleman demonstrated his pedigree by holding up his sword arm to display the filigree of blue-blooded veins beneath his pale skin – proof that his birth had not been contaminated by the dark-skinned enemy.

Sangre azul, blue blood, was thus a euphemism for being a white man – Spain's own particular reminder that the refined footsteps of the aristocracy through history carry the rather less refined spoor of racism. Whenever the Rothschilds went to visit the first, Victorian, Duke of Westminster, they used to notice the strange difficulty that he and the rest of the Grosvenor household had in remembering the name of the Duke's favourite gun dog, Joe – for Joe's name had, in fact, been changed for the weekend. Normally he was known as Jew.

The Spanish concern with racial purity stems, of course, from the fact that Spaniards mingled and married freely with their Arab conquerors in the early days of the Moorish occupation, so no matter how vividly his veins show through his skin, no Spaniard can swear his ancestry lacks Moorish blood – or Jewish blood either, for that matter.

There was certainly Jewish blood in the veins of the forefather who built the Duchess of Medinaceli's magnificent palace in Seville, but he is not the forefather with whom the Duchess really likes to start counting. Her family prefer to trace their pedigree back to the bluest blood of all – the Kings of Castile and Léon whose twelfth- and thirteenth-century campaigns against the Moors started giving the reconquest of the peninsula real impetus.

King Alfonso X of Castile, nicknamed 'the Wise', had two sons – Sancho, nicknamed 'the Brave', and his elder brother Fernando, nicknamed 'la Cerda' – 'the Bristle' – on account of one solitary black whisker that sprouted with rare vigour from his otherwise hairless chest. With the aid of this singular talisman Fernando was hacking out a reputation for himself as a warrior, inspiring the armies of Castile in their crusade against the Moors – until 1275, when he was killed in battle, leaving his inheritance to two small sons.

The elder of these sons, Alfonso, was now, by rights, heir to the throne of Castile, and his grandfather brought the boy up as his successor. But the dead Fernando's younger brother, Sancho, disputed this, and on the death of the old king in 1284 Sancho took the throne for himself.

So young Alfonso de la Cerda acquired a new nickname, 'Alfonso el Desheredado' – the disinherited – and he confirmed this in the course of three consecutive reigns in which he tried, and failed, to recapture the succession. He evidently did not have his father's bristle.

But the hereditary vigour did re-emerge in Alfonso's grand-daughter Isabella, a spirited lady who was first widowed at the age of twelve. Married and widowed again, she subsequently managed to arrange a third marriage for herself, at the age of forty-six, to Bernardo de Foix, himself the illegitimate son of a French count, and together Isabella and Bernardo set about establishing a noble dynasty. In her late forties Isabella succeeded in producing a son, while Bernardo, a rough but effective soldier of fortune, secured for his descendants the title Count of Medina-celi – Medinaceli being a hill fortress on the border of Castile. So much for blue blood.

Today the town of Medinaceli is forlorn and decayed. The road winds up a dry hillside to the bald rocky plateau whose military usefulness was first realized by the Romans – there is still a Roman arch at the entrance to the town – then the tarmac peters out into dust and pebbles. It takes some searching to dig out an old priest who will unlock the church in whose crypt lie the coffins of fourteen Medinaceli, and when, climbing up inside the church tower to look at the view, you feel a hint of resistance beneath the sole of your shoe, there follows a saddening, delicate splintering. It is so long since anyone walked up to the belfry that birds are nesting on the steps, and they have laid their eggs there.

Seen from above, the town takes on the air of a film set – and, it seems, the greatest excitement the locality has known for generations was when a film company came there some years back to shoot a tortilla-western. A few of the original peasant dwellings have been feebly gentrified by foreigners and week-enders from Madrid, just ninety miles distant, but most of the place lies derelict, peopled only by long-haired shadows with pallid complexions and open sandals who, if they see you coming, turn off down another path.

Occupying one long side of the open square is the palace of the family which takes its name from this shell that used to be a town. The Counts of Medinaceli were raised to dukes in 1479, and in the eighteenth century they built themselves this sweeping, balconied summer residence. It was a refuge for bewigged and ruffed grandees, happy to escape from the dust and heat of Madrid into the relative cool of the hills.

But today the palace lies even more derelict than the rest of the town. Its roof has fallen in, and the main courtyard has surrendered to a jungle of weeds and brambles. A few years ago some radical souls commandeered a wing of the palace to serve as a community cinema and as a play centre for the children, but now the building cannot even support this vestigial use. The ceilings that survive are too unsafe. The Duchess of Medinaceli offered the local council a long lease on the palace for one peseta, providing they would spend their own money on its restoration. But the mayor decided there were better uses for hard-scraped rates and taxes. So the summer palace just stands there, crumbling a little more with every passing year.

The family themselves are embarrassed. Ignacio, Duke of Segorbe, youngest of the Duchess's sons and chief custodian of the family heritage, says that he would like to organize a rescue, but that the means are not there.

'We cannot afford to repair it. The village cannot afford to repair it. The government cannot afford to repair it. So what can we do?'

The only remaining answer, to sell the palace off to whatever visionary, multi-millionaire or madman would dare to dedicate himself to the endeavour of restoration does not seem feasible either, since the Medinaceli are not prepared to sell it freehold. They are only prepared to grant a lease. Their palace may be a ruin, but at least it is a family ruin.

The home where Doña Victoria Eugenia, Duchess of Medinaceli, prefers to spend most of her time is definitely a less mournful place. The Casa de Pilatos in Seville is more the style of setting you expect of a lady who is twelve times a Grandee of Spain – though in terms of architecture it represents the most exuberant denial of blue blood imaginable: Moorish tiles, Greek statues, Roman busts, Gothic stoneware – if ever a building were a mongrel, it is the Casa de Pilatos. Standing in one corner you could imagine yourself in a mosque at Marrakesh; in another, you have been transported to the private library of an English country gentleman. The sheer energy of the cultural interbreeding makes analogies of mixed marriage inappropriate. The Casa de Pilatos is an ethnic orgy – and that is only fitting, given the origins of the man who laid its foundations.

CASTLES
IN SPAIN
THE TITLES OF
THE DUCHESS
OF MEDINACELI

DUKE
MARQUIS
COUNT
VISCOUNT

Don Pedro Enríquez was a landowner and entrepreneur who developed a flourishing business in soap. His soap factories stood on the banks of the Guadalquivir River outside Seville, and he was descended from the liaison between Alfonso XI of Castile and his Jewish mistress.

There was comparatively little anti-semitism in Spain during

71

the years of the fiercest fighting with the Moors. Between the peasantry and the still largely military aristocracy, the Jews constituted an able middle class of doctors, lawyers, administrators and merchants – and the funds for the final and glorious reconquest of Granada in 1492 were largely provided by Jewish financiers.

But Jewish expertise and prosperity provoked in Spain the animosity which it encountered elsewhere in Europe, and local prejudice was intensified by the doctrines of blue-bloodedness fostered by the long campaign against the Arabs.

The notion of Spanish racial purity held no more validity vis-à-vis Jews than it did with the Moors. Like Don Pedro Enríquez, the great King Ferdinand the Catholic himself had recent Jewish blood in his pedigree. But as success against the Arabs made the Jews less and less necessary to the Christian community, so prejudice and pogroms intensified against them, and the decree finally banishing all Jews from Spain unless they converted to Roman Catholicism was issued in 1492, the very year of final victory over the Moors.

Ex-Jewish Catholics were known as *conversos* and a number of them, rabbis amongst them, distinguished themselves by becoming more Catholic than their former persecutors. Torquemada, the first Inquisitor General, notorious for the tortures which he inflicted on *conversos* whose conversion was suspected of not being sincere enough, was himself a new Christian of Jewish descent, and Don Pedro Enríquez profited from Torquemada's autos-da-fé to acquire the land on which the first foundations of the Casa de Pilatos were laid.

Conversos who fell foul of the Inquisition forfeited their lands as well as their lives, and when a small palace on Seville's Calle Imperial fell vacant for this reason, Don Pedro Enríquez snapped it up. He bought up one plot of land next door to it, then another, and another, until, by the beginning of the sixteenth century, he had reached the next street westwards in the block and owned a broad belt of land on which he could really build in style.

Don Pedro died in 1514. He had married well, into the de Ribera family, and his son Fadrique, bearing the grand surname Enríquez de Ribera, acquired a prestigious title shortly after his father's death. He was created Marquis of Tarifa and he promptly

72

set about constructing an ancestral home appropriate to his new dignity.

The curious name Casa de Pilatos comes from a pilgrimage that Don Fadrique, Marquis of Tarifa, undertook in 1518 to the Holy Land via Italy. Ostensibly the excursion was inspired by genuine piety, but it also took the form of a cultural grand tour, for the young Marquis returned to Seville with all sorts of artistic ideas as to how his new home could be embellished in classical fashion – and among them was the notion that its design should be modelled upon the palace of Pontius Pilate in Jerusalem.

How the Marquis developed this fancy is uncertain. The building where Pilate washed his hands can no longer have existed in sixteenth-century Jerusalem – though that would not have prevented some enterprising local guide from pointing it out to a wealthy Spanish tourist.

The most likely explanation stems from the reconstructions of Calvary being built outside Spanish towns as they were reconquered from the Moors. These artificial hills, complete with a trio of crosses hung with lifelike cadavers, were like twentieth-century war memorials, cloaking the naked celebration of victory with more seemly robes, and every Easter a young Christ from the town would process out to the shrine, stopping at the stations of the cross along the way. The first station in every Holy Week procession symbolized Pilate's house, and in Seville that stop occurred beside the land on which Marquis of Tarifa was building his new palace.

Yet the resemblance between the Casa de Pilatos and the *praetorium* of a Roman governor begins and ends with its name, for its character derives from its whimsy, not from the faithfulness of its historical reconstruction. One day in 1528, several dozen marble columns, some marble fountains and one thirty-foot-tall triumphant arch were unloaded onto the banks of the Guadalquivir. They had been brought back from Genoa in the holds of the family soap ships as dead weight, and they were the beginnings of the grand courtyard which the Marquis had dreamed up on his way back from the Holy Land.

By the standards of holiday souvenirs the pillars were bulky, and by the standards of architectural practice they were eccentric to say the least. Classical columns are traditionally carved with a slight bulge in the middle to counteract the visual illusion of concavity created by a straight, upright object. But this *entasis*, or stretching of the Marquis of Tarifa's columns would have made them roll in the holds and unbalance the family ships. So they had been carved straight, and it is this that gives the pillars of Pilatos their endearing, but definitely un-Roman fragility as they uphold the Moorish arches in the main courtyard (see picture following p. 208).

This idiosyncrasy is enhanced by the fact that no two arches are exactly the same. For reasons never explained, the pillars are placed haphazardly around the courtyard, some almost rubbing shoulders, some far apart. But the arches do, at least, match from one floor to the next, for this was the point of building the courtyard in two tiers. In the sixteenth century the family would inhabit the cool, tiled ground-floor rooms in summer, then move upstairs in autumn to the warmer, tapestry-hung chambers, the impact of this biannual migration being softened by the pattern of the downstairs wall tiling, designed to look like the tapestries above.

Today the Duchess of Medinaceli and her family all live upstairs, surrendering the lower floor of their palace to tourists earnestly analysing what is Roman and what is Moorish in the long, shaded arcades – or just happy for the chance to escape from the hot Seville sun. The Duchess's sons all have apartments around the palace, and the youngest of them, Ignacio, Duke of Segorbe, has converted a pigeon loft over the family archives into a futuristic penthouse (see picture following p. 208).

He remembers how, one day as a little boy, he was playing football in one of the upper arcades of the main courtyard, when his ball knocked a piece of whitewash off the wall. A face was peering out, and picking away at the whitewash around it, the young Duke of Segorbe uncovered part of a sixteenth-century fresco – though his mother's delight at the discovery was somewhat tempered.

'It cost a fortune to have the rest of the fresco uncovered and to have it restored.'

The Duchess was scarcely more amused in the 1960s when

the Moorish atmosphere of the Casa de Pilatos suggested itself to the producers of the film *Lawrence of Arabia*. The strange mixture of east and west made it an ideal location for the British headquarters in Jerusalem where Peter O'Toole, in Arab dress, gets ostracized by his fellow officers. Somehow this sequence took longer to film than anticipated, and the cameras and crew stayed several weeks more in the Casa de Pilatos than they had originally arranged – without paying any extra fee.

The Duchess would not have minded if the sequence had involved Omar Sharif, who shares one of her chief passions in life. But he was elsewhere, and Peter O'Toole was not interested in playing bridge.

It is comparatively easy to get to the top. . . . But constant watchfulness and an alert and abiding energy are necessary to preserve through the centuries what a distant ancestor acquired. . . . Families that have long been able to survive that test are usually families in which the majority of individual members, at least, have been able to maintain a sense of restraint and proportion, and to resist the temptation to yield to impulsive desires.

GAETANO MOSCA,
The Ruling Class, 1939

I have been accused of being undignified. That is quite true, I am. If you take your dignity to a pawnbroker he won't give you much for it.

JOHN RUSSELL,
13th Duke of Bedford, 1971

V · CORRECT
ADDRESS

Aﬀﬁﬀ the endless gilded chambers hung with florid tapestries and baroque chandeliers it is quite a relief to enter the private sitting room of Prince Johannes von Thurn und Taxis. It is decorated in calm, cream tones, with modern furniture, and there are just a few small paintings on the walls.

The elderly relative whose portrait hangs above the fireplace obviously occupies a place of honour. The family likeness is not apparent, but he must have been the subject of quite recent conversation, for the three-year-old Princess Maria Theresia von Thurn und Taxis points up to him from time to time and calls him 'Franz'. The little girl smiles familiarly at the old man, as if he had come to call only a day or so ago – which is strange, because Franz von Taxis, the founding father of the Thurn und Taxis dynasty, died in 1517.

Most of us have old snapshots – if we have anything at all – to tell us what our grandfather or our great-grandparents looked like. A faded sepia image whose features echo with some eerie resonance of our own stares out briefly across the decades before we close the album, and unless it happens to be currently fashionable to put such memorabilia on display in farmhouse-style kitchen, or bathroom, the dead relatives are pushed back in the attic and forgotten about until the next spring cleaning.

But aristocrats like to hang their dead around them all the time. There may, occasionally, be artistic justification for this, if the forefather was painted by Gainsborough or Van Dyck. But it is remarkable how many of the portraits hung in aristocratic homes look as if they were executed by some local graduate of painting-by-numbers.

Art and aristocracy do not make happy bedfellows. The only British painter ever to be made a peer of the realm, Lord Leighton, died the day after his peerage was announced (in 1896). Picture collecting began to be incorporated into the noble ethos in the sixteenth century, and by the nineteenth century every gentleman was expected to have some paintings on his walls as a token of 'good taste'. It was a concept which mattered more and more to aristocrats as opportunities diminished for distinction on the battlefield – and the Liechtenstein family, in particular, cultivated their reputation as connoisseurs: in the seventeenth and eighteenth centuries they built up a hoard of art treasures which outdazzled certain royal collections.

But on the whole it was considered bad form to take art too seriously. 'Damn fellow, he admired my chairs,' growled the 17th Earl of Derby after one of his guests had waxed lyrical over the delicate furniture at Knowsley. When Boughton House in Northamptonshire was reopened in 1947 it was discovered that the Duke of Buccleuch had been happy to leave fourteen Van Dycks, for the duration of the war, in one of the lavatories. They were beautiful pictures, but they did not depict members of the family. The rather more mundane Buccleuch portraits, on the other hand, had been treated with considerably greater reverence. Ancestral paintings do not, on the whole, grace great halls and staircases for the sake of art – they are there for the sake of the ancestors.

It is consciousness of ancestors which gives aristocrats that sense of identity which is particular to them – the feeling of being members of a community, a team almost. Gerald Grosvenor frequently likes to describe himself as a 'caretaker' of the family assets which he has inherited and which he must pass on in as good or better state than he received them. If all the generations of a noble dynasty could meet up to talk it would be rather like the annual get-togethers for executives of multi-national corporations, where the Vice-President, Africa meets up with the Vice-President, Middle East to compare notes: the marquess in charge of the late nineteenth century could swap notes with the baronet who tried to shepherd the family through the Civil War, discussing how their particular stewardships were affected by the circumstances of their time.

Perhaps that is why religious feeling survives more strongly among aristocrats than it does among most other classes in the 1980s. Those who put their ancestors away in the attic are not likely to be naturally receptive to the idea of an eternal brotherhood from which all come and to which all return. But such an idea is more likely to appeal to those who, like the little Princess Maria Theresia von Thurn und Taxis, have been brought up to consider the dead around her as ever-present members of the family – even if they do sport funny clothes and hairstyles, and have not been around much recently.

Franz von Taxis was a successful entrepreneur in the Low Countries around the turn of the sixteenth century, hailing originally from Bergamo in northern Italy where the courier routes through the Alpine passes came together. Carrying letters was the family business, and sometime around 1500 Franz von Taxis moved his headquarters to Brussels, for he saw the possibility of his mail operations expanding there as a result of the marriage that Maximilian von Habsburg had contracted a few years earlier to the heiress, Maria of Burgundy.

Maria was heiress to Charles the Bold, ruler of Flanders and Artois – modern Belgium and Luxembourg – and her marriage to Maximilian was one of the major stepping stones which took the Habsburg family to their remarkable domination of Europe in the sixteenth century. The Habsburgs were Germanic nobles of traditional military origin – their name derived from their first family stronghold in what is today the Swiss canton of Aargau, the Habichtsburg or 'Hawk's Castle'. They had secured large areas in and around the Austrian Tyrol from the old Dukedom of Bavaria and, by fostering the support of other German aristocrats – notably the Liechtensteins – they had won for themselves the inheritance of Charlemagne, the succession to the Holy Roman Empire.

Holding the glorious and historic title of Holy Roman Emperor in the fifteenth and sixteenth centuries meant, in effect, being the German king. The Emperor commanded the allegiance of the several hundred margraves, dukes and princes whose little states made a patchwork of central Europe until Bismarck's unification of Germany at the end of the nineteenth century, and succession to the crown was by election. But once the Imperial title had been secured by Maximilian's father Frederick in 1452, it remained effectively the property of the Habsburg family, and it provided the basis for the extraordinary expansion of their power into the Netherlands, Spain, Italy and beyond.

The Habsburgs' secret of success was clever dynastic marriage – to which their portraits bear witness, uncannily reproducing the prominent jaw and lower lip of Maximilian's father from genera-tion to generation – and the late fifteenth-century alliance between Maximilian and Maria of Burgundy was the match that transferred their previously German powerbase onto the international stage.

The Taxis had been carrying Habsburg letters for some time between the Tyrol, northern Italy and Rome – so when Maximi-lian went north his postmen followed him. Merchants had always earned extra money or done favours for friends and rulers by transporting letters with their consignments of goods. But working out of Bergamo the Taxis had extended this principle, organizing courier routes and relay stations through the Alps which dealt in nothing but mail, and the Habsburg need to communicate between their Austrian and Netherlands headquar-ters led Franz von Taxis to extend the family's courier system still further. He set his post offices and relay stations at stages corresponding to the distance that one fresh horse could travel, and the Taxis courier would blow on his horn as he rode over the hill to warn the courier waiting in the valley below to get

Johannes Baptiste
de Jesus Maria Miguel Friedrich Bonifazius Lamoral,
11th Prince of Thurn und Taxis, born 1926

Founder of the dynasty, Franz von Taxis (1459–1517),
postman to princes

<small>LEFT:</small> *The library, Schloss St Emmeram, Regensburg*

Gloria, Princess of Thurn und Taxis, born in 1960,
Countess of Schönburg-Glauchau

Schloss St Emmeram, Regensburg, one room out of
five hundred

Pater Emmeram, uncle of Prince Johannes von Thurn und Taxis. LEFT: *His church, Neresheim Abbey, near Heidenheim, Baden-Württemberg. His father gave it to him when Pater Emmeram took Holy Orders*

*Schloss Taxis, Dischingen, the summer castle of
Prince Johannes von Thurn und Taxis; he has ten
others*

saddled up; then the mail bags would change hands outside the stables, and the first courier would rest a little before returning home, carrying back a fresh load of mail to his own base.

Initially the Taxis couriers carried letters exclusively for the Habsburgs and their officials. But it was not long before the ambitious dynasty found itself in debt – and postman's bills were not a priority. So the Taxis family, faced in turn with debt, started carrying private letters to cover their expenses, and it was the least the Habsburgs could do, in return for the effectively free transmission which they now received of their own mail, to grant the obliging postmen a monopoly of courier rights in their territories.

With official endorsement and protection, the Taxis couriers were to become the free enterprise post office of the Habsburg domains. In 1505 Franz von Taxis was appointed Postmaster General to the Habsburg court in the Netherlands – and this was just the beginning. Maximilian's policy of empire building through marriage had resulted in the betrothal of his son Philip to Joanna, daughter of the Catholic monarchs Ferdinand and Isabella of Spain, and from this union came Charles V, destined to rule over Spain as well as over the Low Countries and the rest of the Habsburgs' German, Austrian and Italian possessions.

So the Taxis communications system became necessary south of the Pyrenees as well, and in 1505 Franz von Taxis obtained the official contract for mail travelling between Brussels and Castile. He was paid 12,000 livres a year to maintain communications between the Spanish court, the Netherlands, the French court and the court of the Emperor Maximilian wherever he might be in Germany and as Spanish antennae spread out in turn towards the New World, so letters from the Taxis system crossed the Atlantic with it – well on its way to becoming an intercontinental business whose like the world had never seen.

'We were the IBM of our time,' says Prince Johannes von Thurn und Taxis today. 'We weren't noblemen behind a bush in a quaint little castle, going shooting and fighting our neighbours. We weren't generals, sacrificing sons for national pride and making mothers unhappy. We weren't bastards of kings, only titled because of who our fathers were. We had other ideas in our heads. We were interested in communication. We started a new thing – connections of human understanding.'

The impact which printing had upon Renaissance Europe is well known. But the speeding up of communications that the Taxis couriers represented also played its part in the spreading of ideas through the tumultuous decades of the Reformation. The Taxis could get letters along their primary run, from Brussels to Innsbruck, in five and a half days in summer and six and a half in winter; from Brussels to Paris took forty hours, and Brussels to Toledo took twelve days.

'I sometimes wish,' says Prince Johannes, 'that I could get my letters delivered as quickly as that nowadays.'

The success of Franz von Taxis depended upon his relationship with the Habsburg family, for though there was nothing to stop other merchants carrying letters and parcels informally as they had always done, the Imperial monopoly meant that potential rivals could not set up post offices and exchange points to carry mail any further. It was not worth anyone trying to compete inside the massive Habsburg domains, and even French and English letter carriers had to tie into the Taxis network on the continent.

Franz von Taxis was effectively postman to the civilized western world. No wonder that in his portrait, hanging above the fireplace in the modern palace of Schloss St Emmeram in Regensburg, he pushes forward his Imperial scroll of office, as if to explain the pile of gold ducats over which he proudly broods, firm featured, fleshy, and almost totally lacking a neck.

But the Taxis courier system had always been a family affair. Brothers, cousins, and nephews were distributed around Europe as new post offices opened up, and in the best Italian tradition the major money-spinning branches were only entrusted to relatives. Wherever there was a Habsburg who mattered, there would be a Taxis stationed close by, so when Franz von Taxis died in 1517 the business passed smoothly to his nephew Johannes Baptista, who continued its expansion.

'I speak Spanish to God, Italian to women, French to men – and German to my horse.' Thus Charles V, grandson to Maximilian and inheritor of his grandfather's empire building by marriage.

In 1519 Charles succeeded Maximilian as Holy Roman Emperor which gave him authority over most of Germany; he was already ruling over the Low Countries; as King of Spain his writ extended to the Spanish possessions in the New World and Italy – Lombardy, Sardinia, Naples and Sicily; and in addition to all this he also held title to Bohemia, Moravia, Croatia and Hungary which, after 1526, he was to delegate to his younger brother Ferdinand. No one in modern history has inherited more of western Europe than Charles V, and crucial to Charles's success in maintaining some sort of control over his vast domains was Johannes Baptista von Taxis.

The obvious way to recognize this importance was with a noble title. Kings and emperors had been bestowing nobility without land for some time, nor was military usefulness any longer the criterion for aristocracy. In 1514 the Habsburgs raised their bankers, the Fuggers of Augsburg, to the level of count.

But it took some time for the Taxis family to reach this rank. They had some pretensions to minor nobility, as the 'von' in their name indicated. It came from their original Italian surname de Tasso, and its Germanic status was formally recognized by the Emperor in 1512. The son of Johannes Baptista, Leonhard, was made Baron of the Empire in 1608, at the end of a career whose unusual length had embraced Philip of Spain's wars against the Dutch and the English. But not until 1624 was Leonhard's son Lamoral elevated to the ranks of the Imperial Counts.

The problem was that the grandest German aristocrats jealously guarded their status as *landadel* or 'landed noble', the link with the military and feudal origins of aristocracy which set them apart from parvenu nobles whose wealth came from 'trade'. To be *landadel* meant that you were of warrior stock with forefathers who rode through the forests with Siegfried or Sir Perceval – you could pick your myth – and it was bound up in the semi-royal status so many Teutonic noblemen enjoyed as rulers of semi-independent states.

This hierarchical sensitivity has been preserved into the twentieth century. In Britain today few people could range dukes, marquesses, earls, viscounts and barons in order of precedence, and fewer still could care. In Germany the *Almanach de Gotha*, the *Debrett* of Europe's royals and higher nobility, grades titles into separate classes according to the refinement of their pedigree – 1A, 1B, 2nd and 3rd – and with these distinctions go elaborate rules. Families in Section 1A of the *Gotha* look down on the top rank of British aristocracy, the dukes, because British dukes are allowed to perpetuate their dynasties by marrying barmaids and actresses – and have not infrequently done so. A German duke wishing to marry a barmaid would be required by his house rules to make his marriage only a morganatic one – his spouse and offspring being barred from the family title and inheritance – and, in this vein, certain German relatives of HRH Prince Philip have been heard to express surprise that he allowed his son to marry a girl who was only an earl's daughter.

In the seventeenth century this refinement of noble distinction was reaching full flowering as the *landadel* sought to protect their status against the new sources of wealth and power represented by families like the Taxis and the Fuggers, and the Taxis might have been perpetually foiled in their social ambitions if it had not been for one enterprising woman – Countess Alexandrine von Taxis, the wife of Lamoral's son Leonhard.

Countess Alexandrine was a formidable lady who took over the family postal services after the early death of her husband in 1628, and she proceeded to run them with consummate skill through all the disruptions of the Thirty Years War. Her simple remedy for the Taxis's lack of pedigree was to create one. Everyone has notable ancestors in their pedigree – after all in the last resort one can always go back to Adam and Eve – and the experts whom Countess Alexandrine commissioned came up with what she wanted by going back to the early years of the twelfth century.

Delving into the northern Italian origins of the family, the genealogists somehow managed to make a connection between Franz von Taxis and the Torriani family, a clan of warriors who had been rivals of the Visconti in Milan and who had exercised despotic rule over Lombardy until 1311 – authentic sword-wielding knights as ferocious as any Siegfried. These were ancestors to be proud of, a dynasty of warrior princes, and if they were regarded as the main trunk of the family tree, it became possible to claim that the Taxis stemmed from the most authentic noble stock – *landadel*, with an Italian flavour.

So in 1645 Countess Alexandrine had the results of her researches made up into a book with illustrations by van der Horst, a pupil of Rubens, and she also applied for a change in the family surname. Torriani, or della Torre, means 'tower', and the old German for tower is *Thurm*. So the plain von Taxis family became von Thurn und Taxis.

Today Countess Alexandrine presides over the state dining room in the Regensburg palace of the Thurn und Taxis. She is woven in tapestry, almost life size on a white battle charger, and rearing up beside her on the same tapestry is her husband Leonhard. His black horse is draped with heraldic hangings which display, for the first time, a tower on the family coat of arms – though Leonhard had, in fact, died eighteen years before the tapestry was woven. He had never borne the family's new double-barrelled name, let alone exhibited a tower on his shield.

Still, this was a detail. A double-barrelled name is usually a sure sign that someone, somewhere in the family history, has been anxious to impress – and thanks to their postal service, the newly double-barrelled Thurn und Taxis had the money to indulge this anxiety to the full. Alexandrine and her son Lamoral Claudius commissioned a spectacular series of wall hangings to display the heroic deeds of their previously obscure ancestors the Torriani, and hung them on their walls.

Today these Torriani tapestries line salon after salon in Regensburg. Their classically armoured warriors and tumbling crowds of well-fed horses make impressive decoration, though they display a quite spectacular disregard for twelfth-century historical accuracy since, whatever the truth about the links between the Taxis and the Torriani, it was clearly quite impossible for the tapestry makers to reconstruct the details of skirmishes on the northern Italian plains at four centuries' distance.

Yet the object of the exercise was propaganda, not historical reconstruction. The Thurn und Taxis wanted to persuade their visitors that their family started off in the world doing something rather grander than delivering letters – and they evidently succeeded, for in 1695 the Emperor Leopold I bestowed upon Eugene Alexander, son of Lamoral Claudius, the highest honour in his gift, the rank of Prince of the Holy Roman Empire. It had taken two centuries, but the postmen had become princes.

How often have I wondered at the difference between the stately beauty of a great house, so exalting and tranquillizing, and the fierce restless unscrupulous character of the men who were so often responsible for its original building.

LORD DAVID CECIL,
Library Looking Glass, 1975

It is a matter of common observation that those who most distinguish themselves by an insensate squandering of the fruits of human toil are the ones who have most recently attained the fruits of human power and wealth.

GAETANO MOSCA,
The Ruling Class, 1939

VI · STATELY
HOMES

THERE is no mains water at the Chateau de Courances. When the Marquis de Ganay offers you a scotch on the rocks, the rocks have been frozen from the chateau's own spring – and that is not a consequence of outdated plumbing. It is a deliberate matter of pride and of digestion, for the springs of Courances yield refreshment as soft and salubrious as any other *source* in France, that country which chews and savours its mineral waters as seriously as it tastes its wines. Modern Parisians who care for their digestive tract bring jerry cans to fill up with the waters of Courances. They take them home to sip in preference to the capital's processed tap water – and three centuries ago, whenever the kings of France came to their hunting lodge at Fontainebleau, it was the waters of Courances that they called for to drink.

The game-rich forest of Fontainebleau, forty miles south of Paris, attracted the French kings and their nobles as early as the twelfth century. Philip the Fair was born there – and he died there forty-six years later, following a fall from a horse. But it was François I, the contemporary and rival of the English Henry VIII, who started turning the royal hunting lodge into one of the great palaces of Europe, and his son Henri II continued the work, commissioning the chateau's curlicued ballroom with its sinuous monograms of Cs entwined around Hs – tributes, on the face of it, to Henri's wife Catherine de Medici, but seen by malicious eyes as double Ds, in honour of Henri's mistress, Diane de Poitiers.

Whenever the royal court was in residence at Fontainebleau, Flemish drays would lumber the twelve miles through the forest, dragging purpose-built wooden tankers filled with the waters of Courances. Henri II's Finance Minister, Cosmo Clausse lighted on the spa as a convenient and healthy spot for a house, hiring Gilles le Breton, the king's builder, to do the work. Since Cosmo Clausse supervised all the king's building bills, it may be presumed that the minister got his chateau at a bargain price – the notion that office holders should not enjoy the fruits of office had not yet started to complicate the ethics of public life.

Gilles le Breton built Courances during the French Wars of Religion – times of bitter civil war and bloodshed – and the chateau was remodelled a few decades later during the reign of Louis XIII and the Fronde, another period of disorder. But as a classic example of Louis XIII architecture, the Chateau de Cour-ances has no ramparts or battlements. There was no point in such things. The widespread use of gunpowder had made domestic fortifications virtually redundant by the end of the sixteenth century, for even a nobleman bold enough to buy his own cannon in defiance of the royal monopoly on gunpowder risked seeing his castle reduced to rubble. The fortified noble stronghold had had its day. Since your home could no longer be your fortress, you might as well build it as you fancied – and surrender it meekly if ever the soldiers came.

So began the age of the country house as a pleasure resort. The French kings came to Fontainebleau for relaxation, and the Chateau de Courances was built in that spirit – for fun. It did have a moat but, lacking a drawbridge, this was an architectural fancy, not an item of defence. With two solid fixed stone bridges crossing it, the function of the water was purely to act as a mirror,

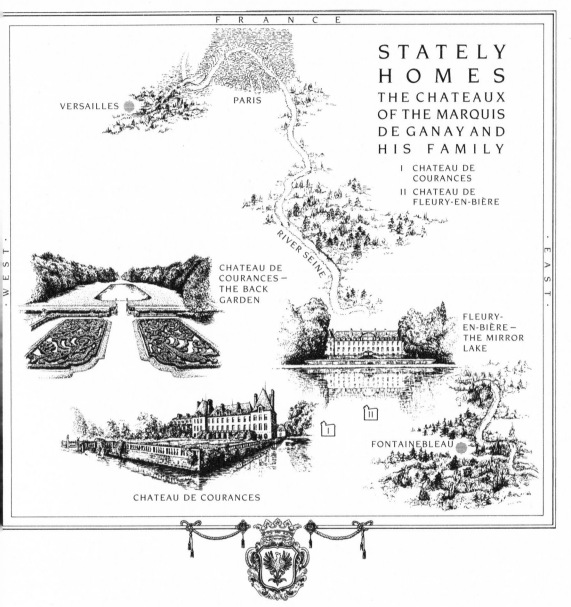

STATELY HOMES

THE CHATEAUX OF THE MARQUIS DE GANAY AND HIS FAMILY

I CHATEAU DE COURANCES

II CHATEAU DE FLEURY-EN-BIÈRE

FRANCE

VERSAILLES

PARIS

RIVER SEINE

WEST

EAST

CHATEAU DE COURANCES – THE BACK GARDEN

FLEURY-EN-BIÈRE – THE MIRROR LAKE

FONTAINEBLEAU

CHATEAU DE COURANCES

reflecting the shimmering pink and grey of the chateau for visitors as they clattered into the courtyard in their carriages.

The house was devised to be a visual experience, and its harmony of brick, slate and dark green foliage was designed in the classic tradition of the Ile de France – the French heartland round Paris so-called because the Franks founded the first France there inside a boundary of rivers, the Seine, Marne and Oise. It would have been a departure from Ile de France style for Courances to have any other colours than brick, slate and green – flowers would have been very vulgar – and the Ganay family maintain that style to this day. They do have some trees that display spectacular yellow, red and cream foliage, but these are all segregated in a garden of their own in a remote corner of the grounds – strictly out of sight of the chateau.

The gardens of Courances were laid out to the plans of le Nôtre, who later designed the Sun King's gardens at Versailles and whose work was the logical consequence of houses ceasing to be fortified. Le Nôtre remodelled the landscape not for the sake of agriculture or defence, but in order to make his patrons' home look grander. So the 'Turkish carpet' of low clipped box hedges arabesqued to the rear of Courances (see illustrations following p. 112) was intended to be seen from the salons on the main reception floor as an extension of the house rolling out into the countryside – and, from the outside, the green geometry of the gardens was designed to display the structure of the chateau itself in all its splendour, for if the aristocratic home could no longer intimidate, it could at least impress.

The aristocratic country house was never just a big house in the country where rich people happened to live. When fortified, the stately home had been a very obvious component of aristocratic power, and even when designed for pleasure, without fortifications, the visual display of the big house was still intended to reinforce the lord's authority over the local population. It maintained his status in the eyes of his noble equals, and it might also impress any of his royal betters who came to call.

For the aspiring aristocrat a grand country home represented a bid for status – and Cosmo Clausse was very much an aspirant. He was trying to execute the crucial leap from transient royal servant to permanent member of the aristocracy, and he built Courances in the same tradition in which English politicians like the early Cecils or, later, Sir Robert Walpole, sought at Burghley, Hatfield and Houghton to convert their short-term political prominence into long-term, tangible form. No matter how much power these great men exercised in the affairs of their nation, swaying the destinies of hundreds of thousands, if not millions, they were, somehow, not satisfied: they could not feel they had really arrived until they had built themselves a country house where they could impress a few dozen friends and lord it over a few hundred farmers and yokels.

So the ethos of the castle lived on after its battlements and towers had been demolished. A big house dominating its local countryside was still the hallmark of aristocracy – but with a difference, for if noble status was vested in land which anyone could purchase, why not cut short the process and purchase nobility itself?

Elizabeth I was mean with titles as she was with everything else. Apart from allowing one lord (Willoughby de Eresby) to inherit a title on his mother's side, and promoting another (Howard of Effingham) to the rank of earl, she only created one new peer (Lord Howard de Walden) in the last thirty years of her reign. After the execution in 1572 of the Duke of Norfolk, England's last surviving duke, the country was totally dukeless, and Elizabeth I, at least, did not exhibit any great sense of loss.

Her successor, James I, was less parsimonious. Short of money within months of his accession in 1603, he searched round for new sources of revenue and hit upon titles. To start with he only sold baronetcies. He put a job lot of 200 on the market in 1611 at £1095 each, to be paid in three instalments, and, anxious lest he be accused of letting standards slip, he imposed certain conditions on the first 200 bidders – they must have had a coat of arms for at least three generations, and they should also own land worth £1000 a year or more.

But men did not rush to buy. Some old-fashioned feeling seemed to linger that dignities which were put up for sale could not be worth that much. So, at the suggestion of his young favourite, George Villiers, the King decided to improve his marketing, and he delegated to Villiers the responsibility of handling the business.

Villiers was no slouch at collecting honours himself. Thanks to the fascination he exerted over James I, he became the only Englishman ever to pass through all five grades of nobility in his lifetime – baron, viscount, earl, marquess and finally, as Duke of Buckingham in 1623, the duke to end dukelessness, since he was the first man to occupy England's premier noble rank since the execution of the Duke of Norfolk.

Having spread the value of nobility so generously about his own person, the new Duke had little difficulty spreading it elsewhere as well, and between 1618 and 1622 Buckingham managed to sell no less than nine peerages, eleven baronetcies, four knighthoods, the Lord Chancellorship – and one seat on the Privy Council.

The combined wholesale price of these honours was £24,750 – and the ending of the ceremony by which the monarch personally invested all new peers, for since the early Middle Ages English kings had formally strapped a sword around new earls – hence the expression 'belted earls'. This elaborate celebration of girding and banqueting had subsequently been extended upwards to the later titles of marquess and duke.

But even those with the hard neck to buy and flaunt a Buckingham title in the 1620s shied away from the bulk public investiture which bulk buying necessitated. Between 1615 and 1628 the number of earls rose from twenty-seven to sixty-five, an increase of 141 per cent, so the ceremony fell into disuse – and its details were only exhumed in 1964 when Britain's new Labour Prime Minister, the 14th Mr Wilson, ended thirteen years of Tory misrule by creating fifty-three new peers. This was four times more than the annual post-war average and, concerned at the amount of Parliamentary time consumed by the introduction of these new aristocrats (all of them, of course, life peers), the House of Lords asked Garter King of Arms to dig into history to discover what previous ceremonials had existed. In these researches Garter King discovered the details of the investitures sabotaged by the Duke of Buckingham – though even that prodigal royal favourite had only managed, in his best year, to create a tenth of the titles distributed by Mr Wilson.

One of the Duke of Buckingham's baronetcies had been purchased by a Richard Grosvenor Esquire, of Eaton in the county of Chester. Like other members of the squirearchy the Grosvenors had profited from Henry VIII's dissolution of the monasteries to increase their landholdings at a cut-price rate. They had leased, then purchased, the manor of Belgrave next door to Eaton, and they had become active in the local affairs of the community. The newly elevated Sir Richard, the 1st Baronet, was a justice of the peace and chairman of his local Sessions; he was also High Sheriff for Cheshire and the neighbouring county of Denbighshire, mayor of Chester and one of the two Knights of the Shire who represented Cheshire in the House of Commons as MPs. He was clearly a man of some financial acumen, for he did not join the first rush of applicants to purchase baronetcies, but waited until 1622 when the going rate had dropped below the original £1095 asking price.

In other respects, however, Sir Richard was less agile financially. He stood surety for another Member of Parliament, a Peter Daniell of Tabley, who was also his brother-in-law, and when Daniell got into financial difficulties, it was Sir Richard who suffered. He was confined inside the Fleet Prison for debtors in 1629, and remained there until 1638. His bought baronetcy was of no help to him.

A few years later Charles I learned an even harder lesson about the efficacy of titles, particularly when their value had been debased by trading in the marketplace. Concerned to build up royal support as his confrontation with the House of Commons intensified, he bestowed titles with abandon in the months leading up to the Civil War. But when the battle lines were drawn in 1642, it was discovered that of all these new creations, more had sided with Parliament than had lined up with their King.

The Grosvenors had, in fact, sided with Charles I to start with – and they paid for it. A year after the death of the first baronet in 1645 his son, another Sir Richard Grosvenor, was in the Fleet Prison himself, confined by parliamentary order for the support he had given his sovereign. Sir Richard had raised two horsemen and thirteen foot soldiers to fight in the royalist army and his punishment was three years in prison – until love, or rather marriage, came to the rescue; in 1649 the second Sir Richard Grosvenor married the daughter of Sir Thomas Middleton, a general in the Parliamentary Army, and was set at liberty through the good offices of his father-in-law.

How Sir Richard pulled off this fortunate coup while still in prison is not known, but clever marriages had always been a Grosvenor speciality. They owed the lion's share of their estates around Eaton to the well-judged alliance of Ralph, a fifteenth-century Grosvenor, with a local heiress – and, in the England of the 1650s, the family was about to make its cleverest marriage of all.

Mary Davies was barely six months old when her father died. Alexander Davies was a small-time property speculator who had just begun to build up a business of his own when he was struck down in the Great Plague of 1665. He had made only a rudimentary will, and by its terms all his property went to his first born and only child, Mary.

The bulk of the estate was an area of marsh and meadowland outside London, the manor of Ebury, which, until the Reformation, had been owned and farmed by the monks of Westminster Abbey. With the dissolution of the monasteries, Henry VIII sold off the land, retaining for himself the woods that lay to the west of it, and today that deer forest is still owned by the sovereign, though Elizabeth II does not go hunting in Hyde Park.

London was just starting to expand in the middle of the seventeenth century. At the beginning of the reign of Elizabeth I it had still been a walled city, separated from Westminster by meadows through which ran the Strand, the main road connecting the two cities. But during the reign of Queen Elizabeth, property developers pushed out to the north of the grand houses lining the Strand, and by the reign of James I flourishing suburbs had been established in the areas of Piccadilly and Soho.

The manor of Ebury was a few steps further westwards, and its value was bound to increase as London edged outwards towards Hyde Park. But the problem for the widow of Alexander Davies was that she could not realize this value, since her husband's will left his land to his child and his debts to his wife. So to raise ready cash, Mary's mother effectively put her little daughter and the manor of Ebury up for auction, and the highest bidder was Lord Berkeley of Stratton, who offered £5000.

Lord Berkeley of Stratton was one of several Stuart aristocrats who were making their fortune as property developers. He had just built himself a grand mansion in Piccadilly and was energetically acquiring building plots around it. Berkeley Square and Stratton Street are modern reminders of his empire building, and with the manor of Ebury he could have extended his development land as far as the royal park. But Lord Berkeley was too greedy, for in purchasing Mary Davies as a wife for his son he agreed to settle some of his own lands on the infant couple, and when he reneged on this, Mary's mother went elsewhere.

Sir Thomas Grosvenor, 3rd Baronet of Eaton, knew a bargain when he saw one. He repaid the £5000 deposit put down by Lord Berkeley, whisked Mary off to the newly built church of St Clement Danes as soon as she reached her twelfth birthday, and married her on 10 October 1677. Leaving nothing to chance, Sir Thomas put down a further £1000 to buy a reversionary interest in the manor of Ebury, so that the land would become his even if his child bride died before coming of age. On his wedding day the enterprising baronet was twenty-one years old.

Davies Street is the modern memorial to the little girl who made the fortunes of the baronets from Eaton, Cheshire. The most handsome building in the street is the chief office of the Grosvenor Estate, just across the corner from Claridge's, and it is only right that Mary's portrait should occupy pride of place there in the office of the Duke of Westminster – even if the present Duke is less than complimentary.

'No beauty, was she?'

But that portrait in itself (see illustration following p. 16) is an indication that Mary was a good deal less than happy with the fate to which her mother consigned her, for she commissioned it herself after her husband's death in 1700. It was part of a campaign she started to wage as a thirty-six-year-old widow to re-establish her own identity and to recapture her land from the Grosvenor family: even in her husband's lifetime she had been consulting lawyers to challenge what he was doing with her lands.

Mary's most expressive gesture of rebellion in a religious age was to show what she thought of the system which had bartered away her life, by becoming a Roman Catholic. After her husband's death she travelled to Europe to do pilgrimage at Catholic shrines, paying a visit on her journey to James II, exiled for his Roman Catholicism in 1688, and while abroad, she decided to remarry inside the faith – her Catholic husband, Edward Fenton, having a brother who was a Jesuit.

The new Mr and Mrs Fenton naturally hoped to enjoy the benefits of Mary's childhood inheritance, the manor of Ebury, or at least part of it – but they had not reckoned with the Grosvenors. The lords of Eaton had no intention of letting slip what Sir Thomas had purchased in 1677, and they exploited Mary's Catholicism to enlist the Protestant authorities to their cause. They had Mary declared insane – which dealt neatly with both her second marriage and the problem of keeping her out of any more such adventures – and if Mary Davies did finally die mad, kept in custody for the rest of her days, then given the story of her life, that was hardly surprising.

Some years before her death in 1730 the Grosvenor family started developing her inheritance. The arrival in England of the Hanoverian George I had coincided with an explosion of speculative building on the outskirts of London; Hanover Street and Hanover Square, the first developments south of the road to Oxford, had paid homage to the new dynasty. But further west the baronets of Eaton Hall preferred to use the family name.

The site of what today is Grosvenor Square had developed a certain notoriety before it was built upon, for its meadows were the focus of a riotous and disreputable fair to which Londoners travelled out every year in the month of May. Ale-sellers and ladies of easy virtue plied their trades in a shanty town of stalls and tents around the Maypole, pickpockets and footpads lurked in the hedgerows for the unwary, and the whole area had such an unsavoury reputation that people would sniff disdainfully whenever the name of Mayfair was mentioned.

This was the reputation which Sir Richard Grosvenor sought to dispel as he laid out the grandiose lines of Grosvenor Square in the early 1720s. He was the 4th Baronet, the eldest son of Sir Thomas and Mary Davies, but we know nothing of the relationship he had with his poor mad mother. Though she did not die until after the development had started, it does not seem likely that he took her out to see the buildings going up all over the

GROSVENOR
SQUARE, 1983
MAYFAIR, LONDON
W 1

U.S. EMBASSY

ABBEYSTEAD AND EATON HALL.
THE COUNTRY HOMES OF
GERALD GROSVENOR.
SIXTH DUKE OF WESTMINSTER

ABBEYSTEAD

CHESTER

EATON

ENGLAND

LONDON

TO
DAVIES
STREET

THE 'BEND OR' CLAIMED BY SIR ROBERT GROSVENOR IN 1385

land she had brought to the Grosvenors and had then tried unsuccessfully to wrest back.

It was an extraordinary sight – an 'amazing scene of new foundations, not of houses only, but as I might say of new cities,' wrote Daniel Defoe in 1725 when he included Mayfair in his *Tour of the British Isles*. He marvelled at the 'new towns, new squares, and fine buildings, the like of which no city, no town, nay, no place in the world can shew; nor is it possible to judge where or when they will make an end or stop to the building. . . All the way through this new scene I saw the world full of bricklayers and labourers, who seemed to have little else to do, but like gardeners, to dig a hole, put in a few bricks, and presently there goes up a house.'

In reality, this fanciful comparison to a gardener scattering seeds from which buildings sprang, applied less to the builders themselves than to Sir Richard Grosvenor, for, like the best property developers, he spent as little of his own money as possible in launching his development. He produced a grand overall plan around the central squares, with straight streets radiating outwards and then he parcelled the whole area into a hundred or so lots which were let, on long leases, to 'undertakers'.

Some of these 'undertakers' were individuals wanting to build their own homes, but most of them were free-enterprise jobbing builders, who bought up one or more plots in the hope of turning over a good profit on the finished houses.

The façade was the thing. This had to conform to a common plan – thus creating the integrated vistas that remain a feature of Mayfair even after two centuries of rebuilding – and it had to be completed within eighteen months, on pain of losing the lease. But behind the façade the house could be designed to the whim of individual clients who could then live there for a limited term of years which, after a number of experiments, usually came to be set at ninety-nine. After that the entire building had to be vacated and surrendered to the Grosvenors in a decorative order that was as good as new.

The ninety-nine-year lease became the cornerstone of the prosperous empire which the Grosvenor family created on the inheritance of Mary Davies. Other noblemen had let off their lands around London for 999-year leases, and while this displayed a long-term perspective that was truly aristocratic, history cannot yet pronounce on its commercial prudence. Ninety-nine years has so far proved a preferable timespan, for while long enough to tempt £4–£5000 out of purchasers for a good house in Grosvenor Street in the 1720s, and £7000 or more for a house in the square, it was short enough for the Grosvenors to realize their profits inside three generations. They seldom took the vacant possession of a house after the ninety-nine years had elapsed, but as their prosperous tenants saw the end of their leases approaching, they would renegotiate continued residence in return for a lump sum renewal fee and a higher ground rent. By the 1760s the Grosvenor income from their Mayfair estates totalled over £3000 a year – compared to £400, the annual income the land had yielded when it was agricultural.

Grosvenor Square was one of London's smartest addresses from the start. The street the family named after Mary Davies was occupied mainly by tradesfolk – Davies Street properties changed hands for just a few hundred pounds. But the main square and streets of the estate attracted the great of the land. By 1751 there were thirty-nine peers of the realm living in Mayfair as tenants of the Grosvenors, and it was only right that a landlord to aristocrats should enjoy some degree of aristocracy himself. In 1761 Sir Richard Grosvenor, the 7th Baronet, was created Lord Grosvenor, and in 1784 he moved on upwards. He was given a viscountcy and an earldom. The new Earl Grosvenor kept Eaton Hall as his ancestral home, and he bought himself a racing stable at Newmarket. But in London his town house, naturally, was situated in Grosvenor Square.

Property development was a respectable activity for an aristocrat in the seventeenth and eighteenth centuries. As a leisurely way of making money it avoided the stigma which hard work gave to 'trade', and it also provided the means by which the more nimble members of an essentially rural elite could turn the rise of urban society to their advantage. Bedford, Cadogan, Harley – to this day the names of London streets and squares bear witness to the process by which country gentlemen came to court, bought land around the capital and let it off, as the Grosvenors did. And the same process was going on around the courts of Europe. In Vienna a whole new neighbourhood was created by the noble house of Liechtenstein.

The Liechtensteins had maintained the martial reputation established by Hugo, the family's founding father, in the early

Middle Ages. They defended and extended the lands they had been given in Moravia and Bohemia against invasion from the east, and their names figured prominently on the rolls of honour in medieval battles all over Germany and Austria.

They also displayed a flair for making money. The family ran their eastern estates at a considerable profit, and they put their wealth to good use in the complicated politics of the German Reformation. They became Protestant for a while under pressure from the Anabaptists in Moravia, but their political instincts homed in on the house of Habsburg. In 1620 the Habsburg victory at the battle of the White Mountain near Prague was largely due to the local resources of the Liechtensteins, and for the rest of the Thirty Years War the family supplied men and lent money to the Imperial cause.

Their reward was land around Vienna and they were also ennobled. Three brothers, Charles, Maximilian and Gundackar were all raised to be Princes of the Holy Roman Empire.

The Liechtensteins did not suffer the credibility problem of the Taxis family. Few Teutonic dynasties had such an ancient landed pedigree as the Liechtensteins who, from the start, had lived as princes in all but name upon their eastern estates. But to qualify for full membership of the supreme inner council of Imperial Princes, the Reichsfürstenrat, there was one territorial requirement which all the Liechtensteins' tens of thousands of acres could not satisfy. They had to occupy one of the few dozen ancient Imperial fiefs which had no overlord except the Emperor himself.

When the Thurn und Taxis later encountered the same problem in the early eighteenth century they were to find a parcel of such ancient feudal land, Friedberg-Scheer, in Würtemberg, north of Bavaria. This gave territorial backing to their membership of the Reichsfürstenrat.

In the early seventeenth century the Liechtensteins were not so fortunate. The Emperor had bestowed the rank of Prince upon them, but they had to go shopping for the right sort of land to accompany that dignity, and they searched unsuccessfully for more than eighty years. All their attempts to purchase one of the select groups of territories carrying the magic Reichsfürstenrat status were rejected, and not until 1699 did the Liechtensteins finally track down a seller – Count Ferdinand Charles von Hohenems, ruler of Vaduz and Schellenberg in the upper Rhine valley between the borders of Switzerland and Austria.

It seems unlikely that the Count von Hohenems was much happier to lose his Imperial fief than any other of the nobles whom the Liechtensteins had been courting so long, but he had little choice in the matter, for he had gone bankrupt. Vaduz and Schellenberg were a pair of backward, poverty-stricken counties whose farms yielded scanty profits in good years, and which were devastated in bad years by the overflowing and flooding of the Rhine. They required subsidies from their ruler as often as they yielded him dividends, so when the Count von Hohenems got into financial difficulties it meant hard times for the entire community – and a local ecclesiastic, the High Abbot of Kempten was appointed official receiver. He put the two little counties, whose total area was less than seventy square miles, up for auction – and the highest bid came from the house of Liechtenstein.

In the final years of the seventeenth century the Liechtensteins' family fortunes were in the able hands of Prince Johann Adam Andreas, generally nicknamed 'Hans Adam the Rich' on the basis of the skill with which he ran the family's eastern estates and had developed their land around Vienna. Grandees of the Habsburg court competed to make their Vienna residences palaces in their own right, and Hans Adam proved as good at this as the next margrave. He brought the Italian architect Domenico Martinelli north to build him two palaces, one inside the city on the Bankgasse and the other outside at Rossau, and this fine pair of buildings, filled with a collection of paintings, busts and tapestries to demonstrate their owners' tastes, set the vogue for high baroque in Austria.

Around his palace at Rossau Hans Adam had also developed the land to create an elegant neighbourhood yielding substantial rents, so when he entered the auction for the little counties of Vaduz and Schellenberg, he was able handsomely to outbid his rivals. He paid a total of 405,000 florins for the two counties which, in 1719, were combined and renamed the Principality of Liechtenstein.

As an economic proposition it was an insane price to pay for a few thousand flood-prone peasant smallholdings, but Hans Adam had not purchased the land for the sake of economic return. He did not bother to inspect his purchase, and no other Prince of the family visited the principality bearing the family name until 1842. Hans Adam had created Liechtenstein for the sake of status, and status is something on which a price cannot be set.

Nobility of birth commonly abateth industry.

FRANCIS BACON, 1612

Lord Finchley tried to mend the Electric Light
Himself. It struck him dead. And serve him right!
It is the business of the wealthy man
To give employment to the artisan.

HILAIRE BELLOC, 1870–1953

VII · REVOLUTION

ROBERT Smith, bank manager to William Pitt the Younger, British Prime Minister from 1783 to 1801 and again from 1804 to 1806, was riding one day with his most important customer through the Horse Guards in Whitehall, when it struck him how convenient it would be if he himself could take this short cut to work every day. Could his influential client, perhaps, arrange this privilege for him?

The Prime Minister considered the request and decided that his bank manager was asking too much, but that he would give him a peerage instead. So Mr Smith became Lord Carrington.[*]

William Pitt the Younger had a matter-of-fact attitude towards aristocracy. 'Anyone worth £10,000 a year is worth a

---

[*] The Smiths changed their surname to Carrington in 1839 and then to Carington, with a single 'r', in 1880. Peter Carington, 6th Lord Carrington, born 1919, was British Foreign Secretary 1979–82.

peerage,' he said on one occasion, and he had no difficulty finding men who met his criterion. In Pitt's time as Prime Minister there were 119 creations and promotions in the various categories of British peerage – and there had been only 212 hereditary peers in the House of Lords when he first took office in 1783. It was under his patronage that the Barings started collecting their titles.

'He made peers of second-rate squires and fat graziers,' complained Disraeli in the following century. 'He caught them in the alleys of Lombard Street, and clutched them from the counting houses of Cornhill.'

It was not as though the British aristocracy had much need of reinforcement at the end of the eighteenth century. Legislated out of existence as 'useless and dangerous' a few weeks after the execution of King Charles I in 1649, the House of Lords had enjoyed a remarkable comeback in the century that followed. After the Restoration of 1660 and the Glorious Revolution of 1688–9, kings ruled by the grace of the people, but their governments were invariably aristocratic. Throughout the eighteenth century cabinets contained more lords than commoners, and in Pitt's War Cabinet of 1804 all the ministers were peers or sons of peers.

One reason why it was possible for prime ministers and their governments to rule Britain from the House of Lords was that so many of their relatives sat in the Commons. In the general election of 1754, for example, no less than seventy-seven sons of English peers were returned as MPs to the House of Commons, and this was just the start of it: also elected to the Commons in that year were seventeen Irish peers (who had no seat in the Lords), six sons of Irish peers, thirteen sons of Scottish peers, forty-five grandsons of peers, thirty-three MPs married to the daughters of peers, twenty-two nephews of peers, eight brothers of peers, seven brothers-in-law of peers and one foreign nobleman – not to mention two illegitimate sons of peers and one illegitimate grandson, if such a thing is possible.

This brought the aristocratic element in the House of Commons in the middle of the eighteenth century to a grand total of 230 out of 558 members – and even this figure leaves out of account the election agents and paid retainers who were returned for many boroughs in their noble masters' interest. Almost all other MPs were classed socially as 'gentlemen', old landed stock with which the titled interbred freely – over 70 per cent of peers' sons born between 1760 and 1779 married the daughters of untitled gentlemen. So with the upper crust enjoying so much more than its fair share of power in Britain at the end of the eighteenth century it might, on the face of it, seem surprising that the great revolution of 1789 took place in France and not upon the other side of the Channel.

On 14 July 1789 crowds of angry Parisians stormed the medieval fortress of the Bastille that loomed over the east of Paris, symbolizing all that was wrong with royal France. Inside the dungeons of the fortress they discovered four petty crooks jailed for passing bad cheques, an aristocrat confined at his family's request for incest, and two lunatics, one of them French and the other an Irishman who believed himself to be Julius Caesar. But this did not deter the attackers' righteous indignation at the injustices of the *ancien régime*, and they demolished the fortress stone by stone.

Today all that remains of the Bastille in Paris is the line of its walls, traced out in cobblestones in the open square that bears its name, and Bastille Day, 14 July, has become the country's national day, commemorating that grandiose and bloody hacking to pieces of aristocratic privilege, the French Revolution.

The modern village of Courances celebrates Bastille Day in style. The 385 inhabitants come out onto the little patch of green in front of the *Arc en Ciel* – the Rainbow Inn, the only bar in the village – and they roll up their sleeves for an afternoon devoted to a series of the most cheerfully absurd pastimes: flowerpot smashing, egg-and-spoon racing and shin-skinning contests to climb up the telegraph pole and ring the bell that has been set on top of it for the day.

Children join forces for the three-legged race, black-garbed widows cluster together beneath the plane trees to recall 14th of Julys that they did not spend alone, and the village councillors proudly sport little *tricolores* in their buttonhole. It seems a totally appropriate way for the people of the village to celebrate their release from the tyranny once exercised over them by the lord of the chateau – except that all the games, contests and silly tricks are being organized and supervised most energetically by Jean Louis, Marquis de Ganay, the present-day lord of Courances.

In short-sleeved, floral shirt, and perspiring profusely, the Marquis is acting as starter, referee and finish judge of every race. Technically he is carrying out his responsibilities as elected mayor of the village, but in thirty-five years no one has ever actually stood against him, and as he bestows five-franc pieces on successful contestants from a seemingly endless supply in his pocket, he does not, somehow, carry himself as a conventional municipal officer. His wife, the Marquise, stands with his daughters among the villagers around the fringe of the green, and when his grandchildren take part in the competitions, the Marquis only stretches the rules slightly to make sure that they all end up with a prize – surely any grandfather would do the same. 14 July in Courances is a homely, harmonious and thoroughly good-tempered occasion, and it is really rather difficult to deduce from the proceedings what the storming of the Bastille was supposed to represent.

It was June 1791 when the French Revolution found its way to Courances. The chateau was then occupied by Aymard Charles Marie de Nicolay, 'le Grand Nicolay', Seigneur of nearly a dozen villages, Knight of the Royal Order of St Louis, Councillor to the King – and President of the Chambre des Comptes, the Finance Ministry, as several lords of Courances before him had been: in the three hundred years since the days of Cosmo Clausse the chateau had been occupied by a succession of royal accountants climbing up the social ladder.

Aymard de Nicolay was a pillar of the *ancien régime*. He was aware of the need for reform, but it was not until after the outbreak of the Revolution that he made public his ideas for reforming his own field of responsibility, the Chambre des Comptes, and by then he was too late. Far from satisfying revolutionary appetites he whetted them further. On 13 June 1791, the revolutionary committee in the Courances area received an anonymous denunciation of le Grand Nicolay, and they needed no encouragement to act.

Surrounding the chateau with cannon on the grounds that it

was a suspected storehouse for royalist arms, the local patriots attacked, to discover booty even more disappointing than that which had awaited the stormers of the Bastille. There were an extraordinary number of cues and balls in the billiard room of Courances, but there was nothing else inside the chateau that could remotely be described as an offensive weapon.

On 7 July 1794 le Grand Nicolay stood trial for his crimes against the Revolution, number 81 on the list of enemies of the state brought before the revolutionary tribunal for justice that day. His son, Aymard Pierre Marie Leon, aged twenty-three, 'Nicolay fils, ex-noble' stood alongside him, numbered 83. The documents of the revolutionary court reveal no evidence offered against the Nicolays, father and son. Together with 155 other 'counter-revolutionaries' standing trial alongside them, they were accused, condemned and sentenced, without right of appeal or reply and le Grand Nicolay was beheaded that same day.

His son's execution was delayed until three days later. It was the height of the Terror, when Dr Guillotin's machine was decapitating more than sixty victims an hour, but the Committee of Public Safety felt that the pleasure of watching aristocrats die should not be restricted to one quick afternoon's work.

The roll of the tumbrils and the knitting of the *tricoteuses* beside the bloodstained basket have passed into the folklore of aristocracy – a dreadful reminder of the dangers of getting too close to a king, for since the middle of the seventeenth century, French monarchs had been building up their absolutism by drawing the nobility to their court, cutting them off from their local roots.

'Preserve all the external prerogatives of their rank,' wrote the Sun King, Louis XIV, in 1705, 'and, at the same time, exclude them from a knowledge of all matters which might add to their credit.'

Louis XIV's glorious palace of Versailles demonstrated the elevation of royal power to a level France had never known before. But it also symbolized the dangerous isolation of those noblemen who had chosen to become creatures of his court – aristocrats in name, but in reality a new sort of class, divorced from the land

and from the multitude of local power-bases on which the strength of an aristocracy had originally been founded. So when the French Kings fell, these aristocrats fell with them.

The usefulness of aristocracy in a pre-technological society was to provide some sort of bridge between central authority and the realities of local life. In the absence of newspapers and the electronic media, the aristocrat who shuttled to and fro between his king and his own local people was an invaluable intermediary, and this practical function remained after aristocracy ceased to be an exclusively military institution. The newly rich merchant or politician, eager to get established in his newly purchased country house and to show off the latest trends in living, politics or ideas, proved a very effective channel of communication between capital and provinces – and most of William Pitt's fat graziers clutched from the counting houses of Lombard Street played this role assiduously. Even if the source of his power and wealth was metropolitan, the English nobleman felt he had to play the role of a country gentleman to be worthy of his nobility.

But the French *noblesse* was different. To carry a title meant enjoying almost total exemption from taxes, and while this in itself represented grievance enough in a society whose development was calling for an increasing burden of taxation, it also gave French aristocracy a character all its own.

Medieval French kings who wished to reward their personal servants – cooks, butlers and even valets – sometimes gave them noble status, and since the essence of the gift was the tax exemption it carried, no land was involved. So a curious category of working-class 'aristocrat' developed in France, and this persisted until the Revolution. In the elections of 1789, where men voted by class, seven peasants turned up at their polling station in Poitou claiming *noblesse* and were able to prove their status. They had to be lent swords, and their expenses were paid for them so that they could stay at the local inn in 'noble' fashion. In Britanny similar 'nobles' were to be found who made their living at gamekeeping, wigmaking, mule driving and carrying a sedan chair – inside which, presumably, non-noble passengers were quite frequently transported.

It seems that the proverbial nobleman of Beauce, who stayed

Jean Louis, Marquis de Ganay, master of Courances

Chateau de Courances, near Fontainebleau. Five francs to see the gardens, ten francs to see the house

Philippine, twentieth-century Marquise de Ganay, with a seventeenth-century Lady of Courances

*Courances, bedroom morals. Each panel depicts a
different fable by La Fontaine*

LEFT: *Nursery floor. Family nanny, Miss Blue, with
Ganay grandchild, Emilie*

PREVIOUS PAGE: *Chateau de Courances, the back garden*

*Eldest daughter, Anne Marie de Ganay, in the sitting
room of her wing at Courances*

in bed whenever his breeches needed mending, was an object of some affection in pre-revolutionary France. But the divorce of nobility from social status or function had devalued the concept of aristocracy from an early date. When Louis XIV commissioned his great inquiries of 1666 and 1696 to establish the authenticity of current French titles, he was not motivated by a high-minded wish to preserve the quality of his aristocracy: the surveys have since proved to be a useful source of genealogical material, but they were originally carried out as campaigns against tax evasion. Bogus nobles paid no taxes, and that worried Louis XIV. If they were allowed to get away with it, nobody would bother to pay for titles any more.

James I and the Duke of Buckingham had at least insisted that those who bought titles had land and some sort of lifestyle to complement their purchased status. In France the commerce in nobility was a matter of pure finance. The king mortgaged future income for the sake of ready cash and the purchaser regarded his title as an investment on which he had to make a good return. So when he did acquire land, the new nobleman exploited the local seigneurial privileges that went with it as if they were a business, compelling his villagers to use his mill or smithy, and charging for the compulsory service as he would for any other commercial monopoly.

It was this neocapitalist exploitation of feudal traditions by bourgeois newcomers which provoked some of the fiercest complaints in the *cahiers* of grievances that were drawn up all over France in 1789. Old-fashioned seigneurs who lived in traditional fashion on their estates aroused comparatively little hostility – and many rural aristocrats who had established themselves in their local community managed to ride out the entire Revolution quietly in their chateaux. In the area of the Vendée, north of Bordeaux, these rooted aristocrats even made common cause with the local peasantry to rebel against the arbitrariness of the central revolutionary committees in Paris, out of touch with the provinces, and principally bourgeois.

This was the essence of the French Revolution – a transfer of power not from rich to poor, but from rich to rich. There were some areas, especially in the north, where peasant landholdings increased as a result of the Revolution, but this was not a universal pattern. In one department in the west the number of noble estate owners diminished – as might have been expected – but the average size of the estates in that area actually increased.

'Liberty, equality, fraternity!' wrote Hippolyte Taine. 'Whatever the great words with which the Revolution was ornamented, it was essentially a transference of property.'

When hereditary titles were formally abolished in June 1790, the Marquis de Ferrières wrote to his wife telling her she should no longer address letters to him as 'Monsieur le Marquis' and that she should stop their daughter and son-in-law being called Count and Countess: the family coat of arms in the local church should be obliterated, he instructed. But, being a cautious man, the ex-marquis suggested that one coat of whitewash might be enough – and history rapidly endorsed his prudence. Only fourteen years later Napoleon founded his Empire upon the ruins of the Revolution, and the Caporal from Corsica started handing out hereditary titles of his own.

The rise of Napoleon conclusively disproved one ancient aristocratic myth – that noblemen make the best soldiers. Social status had been jealously protected inside the royal French army: and a man needed seven proofs of nobility in order to qualify as an officer. But purged of its aristocrats, and led by men whose career was determined by their military ability and not by the eminence of their birth, the revolutionary armies swept across Europe to victories on a scale unknown for France, before or since – and when Napoleonic marshals who had risen from the ranks were dignified as Imperial Princes, well, that went back to the very origins of nobility.

Napoleon enjoyed a good aristocrat when he met one. Prince John of Liechtenstein cut an impressive figure in his white and gold uniform as an Austrian cavalry general, and Napoleon took a liking to the Prince when he met him after the battle of Austerlitz. Prince John negotiated the ceasefire after Austerlitz as the representative of Austria, and a few months later he played a similar role at the treaty of Pressburg which marked the end of the Holy Roman Empire in 1806. Henceforward Habsburg authority was confined south and east of Austria, while the German territories over which they had formerly claimed suzerainty became sovereign states, associated, under French supervision, in a new grouping – the Confederation of the Rhine.

Liechtenstein did lie on the Rhine, but it was physically separated by Switzerland and Austria from the other members of the Confederation, and the little Principality's inclusion alongside comparative giants like Bavaria, Saxony and Baden was due entirely to the respect which Napoleon developed for Prince John. The two men fenced and argued for days on end across the negotiating table, John offering at one stage to surrender the famous Liechtenstein collection of art treasures to the Emperor if he would modify his demands on Austria, and Napoleon's unsolicited, not to say capricious, decision of 1806 to include Liechtenstein in the Rhine Confederation was a salute to a worthy opponent.

The prince was outwardly unmoved. He refused to give his personal adherence to the new Confederation, and a few years later he was at war again against Napoleon's armies, leading the Austrian cavalry at Aspern, Wagram and Znaim. But membership of Napoleon's Rhine Confederation turned out to be the qualification for membership of the German Confederation which replaced it in 1815, and it was membership of this grouping until 1867 which gave the little Principality of Liechtenstein the independent status and identity which it has retained to the present day.

The Thurn und Taxis family did not fare so well at the hands of Napoleon, for they had placed their postal services at the disposition of the Habsburgs and their allies fighting the French – and they paid for it. Napoleon abolished their monopoly in all the territories that he conquered.

In England alone did aristocrats escape the turmoil and upheaval that accompanied the progress of the Revolutionary and Napoleonic armies across the map of Europe for nearly a quarter of a century – and among England's aristocrats the Grosvenors fared better than most. This was the time when their ninety-nine-year leases in Mayfair started falling in, and from 1789 to 1809 the renewal fees paid by their tenants to obtain new leases totalled some £180,000. In these early years of the nineteenth century Grosvenor rents were increasing at a most profitable rate, and the family were also starting to develop new parts of their estates.

In the 1760s George III had bought the London residence of the Duke of Buckingham as a home for his wife, and Buckingham House, facing eastwards down the Mall towards London, became known as the Queen's House. Then in 1825 George IV decided to replace the Queen's House with a magnificent new palace, and for this he commissioned the architect John Nash who had designed the Brighton Pavilion for him when he was Prince Regent, and who had also transformed the face of central London with the sweeping white stucco terraces of Regent's Park and Regent Street.

The King's plan was to move his court along the Mall from St James's Palace to his spacious new residence, then known as the New Palace or Pimlico Palace (the building was not called Buckingham Palace until the reign of Queen Victoria), and the Grosvenor family realized immediately what this could mean for them. The developed acres of Mayfair were only part of Mary Davies's inheritance. The manor of Ebury also included several hundred acres of Pimlico running down from the gardens of the old Buckingham House to the River Thames – and this was the ideal spot to build a suburb for the courtiers and ambassadors who would want to live close to the new royal palace.

The Grosvenors had been earls since 1784, thanks to William Pitt; for, working very precisely to his £10,000 per peerage criterion, Pitt had given Richard Grosvenor not one, but two titles within weeks of first becoming Prime Minister. The lord of Mayfair, who had been a baron since 1761, became Viscount Belgrave, after the manor he owned next door to Eaton in Cheshire, and also Earl Grosvenor – even if this did not impress the connoisseurs. In 1808 *The Biographical Peerage of England* described the first Earl Grosvenor, a racing enthusiast, as 'better known in the annals of gallantry and Newmarket than anywhere else, and it must be confessed that peerages appear of little value as long as it is observed that they can be obtained by such qualifications.'

The first earl had become notorious when divorcing his wife,

Henrietta Vernon, in 1770. He cited the King's brother, the Duke of Cumberland, for adultery – and he won. The jury awarded the earl £10,000 damages with an indifference to royal dignity that no French court would dare to have shown before the Revolution.

But it was as a racehorse breeder that Richard Grosvenor really made his name. His stud was acknowledged the finest in England, and he helped make the name of the man he commissioned to paint his finest horses, an artist from Manchester called George Stubbs: Stubbs's painting of *The Grosvenor Hunt* (see illustration following p. 16) succeeded in blending family prestige and artistic feeling with rare skill. Earl Grosvenor's death, declared the *Gentleman's Magazine* in August 1802, 'will be much regretted on the turf'.

His son Robert, the second earl, kept up the Grosvenor Stud. But, educated at Harrow and Cambridge, and on two grand tours of Europe, he fancied himself as a man of learning and earned the nickname 'Lord of Greek' when he shocked the House of Commons in his maiden speech by quoting Demosthenes in the original. *The Biographical Peerage* was not impressed with the new earl's classical attainments: 'He has much more solid pretensions to distinction,' declared the editors. 'He is immensely rich.'

It is certainly for his business sense that his modern descendants have cause to remember Robert, the 2nd Earl Grosvenor. In 1826 he secured a private Act of Parliament giving him permission to lay out roads, streets and squares on his property behind the Pimlico Palace, and within months the builders were at work. Earl Grosvenor had the marshes drained, had the clay dug off to be baked into bricks, and then he leased out Pimlico in lots just as Sir Richard Grosvenor had done in Grosvenor Square a hundred years earlier. White stucco was the rage since Nash's confections around Regent's Park and in Brighton, and it was a Brighton builder, Thomas Kemp, the begetter of Kemp Town, who took on some of Pimlico as an 'undertaker', though the chief developer of this southern swathe of Grosvenor land was the builder Thomas Cubitt. His teams of workmen were to labour more than thirty years creating streets, squares and terraces in that part of London, and the Cubitt sign board became such a feature of life there that the area became nicknamed, for a period, 'Cubittopolis'.

But this name did not stick. The Grosvenors had used their own surname in every way they could devise up in Mayfair, and to start with, beside Buckingham Palace, the 2nd Earl Grosvenor was able to draw on the family connections of his wife Eleanor, the daughter of the Earl of Wilton – family name Egerton. But having spun out Egerton to a Crescent, Gardens, Place and Terrace, and Wilton to a Crescent, Mews, Place, Road, Row, Street and Terrace, the Earl was rather at a loss. So he turned to a new source of supply, the family estates back in the northwest, and this was how the streets and squares of London, SW1 bear names like Eaton, Chester, Eccleston (the village beside Eaton), Kinnerton and Halkin – though this last spelling was a slight variant on that of Halkyn Castle, a property which the Grosvenors owned just over the Welsh border.

It was a triumph indeed for London's grandest addresses to echo the humble Cheshire origins of the squires of Eaton Hall, and the nicest irony was reserved for the area's grandest address of all, since Belgrave Square was named by Earl Grosvenor after a tumbledown village next door to Eaton.

Today, Belgrave, Cheshire, is an unprepossessing hamlet. But something in the ring of the word has caused Belgravia to become the name of London's most expensive and prestigious residential neighbourhood – even if the post office declined to recognize it for many years; in the 1830s a letter addressed to Thomas Cubitt, Eaton Place, Belgravia, was despatched straight off to Vienna, on the grounds that such an outlandish name could only belong to some obscure and remote province of the Habsburg empire.

Earl Grosvenor could have continued the joke when he was raised one rank higher in the peerage in 1831. Marquess of Belgravia would have been a cheerful title – exotic and displaying a certain sense of fun.

But, conspicuously lacking a sense of humour, the 'Lord of Greek' chose to be known as Marquess of Westminster, which was totally accurate insofar as he was the largest private landlord in Westminster, but which, somehow, laid claim to just a little too much. The new Marquess seems to have been quite oblivious to the irony in all his Cheshire street names, and a letter which

BELGRAVIA
THE PROPERTIES
OF THE DUKE OF
WESTMINSTER
IN LONDON SWI

BELGRAVE
SQUARE

EATON
SQUARE

PRESENT DAY ARMS   OF   THE   GROSVENOR FAMILY

he wrote in May 1804, while he was still plain Earl Grosvenor,
to his father's benefactor William Pitt, displays insensitivity, not
to say ingratitude, of extraordinary proportions.

The Earl was most unhappy, he informed the Prime Minister,
about the number of peerages being bestowed upon lawyers and
officers in the armed forces:

In regard to the former, from their advanced age when created peers, the increase of Law Lords becomes obviously much too rapid, and in both cases their heirs . . . being seldom possessed of much landed property, become naturally too dependent on the crown. As to those who have distinguished themselves in the service of their country, there are other methods of rewarding them. . . .

The man whose father had been created a baron, a viscount and an earl, who had himself been raised to the rank of marquess, and whose grandson was to become a duke, complained: 'It has long been a matter of regret with many, and myself among others, that the peerage should have been so much increased within the last half century.'

The Peerage is not destitute of virtue.

W. S. GILBERT, *Iolanthe*, 1882

On the whole, Englishmen are made
dukes as a reward for being rich or royal
. . . though dukedoms have sometimes
been bestowed for merit.

NANCY MITFORD,
Noblesse Oblige, 1956

An English Peer of very old title is
desirous of marrying at once a very
wealthy lady; her age and looks are imma-
terial, but her character must be irrepro-
achable; she must be a widow or spin-
ster − not a divorcee. If among your
clients you know such a lady, who is
willing to purchase the rank of a peeress
for £25,000 sterling, paid in cash to her
future husband, and who has sufficient
wealth besides to keep up the rank of a
peeress, I shall be pleased if you will
communicate with me in the first instance
by letter.

Advertisement in the *Daily Telegraph*,
February 1901

VIII · NOBLESSE
OBLIGE

INHERITED titles are expressly forbidden by the American Constitution. Article I, Section 9, No. 8 reads: 'No title of nobility shall be granted by the United States.' But this has not prevented white Americans proclaiming themselves John Smith III or IV, while the absence of official titles has enabled black jazz musicians cheerfully to dub themselves Count, Earl and Duke – the order of precedence being a matter of opinion.

Nor has the banning of titles succeeded in abolishing inequality. As early as 1860 censuses showed that the richest 1 per cent of Philadelphia owned 40 per cent of the personally held wealth in their communities, while equivalent figures for the upper hundredth elsewhere showed them owning 37.6 per cent in St Louis, 38.5 per cent in Baltimore and 43 per cent in New Orleans.

These prosperous New World elites have sometimes been described in terms of 'aristocracy', but the highest distinction to which they could aspire was, in fact, plutocracy. The achievement of wealth and success had been reigning values in American society from the start, so the rich and powerful were always treated by their fellow citizens with a certain esteem. But this was not the forelock-tugging deference granted to the European noblemen in the nineteenth century: being a landowner was nothing special in a continent whose land was still mostly waiting to be owned. There was no mechanism by which America's nineteenth-century patrician could take on the charisma of a rural 'aristocrat', lording it over the local community, unless he lived in the south and purchased slaves, and if an American business dynasty had a country residence it was no more than that – a residence in the country. For status, they had to be content with showing off their mansion in the smart part of town.

Around the middle of the nineteenth century, however, a neat way of gaining status without infringing the Constitution presented itself to America's plutocrats. If they could not have a title themselves, they could buy one for their daughters by marrying them into the European aristocracy. They could enjoy the snobbery of having a countess in the family and, far from betraying the New World ethos, they could also relish the satisfaction of having bought out the upper crust of the old societies that they, or their recent forefathers, had been driven to leave by poverty or lack of opportunity.

As in all things, the Americans went to it earnestly, becoming experts at the subtle gradations of European nobility – and the relative prices they commanded. 'Dukes are the loftiest kind of noblemen in England,' explained one New York newspaper in 1886. 'There are only twenty-seven of them in the whole United Kingdom. Of these, there are only two available for matrimonial purposes. These are the Dukes of Manchester and Roxburghe. The Duke of Hamilton is already spoken for, the Duke of Norfolk is an old widower, and the Duke of Leinster is only eleven years old.'

There was great excitement when the Duke of Sutherland, whose estates, it was reported, ran from sea to sea across the Scottish county of Sutherland, visited New York. 'Attention, heiresses, what will you bid?' demanded *The World*.

For a dollar a year parents keen to enter the title-buying business could receive a directory of eligible bachelors available for their daughters. In 1890 the list ran from Abercromby to Uzès:

The Rt Hon John Abercromby; eldest son and heir to Lord Abercromby; 48 years old; educated at Harrow; formerly captain of the Rifle Brigade; divorced from Baroness von Heidenstam of Sweden; has no children; entailed estates amount to 16,000 acres yielding an income of $75,000. Family seats: 3 castles in Scotland. . . .

The Duc d'Uzès; is in his 20th year, exceedingly wealthy and holds the title Premier duke of France. The Duke owns the whole of the town of Uzès in the valley of the Rhône. His mother is the heiress of the celebrated Veuve Cliquot of Champagne fame. Family seat: Chateau Uzès, Uzès, Rhône.

Where available, this directory gave details of special circumstances which might incline the nobleman to accept a well-judged offer – 'the Earl of Ava's entailed estates do not, owing to mortgages, yield their nominal income of $100,000' – and by 1915 the publication *Titled Americans* was able proudly to list the names of nearly 500 American girls who had married into the European aristocracy: 42 American princesses, 33 marchionesses, 136 countesses, 19 viscountesses, 64 baronesses, 46 ladies who were wives of baronets or knights, and 17 duchesses – including the Duchesses of Manchester and Roxburghe.

Thomas Mann wrote a whole book on the theme – *Königliche Hoheit*. Only by embracing the wealth of the New World could the values of the old be preserved and renewed, he believed, and many a nobleman who had never heard of Thomas Mann agreed: the 8th Duke of Marlborough married one American girl, while his son, the 9th Duke, married two* – though the local villagers took some time to get accustomed to duchesses with an American accent.

'Your Grace will no doubt be interested to know,' sniffed the Mayor of Woodstock to Consuelo Vanderbilt, first of the 9th Duke's foreign wives, 'that Woodstock had a mayor and corporation before America was discovered.'

---

* Thomas Mann's theory was vindicated by the marriage of the 8th Duke's brother, Lord Randolph Churchill, to Miss Jennie Jerome of New York. Their elder son was Winston Churchill.

The French aristocracy recruited dollar princesses as assiduously as the British. In 1887 Charles de Talleyrand-Périgord, Duc de Dino, collected a dowry of $7 million on his marriage to Adele Sampson, and in the following year the Duc Elie Decazes picked up $2 million when he bestowed his hand and title upon Isabelle Singer, heiress to the sewing machine fortune. 'SHE PAYS ALL THE BILLS – HE THINKS HIMSELF CHEAP AT THE PRICE,' commented a headline in the *New York Tribune*.

Both these coups were outclassed by the Comte Boni de Castellane, who netted $15 million from Anna Gould, daughter of Jay Gould, the 'Great Bear' of Wall Street – though she then divorced him and married another Talleyrand, the Prince de Sagan; Rothschild heiresses were married by the Duc de Gramont and the Prince de Wagram; the Duc de Richelieu got a Heine, the Marquis de Plancy got an Oppenheim and the Marquis de Breteuil married a Fould.

The Ganays got themselves two heiresses. Jean, the 6th Marquess, married Berthe de Behague, granddaughter of a wealthy Austrian banker, the Baron de Haber – and Jean's son, Hubert, found a fortune still further afield. Marie Rose Bemberg was the grand-daughter of Otto Pieter Bemberg, a German of moderate means who had gone on an equatorial cruise for the sake of his health in the middle of the nineteenth century, settling in Argentina and founding there a financial empire that comprised ranches, dairy and meat-processing factories, as well as the largest brewery in Buenos Aires. He then decided to set up a bank in Paris, and that was how his granddaughter, Marie Rose Bemberg, came to meet Hubert, Count de Ganay and future Marquis.

The Ganays were made by these two lucrative marriages. They had had nobility of some sort since 1300 in their native Burgundy – Ganay is the name of a village there – and they achieved distinction in the sixteenth century when Jean de Ganay was made Chancellor of France by Louis XII. But they were not rich or important enough to feature in the annals of the Revolution, and it was not until the end of the nineteenth century that they established their present-day connection with the Chateau of Courances through the Marquis Jean's marriage to Berthe de Behague.

Confiscated for a period during the Revolution, Courances had been regained by the Nicolay family, and with the restoration of the monarchy after the fall of Napoleon, Aymard-Charles Marie Théodore de Nicolay, youngest son of le Grand Nicolay, had tried to pick up the pieces of his life in the family home. But the executions of his father and brother when he was only eleven had hurt him at an impressionable age, and a second family tragedy that occurred in the spring of 1830 seems to have unhinged him still more.

It was Easter Sunday, and because two of the Marquis's daughters had measles, they were left at home while the rest of the family and most of the household went to church in the village. But somehow, while the chateau was practically deserted, two farm labourers broke in, and when the Marquis and Marquise de Nicolay arrived home, they discovered that their little girls had been brutally assaulted and raped.

Horrified, the parents called for their carriage to transport their family as far away from the trauma as they could possibly get and, once away, the Nicolays could never, somehow, be persuaded to return to Courances again.

The Marquis seems to have blamed France itself for the misfortunes that had befallen his family, for he went to Switzerland to start a new life, and while he could not bring himself to part with Courances, he also begrudged the cost of guarding and maintaining a place that had come to represent so much unhappiness for him.

So by the time the Marquis de Nicolay died in his self-imposed exile in 1871, Courances was a ruin. Vandals had thrown stones through the windows. Slates were dislodged from the roof, and there was even a tree which had seeded itself and started to grow in the dining room. The chateau was a forlorn and ghostly shell when it was purchased in 1872 by the Austrian Baron de Haber – and it was he who, with his daughter Fanny, started devoting his fortune to the task of rebuilding Courances in its original Louis XIII style.

The chateau was so broken down that it would have been cheaper for Haber and his daughter to demolish it entirely and to rebuild in the currently fashionable *style Napoléon III*. But when

Haber had bought the ruins of Courances he had been buying more than a building site. He wanted to purchase history. So, with his daughter's help, he searched out the original plans of the chateau and the designs of the le Nôtre-inspired gardens.

The Nicolays had softened the geometrical lines of the park in imitation of the romantic 'natural' style of English landscaping popularized by Capability Brown. But the Habers went back to the original classical severity of raked gravel walks around Turkish carpets of low box hedges, and they restored the primacy of the precisely regimented avenues of plane trees that give such drama to the vistas of the chateau today.

After Fanny Haber's death her fortune and Courances passed to her daughter Berthe, whose marriage to the Marquis Jean bestowed the benefit of both upon the Ganay family, and when their son, Hubert, married Marie Rose Bemberg, the wherewithal was guaranteed to keep the ready-made ancestral home going in style to the present day. But, maintained by the sales of Latin American beer, butter and bully beef, reconstructed and inhabited for little more than a hundred years, and occupied by the Ganay family for even less – the historic Chateau de Courances is not quite as historic as it might at first sight appear.

Helen, elder daughter of Max von Wittelsbach, Duke in Bavaria, was Germany's most eligible bride at the beginning of the 1850s. Twenty years old and of impeccable pedigree, she was a match fit for a prince, or even an emperor – and in the summer of 1853 the young Franz Josef, newly crowned Emperor of Austria, came to Munich to pay court to her.

Helen's qualifications had been assessed in advance by the Emperor's representatives, and her father had given his approval in principle to a marriage. But when the dashing young Franz Josef arrived, he found that Helen did not live up to the expectations which his ambassadors had aroused.

Franz Josef was much more attracted by Helen's vivacious younger sister 'Sissi', who was only fifteen. In a matter of days the Emperor had fallen head over heels in love with her, and the following spring the couple were wed. So little Sissi became Elisabeth, Empress of Austria – and her jilted elder sister was required not simply to smile graciously at her wedding; she had to curtsey as well.

Helen could not find a substitute husband with rank to match that of her new brother-in-law. But she did succeed in finding someone who was almost as rich, Maximilian Anton von Thurn und Taxis, and Helen married him in August 1858, five years to the month after the Emperor Franz Josef's ill-starred mission to court her.

The Thurn und Taxis fortunes had revived somewhat after their sufferings at the hands of Napoleon. There was no longer a Holy Roman Empire to which they could be postmasters, but they remained close to the Habsburgs, and they had secured postal rights in several of the newly autonomous German states. In 1852 they had started issuing their own postage stamps.

They did not enjoy the luck of the Liechtensteins, whose little Imperial fief had been given sovereign status in Napoleon's Confederation of the Rhine and in the German Confederation that followed it. Sovereign authority over the Thurn und Taxis fief had been taken over by the ruler of Württemberg that surrounded it.

But the Thurn und Taxis remained freehold owners of their estates, and they purchased more elsewhere. Owning substantial acreages in Prussia and Bavaria, the family had more land to their name than many of the German rulers who had kept political control of their own little principalities, and they themselves were treated as princes in the city which had come to be their home – Regensburg, formerly Ratisbon, northeast of Munich on the banks of the River Danube.

It was here that Helen von Thurn und Taxis set about creating a palace where she could live in a style to rival that of her sister Sissi. Her husband died after less than ten years of marriage, leaving her with two small sons, and since the elder inherited the family title while still a minor, Helen reigned over the family palace as regent for the best part of twenty years, until her death in July 1890.

The Thurn und Taxis had built their first great palace at Frankfurt when they became princes of the empire, commissioning the court architect of Louis XV to design them a baroque residence near their postal headquarters. By the 1740s the family were living there in splendour, with eighty horses in the stables, a hundred and sixty servants, a master of ceremonies, gentlemen-in-waiting and a private orchestra. This way of life had grown even grander when the family was appointed to represent the Emperor in Regensburg at the Everlasting Diet of the Empire – the Habsburgs' grandiose attempt at a federal German assembly which ceased to be everlasting in 1806, along with the empire as a whole.

The Thurn und Taxis liked Regensburg, however. They had links with the princely family of Bavaria, and in 1812 they took over Regensburg's biggest building, the former monastery of St Emmeram – a rambling collection of cloisters and Gothic arches, knitting together endless little jewel-like chapels. They brought their furniture and fittings across Germany from their old palace in Frankfurt, and out of the unlikely combination of medieval monastery and secular baroque pleasure resort, the family succeeded in creating the splendid anachronism which is today the residence of Helen von Thurn und Taxis' great-grandson Prince Johannes.

Most of the grand chambers in the Frankfurt palace had been two metres higher than the monastery rooms in Regensburg, so the elaborate double doors that were transported across Germany had to lose their upper quarters. Their redundant panelling was redistributed to other corners of the building, and this has left parts of Schloss St Emmeram with a legacy of oddly shaped ceilings and unexpected little staircases improvised to adjust for the varying ceiling heights of the storeys below.

But in the 1880s work started on a new southern wing which more than doubled the size of the palace, and before her death Princess Helen saw installed a glorious chandelier-hung ballroom in the eastern wing with a canopied chamber leading off it, whose function was rather less obvious.

Though the room was dominated by a plump crimson and gold chair elevated on a dais, no member of the Thurn und Taxis family ever sat in the chair – in public at least – and there were two rival interpretations of the chamber's function. The family explanation was that it commemorated the seat which earlier

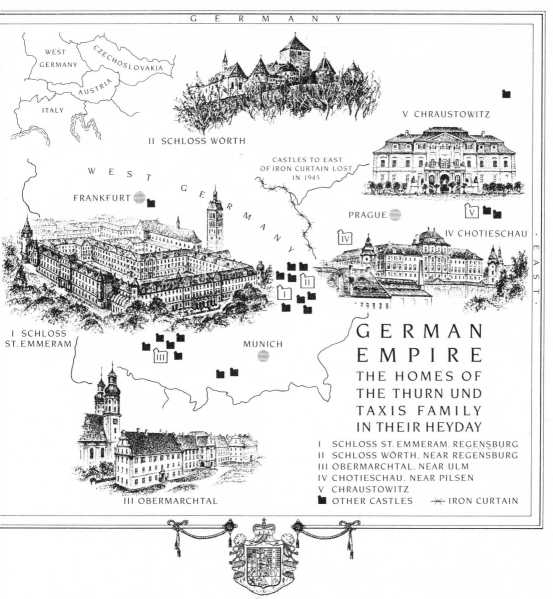

WEST GERMANY

CZECHOSLOVAKIA

AUSTRIA

ITALY

II SCHLOSS WÖRTH

V CHRAUSTOWITZ

CASTLES TO EAST
OF IRON CURTAIN LOST
IN 1945

WEST

FRANKFURT

GERMANY

PRAGUE

IV CHOTIESCHAU

EAST

I SCHLOSS
ST. EMMERAM

MUNICH

III OBERMARCHTAL

GERMAN EMPIRE

THE HOMES OF
THE THURN UND
TAXIS FAMILY
IN THEIR HEYDAY

I   SCHLOSS ST. EMMERAM. REGENSBURG
II   SCHLOSS WÖRTH. NEAR REGENSBURG
III OBERMARCHTAL. NEAR ULM
IV   CHOTIESCHAU. NEAR PILSEN
V   CHRAUSTOWITZ
⬛ OTHER CASTLES   ⚡ IRON CURTAIN

Thurn und Taxis had occupied when they presided over the Everlasting Diet. But rumour suggested, less kindly, that it clearly mattered greatly to someone in the family that Schloss St Emmeram should have a throne room to match sister Sissi's in Vienna.

Certainly the baroque silk liveries that make the servants of

Schloss St Emmeram today look like attendants in a royal palace were manufactured in the time of Princess Helen, just three generations back. With their knee breeches, buckled shoes and powdered wigs their design goes back to the eighteenth century, but they are, in fact, rather like the Chateau de Courances – not quite as historic or ancestral as they might seem.

The nostalgic attempts to regenerate the past at Courances and Schloss St Emmeram demonstrated the insecurity felt by the aristocrats of late nineteenth-century Europe.

On the face of it, the nobility was as powerful as ever. In France the middle classes had proved incapable of stamping their authority on the society which they had led into revolution, and the first half of the century was a history of monarchic and imperial revivals in which aristocrats played a prominent role. All over Europe politics continued to be dominated by the titled. The century's two great movements of national unification, in Germany and Italy, were masterminded by aristocrats – Otto, Prince von Bismarck and Count Camillo di Cavour – and in Britain the reign of Queen Victoria was rounded off by fifteen years of government under the leadership of the 3rd Marquess of Salisbury, who found it possible to act as chief executive of the world's most powerful country while sitting in the House of Lords.

But the signs of change were there to see. In 1870 France established her Third Republic, and in 1872 Britain substituted the secret ballot for the public hustings at which noblemen had been able to keep an eye on how their tenants voted. In 1885 the removal of the property qualification established universal male suffrage, and while the working classes had still to realize the power this gave them, the middle classes were already laying claim to their rights.

One measure of this was the growth of professional associations, through which the more highly skilled among the middle classes sought to give dignity and exclusiveness to their calling. 1800 had seen the foundation of Britain's Royal College of Surgeons; in 1818 the civil engineers gentrified their profession, and in 1825 the Law Society was formed; in 1834 it was the turn of the architects, in 1841 the pharmacists, and the British Medical Association was founded in 1856.

In 1871 the first civil servant was elevated to the House of Lords – Frederick Rogers, Lord Blachford – to be followed by Lords Cottesloe and Hammond in 1874 and half a dozen other civil servants before the century was out. The widening of the franchise made political parties more and more dependent upon financial contributions, and while it was still not quite possible nakedly to buy a title, contributions to party funds produced some novel recruits to the House of Lords: a stationer and newsagent, Viscount Hambleden (of W. H. Smith); a steel manufacturer, Lord Wimborne; two cotton manufacturers, Lords Cheylesmore and Rochdale; and three brewers, Lords Hindlip, Burton and Iveagh, of Allsopp, Bass and Guinness respectively – the trio being collectively known as the 'Beerage'.

The old aristocracy had not lost its grip. When Lord Derby tried in 1873 to disprove the allegation that Victorian Britain was controlled by a minority of rich men, the sweeping land survey he commissioned came to the embarrassing conclusion that 75 per cent of England was still, in fact, owned by only 7000 people. Taking advantage of new sources of wealth had always been a strength of the British aristocrat, and by 1896 no less than 167 noblemen, a quarter of Britain's peerage, were serving as directors on the boards of various industrial and commercial enterprises, almost invariably in a non-executive capacity.

But the dawning of mass democracy brought into being a new sort of popular power which could, if it wished, make the possession of title, money and even land quite irrelevant, and by the end of the nineteenth century British aristocrats were becoming aware, more or less consciously, of the need to justify their existence. Universal suffrage represented a threat to inherited privilege as great as that which the development of the money economy had posed to the knights of the Middle Ages – and the aristocratic reaction to it was similar. Once again, being noble became more than a matter of title: it became a noble way of behaving.

Part of the new aristocratic ethic involved a deliberate return to the age of chivalry. In 1884 the first, and last, British poet ever raised to the peerage was Alfred Tennyson who, in his *Morte d'Arthur* had Victorianized Mallory's fifteenth-century epic of knightly virtues; myths of good deeds and gentility which struck a responsive chord in an upper class dismayed by the dark Satanic mills of industrial Britain. The epic seemed to demonstrate how another elite had kept up standards through an age of barbarity. The Gothic revival enshrined this optimistic theme in art and architecture.

The notion developed that aristocrats should justify their existence by 'setting an example'. Georgian peers and Regency bucks had not worried much about setting an example to anyone. But Queen Victoria and her conscientious German husband were giving monarchy a new lease of life by developing the novel idea that it should be a primary function of the royal family to uphold certain moral values, and the aristocracy took a leaf from the royal book. Increasing numbers of noble lords lent their titles to worthy charities; their ladies paid visits to the worthy poor.

This new earnestness could be represented as a return to the purest meaning of aristocracy – the rule of the best. But it also constituted a concession to the middle-class values of thrift, hard work and duty which underpinned the success of the industrial revolution, and through the nineteenth century these two elements blended to produce the Victorian ideal of the upper-class English 'gentleman'.

Bertrand Russell, himself an aristocrat if never conventionally aristocratic, understood the purpose behind this precisely. 'The concept of the gentleman,' he said, 'was invented by the aristocracy to keep the middle classes in order.' If you enjoy a disproportionate share of a society's wealth and you wish to hold on to it by methods other than violence and intimidation, you have to persuade your fellow human beings that what you own reflects skills and attributes whose value is agreed upon by the people who matter. In nineteenth-century England it was the rising middle classes who mattered, and the aristocratic reaction to their rise was a skilful mixture of concession and outflanking.

At public schools, which were one of the era's great growth industries, new wealth and old breeding were mixed together in a country house setting which made young aristocrats feel at home and gave young plutocrats an ideal to which they should aspire. Wealthy industrialists could enjoy the satisfaction of penetrating the upper crust, while aristocrats could feel reassured that these newcomers were giving aristocratic values their endorsement.

'Look at the bottle merchant's son and the Plantagenet being brought up side by side,' wrote Matthew Arnold. 'Very likely young Bottles will end up by being a lord himself.'

In adult life the process continued in another institution which enjoyed a nineteenth-century boom – the gentleman's club – bastion of those 'sensible men of substantial means' who, wrote Walter Bagehot, 'are what we wish to be ruled by'.

In no other country, noted Matthew Arnold in 1868, 'do the professions so naturally and generally share the cast of ideas of the aristocracy as in England'.

There were those who viewed the moulding of plutocrat and aristocrat into a unified upper class with dismay. Friedrich Engels, waiting vainly for the inevitable revolution he had prophesied with his friend Karl Marx, scorned the British bourgeoisie who were mesmerized, like so many rabbits, by the glamour of aristocracy – while in 1863 Richard Cobden complained, more in amazement than in anger:

We have the spirit of feudalism rife and rampant in the midst of the antagonistic development of the age of Watt, Arkwright and Stephenson! Nay, feudalism is every day more and more in the ascendant in political and social life. So great is its power and prestige that it draws to it the support and homage of even those who are the natural leaders of the newer and better civilisation. Manufacturers and merchants as a rule seem only to desire riches that they may be enabled to prostrate themselves at the feet of feudalism.

A few self-made men stayed true to their origins, but most were only too happy to see their sons pursue a classical education, row at Henley and gain admittance to a world whose red letter days were Ascot week and 12 August – and in this phenomenon, it has been argued, can be seen the seeds of Britain's twentieth-century decline, as compared to the enduring economic enterprise of Germany, where aristocratic distaste for the bourgeoisie stimulated a self-contained urban entrepreneurial elite similar to the American model.

But if this process made the bourgeoisie more idle, it did force the aristocracy to be more industrious, and that proved to be of immeasurable benefit to their health as a class. 'In every country a great proportion of the aristocracy will be idle and fond of amusement and have always been so,' wrote King Edward VII when he was Prince of Wales, 'but I think in no country more than ours do the Higher Classes occupy themselves.' One nineteenth-century American visitor to England judged the philanthropic character of much aristocratic work to be particularly ingenious: 'The enormous amount of unpaid and voluntary service to the state, to one's neighbours in England, results in the solution of one of the most harassing problems of every wealthy nation: it arms the leisured classes with something worthy, something important to do.'

There was no single book setting out the principles of Victorian aristocracy, no code of conduct explaining how the perfect gentle knight could be costumed in a frockcoat and topper. But when contemporaries wished to give flesh to the Victorian ideal of aristocracy, they did have one real life model at whom they could point – Hugh Lupus, 3rd Marquess and 1st Duke of Westminster.

In the final decades of the nineteenth century the grand pillared entrance to Grosvenor House, Mayfair, presented one of the finest spectacles in Victorian London. Seven huge gas lamps illuminated the colonnade spanning the double arched entrance where horse-drawn carriages came and went, and when the Grosvenor family were in residence, the traffic was continuous. Dominating the corner where Upper Grosvenor Street met Park Lane, Grosvenor House looked out grandly over Hyde Park. It was a palace in its own right, and that was only appropriate, for it was the home of a dynasty described in 1865 as 'the wealthiest family in Europe, perhaps . . . the wealthiest uncrowned house on earth.'*

The front courtyard of the Grosvenors' London residence was sprinkled with sand, to prevent horses from slipping. A

---

* This same survey awarded the title of wealthiest crowned house to the family of Liechtenstein, judging the value of their personal landholdings to exceed those of the ruling families of Russia, Austria or Britain.

liveried footman waited by the front door, morning and night, to hand guests down, and as they entered the house, visitors were greeted by a concentration of art treasures that no public gallery or museum could match. Off the hall ran an anteroom graced by Reynolds's picture of *Mrs Siddons as the Tragic Muse* along with Gainsborough's *Blue Boy*, and this anteroom led into a gallery-ballroom on whose walls hung a Velasquez, a Turner and three Titians. Next door was the Rubens room, dominated by the *Adoration of the Magi*, and two other religious studies painted by Rubens for Philip IV of Spain, while another door opened into the saloon on whose walls hung four Poussins, three Claudes and a Rembrandt; seven more Claudes, five more Rembrandts and a couple of Gainsborough landscapes decorated the dining room beyond, and dominating the Grosvenor family as they ate their meals was Van Dyck's *Self Portrait With a Sunflower*.

There were fewer paintings on the private floor above, for that contained the quarters of the Duke and Duchess – art being for public display rather than private enjoyment – and above that was the children's floor with various day nurseries and night nurseries as well as a schoolroom, since little Grosvenors did not go to school: the boys had governesses and tutors until they were old enough for Westminster or Eton; the girls had governesses until they were ready to be married.

Looking after the family was a regiment of servants. The attics were occupied by eight maids' bedrooms – which represented accommodation for at least sixteen maids – and downstairs was the basement which kept the whole establishment running: a housekeeper with still room and china room; the butler, with his pantry and pantry scullery; the steward with his own room and office, a dormitory for the menservants, and the kitchen with its separate apartments – scullery, pantry larder, vegetable larder, meat larder, and individual bake house. There was a brushing room for brushing clothes, a polishing room for polishing boots, and a lamp room where one manservant was employed full time keeping all the oil lamps in order.

With this complex and extensive array of services the Grosvenor family staged some of the most glittering parties in London.

'We always enjoy the entertainments you give at Grosvenor

House so much,' wrote the Prince of Wales to Hugh Lupus – and such royal praise only gave Grosvenor House its due. For grand soirées, the entire garden was lit with fairy lights – the oil-lamp man worked hard that day – and a table stretched from one end of the dining room to the other, candle light reflected on the white linen tablecloths and on the silver racing trophies of the Duke. The art gallery became a ballroom, and one whole side of it was thrown open, with french windows giving onto a balcony and steps that led down onto the lawns.

'Everybody was beautifully dressed,' wrote one of the Duke's grand-daughters describing a ball held at Grosvenor House in the summer season of 1886. 'Mr and Mrs Gladstone were there and the Grand Duke of Mecklenburg. The garden was all lit up with Chinese lanterns and there were tables inside for people to eat at. Then the band played "God Save the Queen" and the Princess of Wales came in and down the middle of the ballroom. She looked very pretty in a mauve gown.'

When Queen Victoria had raised Hugh Lupus Grosvenor to the rank of Duke in 1874, envious gossip interpreted the elevation solely in terms of money. With an income in excess of £250,000 a year, Hugh Lupus was better off than the Queen herself and was something of an embarrassment to his fellow marquesses, for money was an important consideration where the distinction between the ranks of duke, marquess and earl was concerned. In the 1890s the 5th Marquess of Lansdowne was to decline the dukedom he was offered on his return from being viceroy of India because he felt that his income could not sustain the style of life expected of a ducal station.

At least one writer thought that the connection between cash and cachet in the further ennoblement of the Grosvenors was too naked for decency:

To give a fair start in life to a royal bastard, to reward a successful general, to gratify the ambition of a statesman, to add new lustre to a great historic house that has rendered eminent service to the country – these are reasons that we can at any rate understand; but to elevate a man to a dukedom because he happens to be the biggest ground landlord in London is an action which I, for one, cannot admire.

But the author of 'Our Old Nobility' missed the point, for there had been a certain element of abasement in turning England's richest man into its most junior duke. When Hugh Lupus Grosvenor took his place at the state opening of Parliament he had to sit in the lowliest position among his immediate peers – there were twenty-seven senior dukes, and five royal dukes whom he had to look up to – and that remains the position of the Dukes of Westminster to the present day. Dukedoms have been created since, but they have all been for existing members or new recruits to the royal family – like the Duke of Edinburgh.* Among the non-royal dukedoms that of Westminster remains in a subordinate position – a perpetual reminder of how *nouveau* its riches are. Far from glorifying money, Queen Victoria's creation of the new and junior dukedom of Westminster rather helped to put money into perspective.

The very name of the new duke, Hugh Lupus, going back to the first Earl of Chester, demonstrated the family anxiety to emphasize the Grosvenor pedigree at the expense of Grosvenor wealth, and when Hugh Lupus decided to revive the first Georgian earl's exploits on the Turf, his first Derby winner bore a name that proudly reasserted the family's ancient heraldic identity – Bend Or. The Scrope family was no longer in a position to complain.

Still, it was not so much wealth or pedigree which moved Queen Victoria to lift Hugh Lupus Grosvenor into the very top drawer of the British aristocracy as appreciation of his character, for if ever a man embodied *noblesse oblige*, it was he. Educated at Eton and Balliol, where his contemporaries included Matthew Arnold and Palgrave of *Golden Treasury* fame, Hugh Lupus was endowed with all the qualities that went to make up an eminent Victorian. Returned unopposed as MP for Chester at the age of twenty-one, he occupied his Commons seat for more than twenty years in the Whig interest, striking up a friendship with William Gladstone which faltered, but was not destroyed, by the two

* These royal dukedoms are Cornwall (borne by Prince Charles since his mother's accession in 1952), Edinburgh, Gloucester and Kent (these last two created for the sons of King George V). The Dukedom of Fife can be classed as semi-royal, since it was created in 1899 so that Alexander Duff, formerly Earl Fife, should occupy the highest rank in the nobility on his marriage to Princess Louise, eldest daughter of the future King Edward VII.

men's differences over Reform and Home Rule for Ireland, and his political career won him sufficient respect from his Conservative opponents for him to be offered a place in Lord Derby's government of 1866.

He was a tall, handsome serious man, who in later years shaved away the wispy chin whiskers that were the mid-Victorian style. His 'manner was grave, but kind and courteous,' remembered Stacy Marks, the artist the Duke commissioned to decorate his Eaton drawing room with huge paintings of the Canterbury Pilgrims, and his principal pleasures were domestic. The carillon of twenty-eight bells cast for the tall clock tower, which was the focal point of the Gothic embellishments that he added to Eaton Hall, played 'Home Sweet Home' whenever the ducal carriage hove into sight – as well as twenty-seven other tunes which it rang out remorselessly at quarter hourly intervals through the night.

He married twice, and though the infidelities of his first wife, Constance Leveson-Gower, were notorious, he remained faithful to her till her death. She was the mother of eleven children, eight of whom survived childhood, and his second wife, the Hon. Katherine Cavendish, gave him four more. He loved the role of the philanthropic landlord, building for his tenants 48 farmhouses, 360 cottages, 8 schools, 7 village halls, and 3 churches on his Cheshire estates, while he dedicated corners of the Grosvenors' London properties to sanitary low-rent tenement buildings for the working classes.

The Duke's reputation for good works made him immune to conventional Victorian moralizing. He 'could pass from the racecourse to a missionary meeting,' wrote *The Times* in his obituary, 'without incurring the censure of even the strictest'. Only a gentleman so earnest and philanthropic as Hugh Lupus could have got away with inviting a racehorse to the garden party which he gave on Park Lane to celebrate Queen Victoria's Golden Jubilee. The horse was Ormonde, winner of the Two Thousand Guineas, Derby, St Leger and a dozen other races which gave him a national reputation comparable to that of a more modern Westminster horse, Arkle. On 27 June 1887 Ormonde's appearance on the lawn of Grosvenor House, happily munching the best flowers in the garden and lumps of sugar offered by throngs of admiring ladies made the party one of the great private celebrations of that royal summer. The horse was a star guest in an assemblage which also included the Prince and Princess of Wales, the King of Denmark, the King and Queen of the Belgians, the Grand Duke and Duchess of Mecklenburg-Strelitz, Prince Ludwig of Bavaria, the Crown Prince of Sweden and Norway and the Queen of Hawaii.

In Ascot week Hugh Lupus entertained at Cliveden, the Palladian mansion overlooking the Thames and Windsor forest which he inherited from his aunt and first mother-in-law, the Duchess of Sutherland. Infidelities aside, Hugh Lupus's first marriage was another example of the Grosvenors' skill at matrimonial alliance, for if any other duke could match Hugh Lupus as a landowner, it was his first father-in-law. The Duke of Sutherland owned 1,358,000 acres – most of the county of Sutherland in fact – and he had had Cliveden rebuilt to the design of Sir Charles Barry. Queen Victoria loved going over from Windsor to Cliveden, and was most upset when the Duke of Westminster decided to sell the house to the Astor family – Americans.

'It is grievous to think of its falling into these hands!' wrote the Queen in a severe note from Florence where she was staying in the spring of 1893. Hugh Lupus had decided to sell off his Thames Valley estate in order to create a financial settlement for his younger sons and daughters – the Grosvenor family rule always being to preserve the main Cheshire and London estates in a block for the eldest son. But Queen Victoria thought this a poor reason for disposing of 'dear beautiful Cliveden'.

'The Duke must excuse the Queen,' she wrote, 'if she says she thinks he has built too much at Eaton and that if it had not been so, Cliveden might have been retained. He will miss it very much the Queen is sure and the Duchess and the children even more so.'*

---

* After the sale of Cliveden there was some dispute between the Duke of Westminster and William Waldorf Astor over certain works of art and the Visitors' Book which, the Duke said, had not been included in the furniture and effects sold with the house. Cliveden's Visitors' Book contained 200 years of royal and aristocratic signatures. The American, who became a naturalized Briton in 1899 and a Viscount in 1916, eventually returned the art treasures, but the Visitors' Book was something he adamantly refused to part with.

Hugh Lupus's building and rebuilding of Eaton Hall had indeed been a monumental exercise, and Queen Victoria was probably close to the truth when she suggested that the expense had put a strain even on the finances of the Grosvenors. We do not know what sort of buildings the family had inhabited through the years of the Tudors and up to the Civil War. But with the Restoration and Sir Thomas Grosvenor's marriage to Mary Davies, a fine new Charles II house on three floors with two wings had been raised at the end of the mile and a quarter drive which stretched from the ancestral home towards the Welsh hills.

A century later, when the baronets had become earls, this Mark II home was no longer considered grand enough and William Porden was commissioned to present a new design. He offered two alternatives, one Grecian, the other Gothic, and he argued strongly for the Gothic which was, in his opinion, more exclusive, since everybody knew that it was more expensive: it embodied 'Rank and Fortune' and its antique air made it appear 'the work of our ancestors and not of yesterday'. There was only one style to choose, and in 1803 the Grosvenors moved out so that the Gothic tower and pinnacle hoisters could get to work on Eaton Hall Mark III.

Eaton Hall Mark IV had been the work of Hugh Lupus's father in the 1850s, an attempt to tone down the Brighton Pavilion-like curlicues of Porden's Gothic pile. But this seemed a poor compromise to Hugh Lupus, so in the 1870s he embarked on a fifth version of the ancestral home, commissioning Alfred Waterhouse, the leading architect of the day.

Waterhouse was an exponent of Law Court Gothic, famous for the new Natural History Museum in London and for Manchester City Hall, and he gave the Grosvenors exactly what they must have expected – a ponderous blend of mausoleum and municipal monument, which took twelve years to build at a cost of nearly £600,000. Not a single surviving photograph manages to make this lumpish pile look anything less than preposterous, and when he saw it finished, Hugh Lupus himself declared that the best thing to do with it was to rent it out to someone else. He promptly retired to the so-called 'private wing', an unpretentious rectory-sized home in the gardens, and for the rest of its existence the main part of Eaton Hall Mark V* was surrendered by the Dukes of Westminster to the enjoyment of their guests.

Entertaining, however, was what aristocratic homes were all about in the heyday of the house party. Eaton Hall Mark V was the sort of palace that a duke was *expected* to create, for even on the eve of the twentieth century it was still incumbent upon the great aristocrats to provide homes fit for royalty to stay in: Hugh Lupus's guests at Eaton in the last decades of Queen Victoria's reign included the Prince and Princess of Wales (later King Edward VII and Queen Alexandra) as well as their sons, the Duke of Clarence and Duke of York (later George V), the Duke and Duchess of Teck and also their daughter May (later Queen Mary) – the Tecks being relatives, since their eldest son Prince Adolphus, 'Dolly', was married to Hugh Lupus's fourth daughter, Meg. 'A very good connection,' noted Queen Victoria in her letter of congratulation, 'and she will doubtless be well off.'

Eaton Hall boasted its own private railway, connecting it to the local station, and a staff of over 300 men and women. The head gardener alone had forty men under him, and seven of the male staff made up a private fire brigade complete with uniforms and fire engine. Nearly eighty men were involved in the forests and with game – and this was Hugh Lupus's greatest pleasure, for he was proud to have turned Eaton into one of the best pheasant shoots in the country.

But whenever the first Duke of Westminster invited people to come and stay with him for the weekend he never mentioned the shooting. He considered that vulgar. He invited guests for the pleasure of their company and, expecting people to return the compliment, he felt that adding the words 'for some shooting' to his invitation was ungracious – almost a bribe, in fact.

Lord Ernest Hamilton, a noted devotee of game sports, discovered this when he was first invited to Eaton in the middle of the 1890s. He was somewhat disconcerted to see no reference to shooting in the wording of the invitation, and it was only by chance that a friend who knew the Duke's special etiquette advised

---

* Most of Hugh Lupus's Eaton Hall was dynamited in the 1960s. But the clock tower was retained, and beside it the present Duke's father sited the modern Eaton Hall Mark VI.

Lord Ernest to take his guns to Eaton just the same. At dinner on the first night there was no whisper of any sporting activity the following day, but having been coached in the traditions of the place, Lord Ernest turned up for breakfast in knickerbockers and boots.

To his dismay there was no mention made by the Duke as to the day's routine, and after His Grace had eaten breakfast and departed, there was a whispered and nervous conversation between the other guests which, in the absence of firm evidence of sport in the offing, could only come to a despondent conclusion.

About half past ten I was dejectedly smoking a cigarette in the hall, having by that time definitely abandoned all hope of shooting . . . when the Duke strolled dreamily up to me and said 'Brought a gun?'

I replied brightly that I had. As a matter of fact I had brought two.

'Care to come and see if we can pick up a pheasant or two?' he continued.

I said that I was even prepared to do that.

'Then we will start from the front door in a quarter of an hour,' he said.

Lord Ernest had visions of the Duke and himself poking about in the hedgerow with a spaniel, to come home proudly with a couple of cock pheasants in their hands. But when he reported to the front door at the appointed hour he found the Duke and five other guests waiting in a large brake which set off towards woods from which pheasants appeared to be flying in considerable numbers – and as the brake stopped, a group of keepers came up to the guns to request the names of the party.

The moment I had disclosed my name, the keeper attached to me told me that I was No. 3 and pointed to a spot some 200 yards distant which was marked by a cleft stick bearing a card and over which an uninterrupted stream of pheasants were making their hurried and, so far, uneventful exit [from the woods]. I snatched up a gun and did that 200 yards in fairly good time, followed at a considerable interval by my short-winded and perspiring loader. To the right and left of me I could see the other eager enthusiasts, goaded on by the sight of the swarms of fugitive pheasants, running for all they were worth to intercept them, and in some cases, firing as they ran.

Two hours later Lord Ernest went back to luncheon having shot a thousand pheasants with his fellow guests, and he later learned that the Eaton keepers always had orders to start driving the game at 11 o'clock to the minute – whether the guns had appeared or not.

In its 1899 obituary of the first Duke of Westminster, *The Times* paid tribute to the cultivation with which Hugh Lupus took his pleasures, following the pursuits and amusements appropriate to every Englishman of wealth and leisure, while never forsaking his overriding sense of public duty. It was this that made him a 'fine example of the great noble', in the opinion of the newspaper, for rank carried obligations as well as privileges, and in realizing this Hugh Lupus showed himself truly aristocratic.

It was almost impossible to keep a count of the good works sponsored by the first Duke of Westminster. At various times he was president of the Royal Agricultural Society, the Chester Cottage Improvement Society, the Gardeners' Royal Beneficent Institution, five London hospitals, and several dozen other worthy organizations, among them the Metropolitan Drinking Fountains and Cattle Troughs Association whose marbled monuments still ornament London streets: under the presidency of Hugh Lupus the Association built nearly 1500 troughs and fountains to refresh London's livestock and their keepers.

Temperance was a particular concern of his. Alarmed at the tendency of London's hansom cab drivers to warm themselves on a winter's night with a tot of rum, he became a supporter of the Cabmen's Shelter Fund and he personally financed the building of the Maida Vale shelter, which still does its job beside Little Venice, offering cheaply priced food, warmth, tea and coffee to lure drivers from the alternative source of refreshment – the pub.

He was President of the United Committee for the Preventing of Demoralising of Native Races by the Liquor Traffic, and, practising what he preached, the Duke endeavoured to eradicate public houses from those areas of London for which he personally was responsible. To this day the Grosvenor estates in London are only poorly provided with resorts for alcoholic refreshment, and there are just eight pubs in Grosvenor Mayfair, most of them needing to be searched out down back mews and side streets.

The Duke sponsored the enlargement of Hampstead Heath and, in a similar cause, he supported the Sunday opening of museums and art galleries. He was a solemn Christian – he prayed at 9 every morning in Eaton Chapel surrounded by all his household who filed out afterwards in strict order of rank – but he also believed that after six days of hard labour, the working classes were entitled to some sort of relaxation. So when he heard that his agent at Eaton was excluding parties of Liverpool cyclists from the grounds, he rescinded the ban and insisted the estate gates be kept open on Sundays for all comers. If moral and uplifting facilities were not provided for the lower orders they might turn to less desirable recreations.

Of all Victorian aristocrats the first Duke of Westminster could most easily afford to be generous, and he swept through life without stinting his serenely held view of the magnificence appropriate to his station. But his sense of public duty made him very much a man of his times, and when he died in December 1899 at the age of seventy-four, having outlived his eldest son and leaving a grandson to inherit the title, mourning was universal.

'Gone Britain's noblest gentleman,' declared the *Manchester Guardian*.

In Chester flags were flown at half mast, church bells were muffled and all the shops were shut for three hours. It was as if a local prince had passed away, and that is exactly what Hugh Lupus had been. In the Middle Ages such communal sorrowing over the death of a local lord was commonplace. It is difficult to imagine any British town or city doing the same in the twentieth century.

The funeral of Hugh Lupus Grosvenor was a curiously appropriate memorial to the man who earned England's last non-royal dukedom and who thus, given the trend of twentieth-century British politics, will probably go down in history as the last real duke of all. There were no flowers at his burial, just one wreath of immortelles bearing a small handwritten note: 'A mark of sincere respect and regard and esteem from Victoria RI.'

That wreath was placed alone on top of the Duke's coffin. But inside the coffin there was no body, just a small urn containing the dead nobleman's ashes, for in the 1870s Hugh Lupus had included cremation among the worthy causes he espoused. The process was repugnant to many churchmen of the time, but to the Duke it represented progress which should, he thought, be championed for the sake of space, efficiency and low cost to the ordinary working man; he had been instrumental in the opening of Britain's first crematorium at Woking in 1885. So, having worked strenuously to set an example in everything that he accomplished during his lifetime, Hugh Lupus Grosvenor, first Duke of Westminster, felt it only appropriate that he should do the same in death.

Our homes and our cities seemed as safe as the ground under our feet; we could not conceive our relations with people of other nationalities being anything but polite and friendly. When we wished to travel we just bought our tickets, made our reservations, and started for any part of the globe we fancied. Passports did not exist, and we changed our money unrestrictedly into any other currency we required. It now seems incredible.

I remember motoring with friends somewhere in Central Europe during the summer of 1912. The driver stopped outside a small building, and we asked why. 'It's the frontier,' he answered. 'I just have to show a paper about the car.' I do not even remember what frontier it was. In those days all Europe was our playground, and we sped from Italy to Austria, through Germany into Switzerland and so on to France without giving the matter a thought.

THE DUCHESS OF SERMONETA,
Sparkle Distant Worlds, 1947

IX·FLASH GOLDEN

His Grace the 2nd Duke of Westminster – christened with the names Hugh Richard Arthur Grosvenor but generally known to his friends as 'Bend Or' – was so eager to get at the Germans in the summer of 1914 that he enrolled in the French army. Bend Or did not believe that his own countrymen would actually declare war on the Kaiser, and when Britain surprised him on 4 August, it took some complicated reshuffling to extract His Grace from his original commitment. Once extracted, however, Bend Or went to war for King and Country in the style that only an aristocrat could.

It was an unfailing source of amusement to the couturière, Miss Coco Chanel, probably the most distinguished of the 2nd Duke of Westminster's numerous mistresses, that a great English aristocrat should not only be named after a horse, but that he should be so totally unconcerned to hide the misfortune. Yet Bend Or himself was always rather proud to have been nicknamed after the colt that won the Derby for his grandfather, Hugh Lupus, in 1880. According to family legend, some similarity of colour was discerned between the chestnut animal and the reddish fluff on the head of the baby born within a few months of the horse's first successes on the turf, and as a Grosvenor, the 2nd Duke of Westminster knew what 'Bend Or' originally meant. It linked him with the days of Crécy when Sir Richard Grosvenor had flaunted the golden flash across his shield, if only for a season, and the flamboyance with which the grandest twentieth-century Grosvenor went out to do battle in 1914 was in a truly ancient tradition. His Grace arrived at the Western Front in November of that year accompanied by his own private army.

Bend Or had a burning conviction that the future of warfare was mechanical, for he seems to have inherited a bent for engineering from his father, Victor Alexander Grosvenor, eldest son of the great Hugh Lupus. Victor Alexander died in 1884 at the age of thirty-one, thus making his five-year-old son direct heir to the Dukedom. But before his death he had distinguished himself as a railway enthusiast, most frequently to be found, according to his obituary in *The Times* 'in the railway workshops at Crewe, and oftener still driving the "Wild Irishman" between London and Holyhead' – railways being a not uncommon passion for the Victorian aristocracy. The greatest delight of the Grosvenors' prosperous relative, the mine-owning 3rd Duke of Sutherland, had been to drive his private locomotive on his private railway line from Golspie to Helmsdale.

'Now that's what I call a real duke,' his grandson, the 5th Duke, recalls one Scots navvy saying, 'driving his own engine, on his own railway – and burning his own bloody coal!'

Bend Or's maintenance of this tradition had been to build up a fleet of fast cars – he collected a shameless number of speeding convictions in the years up to 1914 – and when war broke out he took one of his Rolls-Royces back to the Rolls-Royce Derby factory to have it modified for battle. The result, with extra metal plating and a Hotchkiss machine gun mounted to the rear, was one of the first armoured cars, and Bend Or decided to take this car and several others with him to do battle with the Germans at his own expense in November 1914.

Mustering his own mechanized cavalry was quixotic enough, but the incongruity of Bend Or's private army was increased by the fact that technically it was on assignment to the Navy, for the senior British generals were little enamoured of new-fangled mechanical gadgets, and they had still less enthusiasm for swash-buckling young dukes coming out to teach them their business. So Bend Or had had to shelter under the patronage of Winston Churchill, First Lord of the Admiralty, a friend he had made during the Boer War, and he led his armoured car squadron with the rank of temporary commander, RNVR. In May 1915 he saw action in the second battle of Ypres, and his metal cavalry distinguished itself when a German attack was met by a counter-charge from the 10th Hussars and the Blues.

'They were assisted,' reported *The Times,* 'by a detachment of the Duke of Westminster's armoured motor cars which did excellent work.'

Bend Or's armoured cars were not really equipped for the mud and trenches of the Western Front, and in the winter of 1915 they were transferred to North Africa to assist Britain's Italian allies fighting the Turks in Tripoli. To drive his Rolls-Royces, Bend Or naturally took his own chauffeur, one of his jockeys, and a number of other servants from Eaton, and on 26 February 1916 the Duke of Westminster's Light Armoured Brigade saw action when they helped Britain's Western Desert Force defeat 7000 Turkish soldiers and Senussi tribesmen. The armoured cars proved their value by rounding up stragglers and capturing weapons with which the Turks and tribesmen were trying to escape, and it was in the course of these mopping-up operations that Bend Or came across the information that was to make his expedition famous.

At the beginning of November 1915 HMS *Tara,* formerly an old Irish packet boat, *Hibernia,* had been torpedoed off the Tripoli coast and its crew taken prisoner by the Senussi. The British Desert Command had heard of their plight, but only through Bend Or's operations of 26 February 1916 was it discovered that nearly 100 men were being held prisoner inland at the oasis of Bir Hakeim. Bend Or took on the mission of rescuing them.

Two Arab guides said that Bir Hakeim was about seventy

miles into the desert, and the Duke of Westminster's Light Armoured Brigade duly set off in that direction. But with 70 and then 100 miles registered on the Rolls-Royces' milometers there was still no sign of the enemy, and at 110 miles Bend Or was warned that his column had exhausted more than half its petrol. At 115 miles from base he was the only man disinclined to turn back.

But before 120 miles was reached the Duke's confidence was rewarded, for the guides recognized the mounds and a tree which told them they were near Bir Hakeim, and Bend Or ordered his twelve armoured cars into formation for the charge.

The Senussi tribesmen were so amazed at the sight of the Duke of Westminster's serried ranks of Rolls-Royces bearing down upon them at full throttle across the sands of the Libyan desert that they quite forgot to turn their guns upon their prisoners, and all the survivors of the *Tara* were saved. Most of the prisoners were suffering from dysentery and malnutrition – Bend Or's armoured column had arrived just in time to save the ship's dog from the cooking pot – and the Duke's supply vehicles became ambulances to carry the invalids back.

It was a daring and famous victory. General Peyton, GOC Western Desert Forces, recommended Major the Duke of Westminster for the Victoria Cross, and the citation for the DSO, which Bend Or was, in fact, awarded, paid glowing tribute to the Duke's personal heroism. The grateful survivors of the *Tara* presented their saviour with a silver model of one of his armour-plated Rolls-Royces, and the clean-cut romance of the Bir Hakeim adventure captured the imagination of a public grown sick of slaughter and stalemate in the mud of Flanders. The Duke of Westminster had proved that knight errantry was not dead.

Europe's aristocrats had entered the lists in August 1914 assuming that battle would be largely a matter of cut and thrust. It all seemed such fun. 'It was generally felt,' wrote Duff Cooper, 'that war was a glorious affair and the British always won.' Left at home, their ladies enjoyed making their own contribution to the national effort.

'Now there is a war on,' declared Lady Ermyntrude Malet,

sister of the 11th Duke of Bedford, to a young cousin who was having tea with her, 'we must learn to do things for ourselves.' And she got up and switched off the light.

Young noblemen rushed into battle eager to prove the oldest, finest meaning of their nobility, and aristocratic influence was exerted shamelessly to jump queues and cut corners. A mother whose connections got her son quickly into the front line was judged 'lucky', and only later did some, like Harold Macmillan, who pulled strings to become gazetted to the Grenadier Guards, reflect that the privilege being so eagerly sought was that of 'getting ourselves killed or wounded as soon as possible'.

It took some time for the realities of modern mass warfare to sink in. Lady Sackville, mistress of Knole, was most indignant that the estate carpenters should all be called up for the army, and wrote to the War Minister to tell him so. 'Do you realize, dear Lord Kitchener, that you are ruining houses like ours?'

Death and the horrors of trench warfare struck down aristocrat and common soldier alike. The flower of youth on both sides butchered each other indiscriminately in the mud of Flanders, and when Margot Asquith went to Ypres with a group of society friends to put crosses on the graves of the sons of the Duke of Richmond and Lord Lansdowne, she saw the true nature of the conflict that had started after the death of an Austrian archduke. The cemetery was no more than a wasteland with sodden scraps of wood stuck hurriedly into the huddled graves. The names scrawled on them in pencil were being washed off by the rain, and when one British soldier, digging a fresh grave, was asked whom it was for, he did not bother to stop digging. 'For the next,' he replied.

Created by warfare during the Dark Ages, Europe's aristocracy was destroyed by the dark age that it brought upon the world from 1914 to 1918. Isolated feats of noble heroism like those of Bend Or or the airborne joustings of Baron Manfred von Richthofen could not obscure the fact that if anyone bore responsibility for the disaster it was the aristocratic classes who had led their societies into war so blithely – and when the time came for reconstruction they were not included. After 1918 it would still be possible to identify the existence and achievements of individual

aristocrats, but whole aristocracies – coherent, landed elites dominating the politics and society of their own particular country –
these were gone forever.

'We were compelled to die,' declared Count Otto Czernin
after the war was over. 'We could only choose the manner of our
death, and we chose the most terrible.'

In the first titanic clashes of the British and German armies
as they met head-on in Flanders, centuries of pedigree were
destroyed in a matter of weeks, and the slaughter continued
remorselessly. Between 1914 and 1918, twenty British peers,
forty-nine direct heirs to titles and a larger number of younger
sons were killed – and the effect of this went beyond blood letting.
Systematically organized death duties had been introduced in
Britain in 1894, and although those men killed in action were
granted exemption on the first £5000 they left, this represented
comparatively slight relief on the full extent of a great noble estate.

Under the impact of death duties and David Lloyd George's
demagogic attacks on the 'land monopoly', some 800,000 ancestral
acres had been disposed of in a flurry of sales before 1914, a
premonition of the Armageddon ahead. Now this accelerated so
that, by the early 1920s, it was calculated that a quarter of English
land was under new ownership.

On 19 May 1920 *The Times* took note of the process in a
portentous article:

We all know it now, not only from the advertisements, not only from various
attractive little descriptive paragraphs, not only from the numerous notice
boards with which the countryside is disfigured, but from personal experience
amongst our friends, if not actually of our own . . . For the most part, the
sacrifices are made in silence. 'The privileged classes', to use an old name, take
it all for granted. It had to be . . . 'England is changing hands'.

Before the First World War less than 10 per cent of British agricultural land had actually been owned by the men farming it. But
by 1927 this had risen to over a third, according to one survey.
The heyday of the aristocratic *rentier* who lived off his tenants was
past. Death duties and the Western Front between them had
proved to constitute a surprisingly efficient method of land
redistribution.

The Treaty of Versailles that gave a new shape to Europe in 1919 was in itself a massive exercise in land reform. One eighth of Imperial Germany, the fringes of Russia and much more of the Habsburgs' Austria-Hungary were redistributed in a chain of individual nation states stretching from Estonia to Yugoslavia – and Teutonic aristocrats like the Liechtensteins were viewed as colonial foreigners by the nationalistic regimes of these new countries. Their grand estates came under attack. Over 70 million acres of eastern Europe, one fifth of the entire farming area, were compulsorily purchased and redistributed by the new national governments established after the Great War, and the Liechtensteins suffered like their fellow aristocrats: their Moravian and Bohemian lands lay in the new state of Czechoslovakia, and they lost 20 per cent of them to land reform programmes – though that still left them with more than two dozen castles to their name.

More serious was the threat that the new forces of nationalism posed to the little principality that bore the family name in the valley of the Upper Rhine. The family still did not live there. The long-lived Prince John II, head of the family since 1858, had presided over reforms abolishing feudal dues and military service for the local inhabitants and he had started to renovate the old castle on the crag overlooking Vaduz. But this was still very much a holiday home, an alpine hunting lodge the family could use when they tired of their great boar forests in the east.

With the fall of the Habsburgs, however, the principality was dragged into the politics and turmoil attending the birth of the new republic of Austria – and this first serious involvement with events outside Liechtenstein's own little sector of the Rhine Valley proved painful. The principality was part of the Austrian monetary area. Their currency was the Austrian crown, and when this collapsed in the runaway inflation that followed the First World War in Germany, Liechtensteiners found that their hard-earned savings had become valueless.

It was a catastrophe by any measure, but it rankled particularly with thrifty farming folk for whom saving was a way of life. Nest-eggs accumulated painstakingly over entire lifetimes were destroyed, and the locals rebelled indignantly against all things Austrian.

The Prince, who had lost the value of his own financial reserves in Austria and who was suffering from the high rates of tax imposed by Austria's new republican government, shared their indignation. So a Liechtenstein delegation made its way to Berne, and in 1923 its negotiations produced a customs treaty which, effectively, transferred the principality from the Austrian to the Swiss sphere of influence. The Swiss government agreed to handle Liechtenstein's diplomatic and economic relationships internationally for a fee; the Swiss would manage Liechtenstein's postal affairs, though the principality could issue its own stamps; and, most important of all, the currency of the principality would no longer be the Austrian crown. Henceforward the solid farmers of Liechtenstein could save their money in solid Swiss francs.

It was one more stage in the process of good luck and self help by which the Imperial fief of Liechtenstein turned itself into a fully fledged, if undersized, sovereign state – a triumph of nationalism in a minor key – and one bonus of its new link with Switzerland was that the 12,000 inhabitants of the principality were now entitled to carry their own Liechtenstein travel documents. Aristocracy could not be entirely dead if one clan of noblemen and their subjects could produce a passport that was emblazoned with the family name.

The three massive empires that had dominated central and eastern Europe at the beginning of the twentieth century were brought crashing down by the war to end all wars, and their emperors crashed with them: Germany, Russia and Austria-Hungary all became republics.

Nancy Mitford was later to write that aristocrats in a republic are like so many chickens who continue to run around after their heads have been cut off. Kings and emperors were essential to aristocratic identity, in her opinion, so in a society which lacks a crowned head, aristocrats must, perforce, themselves be headless.

But she did not give snobbery its due. The French nobility had thrived in the absence of a King. The new post-Imperial Austrian republic went to the lengths of banning all titles and outlawing the use of the 'von' before the name. But the government could not stop servants and friends continuing to render homage to the grand – and in Germany aristocrats were allowed to incorporate their titles as extra Christian names.

The aristocrats who did not survive were the Russians. The *émigré* Russian count or archduke driving his taxi was, proverbially, one of the sights of Paris in the 1920s, his aristocratic polish and breeding proof against even the frustrations of the Parisian rush hour. But legend is the only evidence for the existence of this noble taxi-driving subculture in the French capital after 1917, and it certainly does not exist today.

The Russian aristocracy ceased to exist after 1917 because – unlike their peers in the republics of Germany, Austria, or France – they lost their land. Aristocratic polish and manners may survive one generation of poverty in a garret, or even relative prosperity in a suburban villa, but after that, cut off from the land, the noble identity has nothing to sustain it. An *émigré* title may have some facetious utility in the worlds of fashion or public relations, but for most members of subsequent generations it is an inheritance that is meaningless – not to say pretentious – if it lacks the property with which its status was originally intertwined. It is the loss of land that makes the nobleman headless, not the loss of an emperor or king, and, as calamities go, the latter has usually turned out to be surprisingly survivable.

The British aristocracy certainly did not get much support from their King on the eve of the First World War when they found themselves confronting the House of Commons over the right of the Lords to veto legislation. Edward VII and his son George V prevaricated, but when the monarchy was forced finally to choose sides, it opted against the peers and for the people – and that is the side it has remained on ever since.

Modern British representative monarchy owes its success to having abandoned the old pyramid of privilege, in which the various levels of the establishment were supposed to interlock as a foundation for the throne, and today it floats magically unsupported above British society, for it has realized that the generalized approval it needs to perform its feat of weightlessness means having no links with any one special-interest group – and certainly not with that special-interest group whose hereditary privilege makes it liable to the very attack to which the monarchy itself is most vulnerable.

In 1911 the conflict between the Commons and the House of Lords had been resolved when George V agreed in principle to create an unlimited number of Liberal peers in order to outvote the Tory majority in the Lords. In the face of this threat the Lords had given way, deserting the political battlefield rather than let their social status be diluted by several hundred overnight earls and barons – and that, in itself, was an admission of what their noble lordships had really been fighting for.

But the dilution of their dignity happened anyway. Between 1916 and 1922 David Lloyd George, one of the new non-aristocratic politicians made possible by universal male suffrage, trafficked systematically in aristocratic titles in order to swell his party funds. In one eighteen-month period he nominated a record number of 26 peerages, 74 baronetcies and 294 knighthoods, the majority of them paid for more or less directly – and a minority of them matters of open public scandal.

The 1922 honours list included a baronetcy 'for public services' to one Rowland Hodge, who had been convicted in April 1918 for food hoarding; Sir Joseph Robinson, convicted and fined half a million pounds for fraudulent share dealing, was offered a barony – while Sir William Vestey, managing director of Union Cold Storage, was given a barony for wartime services that were said to have included the gratuitous provision of cold storage facilities for the war effort.

When it emerged that the new baron had, in fact, charged the government the full market rate for these facilities and that, in order to avoid tax, he had also moved his meat-packing firm to Argentina, throwing 4000 British employees out of work, Vestey was unrepentant. The multimillionaire, whose many enterprises included Dewhurst the high-street butchers, confessed that he had, indeed, purchased his peerage since he considered it a just recognition of his own hard work.

It said something about the character of recruits to the British aristocracy throughout the final years of the Great War and the 1920s, that Maundy Gregory, Lloyd George's title tout, did not come up against a man who cared enough about nobility to report his propositioning until 1933. In that year Gregory was sent to jail on the evidence of Lieutenant Commander Edward Billyard-Leake DSO, to whom he had offered to sell a knighthood.

But Billyard-Leake received no noble recognition for his display of public spirit. He died a lieutenant commander, while several hundred of Gregory's less scrupulous customers continued to enjoy their titles. Gregory himself died 'Sir Arthur Gregory', a title which he had awarded to himself and which was accepted by the French amongst whom he chose to exile himself – and it was only appropriate that David Lloyd George should have accepted an earldom shortly before his death in 1945.

Selling titles to buy votes was the logical consequence of mass society taking over the traditional processes of British politics. Lord Grey of Fallodon was moved after the First World War to doubt the whole purpose of his political career when he contemplated what had been wrought by democratization and progress: 'As if anything could be good that led to telephones and cinematography and large cities and the *Daily Mail.*'

The thin distinction between aristocrat and plutocrat had vanished almost completely. Less than one in three new peers – car makers, chain store owners and press barons – bothered to set themselves up as country gentlemen in the old mould, a lifestyle which was in any case becoming increasingly expensive to maintain. Before the Great War country estates, grand houses, suites of carriages and servants were relatively cheap to run. After the war, rising labour costs and taxation meant that noble life in the old style could only be led by those whose wealth was abnormal – and no one displayed that abnormality to a greater degree than the 2nd Duke of Westminster.

It is difficult to estimate the spending power that Hugh Richard Arthur Grosvenor inherited when he became a Duke. At a time when the Prime Minister earned £2000 a year, Bend Or's disposable income, after tax, was probably in the region of a third of a million pounds – £8 to £9 million in modern terms: in 1914 the 2nd Duke of Westminster was reputed to enjoy an income of £1000 *a day.*

'Wealth of such magnitude ceases to be vulgar,' declared

Coco Chanel after she had enjoyed several years of having a great deal of it lavished upon her. 'It is beyond all envy and takes on the proportions of a catastrophe.'

Those who got very close to the 2nd Duke of Westminster knew what his mistress meant. The ability to purchase almost anything damned Bend Or to an existence in which he could enjoy almost nothing, and the private Duke of Westminster was cursed with an eternal hairshirt of restlessness and dissatisfaction that proved a catastrophe for at least two of his wives and for a number of his friends and relatives.

But the public Duke of Westminster, with cigar and spats and a fur-coated beauty on his arm, embodied wealth, glamour and magnificence in the interwar years, and his title became synonymous with everything that a prosperous aristocrat should be.

'Whose yacht is that in the bay?' asks Amanda, in Noël Coward's *Private Lives*.

'The Duke of Westminster's, I expect,' replied Elyot. 'It always is.'

Bend Or had two yachts, in fact. The *Flying Cloud* was his idea of a pirate ship, a pantomime version of a galleon complete with porticoed hatchways, four-poster beds and sails which it took a crew of 120 to master. The *Cutty Sark* was a destroyer, built privately by the Keswick family with the intention of presenting it to the Royal Navy, but it was still uncompleted by the time the Great War ended. So Bend Or bought it for its speed, and he had little sympathy with the numerous wives, mistresses and guests who were rendered seasick by its violent passage through the waves.

'What coastline is that?' invalids would inquire as they rose weakly from their sickbeds.

'The coast of Spain,' was the standard reply that the crew of the *Cutty Sark* were instructed to give, wherever in the world the yacht might be.

Two of everything was the very least to which Bend Or liked to treat himself. When he travelled by private train, it was with two Pullman cars – plus four baggage cars for his luggage and dogs – and when he developed an enthusiasm for boar hunting, he not only bought Mimizan, a shooting box in the Landes near Bordeaux, but also rented St Saëns in Normandy, with a pack of boar hounds at each residence – renting a house on the Riviera to relax in between whiles.

When the second Duke fell in love with a woman, his enthusiasm was equally unbounded. Opening up a crate of exotic vegetables which had arrived in Paris by special messenger from the Eaton hothouses, Coco Chanel was amazed to unearth an emerald brooch. Loelia Ponsonby, daughter of George V's Private Secretary, Lord Sysonby, did even better. Returning from a snipe shooting expedition to Albania as Bend Or's guest at the end of the 1920s, she discovered one evening a new diamond clip pinned to her hitherto plain Pontings hat; a few hours later she found a platinum and diamond cigarette case in her luggage; woken in the night by some discomfort to her ear, she discovered that the trouble was caused by a diamond and emerald brooch which had found its way inside her pillow case; and when, next, morning, she looked in her handbag for her passport to take the steamer at Calais, it would have been almost disappointing if she had not found the diamond and ruby bracelet with long diamond tassel that Bend Or had secretly slipped into it.

The trouble with all these gifts, Loelia Ponsonby found when she got home, was that her friends sneered at her for wearing costume jewellery – diamonds that large could not possibly be genuine.

After accepting such presents, it was only right that Loelia Ponsonby should consent to become the Duchess of Westminster, and her elegant account of her five years as Bend Or's third wife, *Grace and Favour*, is a story of a life on another planet. Wandering round the hothouses of Eaton before her marriage she casually remarked on the absence of any orchids, to discover on her return from honeymoon a complete orchid house, dripping with luscious blooms and presided over by a white coated technician who was busy with pollen and paintbrush propagating more. The new Duchess did not, in fact, spend much time in this orchid house. She had only made her original remark as a conversation filler, and her pleasure in the special orchid which the paintbrush expert eventually created was marred when the Earl of Carnarvon, a house guest, spotted it, sealed in cellophane on the branch, and promptly picked it as a readymade buttonhole for his girlfriend.

It says much for the financial empire built up by the 2nd Duke of Westminster's ancestors that his fortune could withstand more than half a century of the most splendid and luxurious living. But there were losses.

In 1919 Bend Or sold off half the Eaton estate, and he also sold off Hugh Lupus's palace on Park Lane, the great Grosvenor House. He preferred to live in Davies Street – so the five-star hotel which bears the family name on Park Lane today does not belong to the family – and around this time two of the family's most cherished possessions, Gainsborough's *Blue Boy* and Joshua Reynolds' *Mrs Siddons as the Tragic Muse*, also found their way to the auction room.

Bend Or, said the gossips, was selling off old masters to buy new mistresses.

There were excuses for the sale of such assets – the death duties bill on Hugh Lupus's will, the redeployment of capital for new investments abroad. Other aristocrats were doing similarly: the great town palaces of the Devonshires, Lansdownes and Dorchesters ceased to be private residences at around this time. But if Bend Or had not been so extraordinarily extravagant, his own expenses and redeployments could have been met out of current income or through judiciously arranged loans without diminishing capital assets – for the Duke of Westminster, of all people, had the security to support a little borrowing.

In fact, the evidence suggests he was a poor, not to say negligent, businessman, and in her memoirs Loelia Westminster recounts an extraordinary story.

Bend Or's business manager and general factotum was an architect called Detmar Blow (whom Loelia Westminster shields with a pseudonym), and it was Blow's peculiarity always to arrive with business papers at the very moment that Bend Or was off on his travels.

'Just a few papers for you to sign before you catch your train,' he would say, and Bend Or, with one eye on the clock, would scribble his name on the documents without troubling to study them.

But one day this routine was broken, when Detmar Blow tried the same trick as Bend Or was setting off from Scotland to the Wirral by yacht. Wanting to show off his business abilities to his new young wife, the Duke insisted that his business manager should accompany him on the journey and, overriding all Blow's pleas of frailty and seasickness, the stage was set for a long overdue denouement, since on taking the trouble, for once in a while, to read some of the documents he was signing, Bend Or discovered that his trusted agent was disposing of some of the finest properties on the Grosvenor estate on long leases for ridiculously low returns – to the Grosvenors at least.

Detmar Blow tried to make excuses and shift the blame onto others in his office. But inquiries soon revealed that he had for years been privately enriching himself at the expense of his patron – and his patron's negligence was so enormous that it was simply too embarrassing for the embezzlement to be disclosed in any form of prosecution. Detmar Blow was quietly cast adrift to enjoy his fortunes, and the Grosvenor estate set about trying to make good his peculations.

This was the less happy side to the 2nd Duke of Westminster's airy magnificence – and there was another side that was darker still. One of his four wives once described him as part schoolboy, part Roi Soleil. But Bend Or was also part Henry VIII, capable of all the spite which trailed in the shadows of that potentate's bonhomie, for he was cursed with the philanderer's fear that his partners were doing unto him as they had been done by, and his viciousness towards his women could be diabolical. Violet, his second wife, was summoned to his presence after one row to find him in the company of a French whore who was just putting into her handbag a gold powder compact – the centrepiece of a priceless dressing table set which Bend Or had given Violet on their wedding day.

His favourite book was the *Jews' Who's Who*, a scurrilous pamphlet which purported to identify Jewish blood and sinister designs in many of Britain's leading families, and Bend Or fervently accepted these fictions as gospel. He would happily leave gold watches and wallets stuffed with notes anywhere in his houses or yachts, but he had a fear verging on paranoia that this book would be stolen, and he kept it in a secret place he would divulge to no one.

The Duke's greatest venom was reserved for homosexuals. When Noël Coward leaned across the footlights at one of the first performances of *Private Lives*, to deliver personally his memorable line about the yachts of the Duke of Westminster – who was sitting, that night, in the circle – the Duke was doubly insulted, and his persecution of his homosexual brother-in-law, Lord Beauchamp became a tragic *cause célèbre* in the 1930s.

William Lygon, 7th Earl Beauchamp, who married Bend Or's sister Lettice in 1902, was Liberal leader in the House of Lords, a cabinet minister, Governor General of Australia for a time and loaded with all the dignities that go with a career of successful public service – Knight of the Garter, Chancellor of London University, Lord Lieutenant of Worcestershire and Warden of the Cinque Ports. His graceful Worcestershire home at Madresfield Court was immortalized by Evelyn Waugh as Brideshead, and his younger son Hughie is generally acknowledged to have been Waugh's model for Brideshead's central character, Sebastian Flyte. Lord Beauchamp had seven children in all by Lettice Mary Grosvenor – but he was also a homosexual, and Bend Or regarded this as an insult to his sister that he could not tolerate.

Lettice Mary Grosvenor was, in fact, quite unconcerned by her husband's predilections when he was not sharing the matrimonial bed – for her upbringing had been such that she had no idea what a homosexual was, and her brother's efforts to enlighten her might have been amusing had not the news, when Lady Beauchamp finally grasped it, provoked a severe nervous collapse.

It is difficult at fifty years' distance to disentangle precisely what occurred in the scandal that led to Lord Beauchamp's disgrace in 1931, but all are agreed that it was his brother-in-law who played the most active role in bringing it about, notably by passing on to King George V the news that one of his Knights of the Garter was a homosexual.

The King's initial response is said to have been as bemused as that of poor Lady Beauchamp – 'I thought men like that always shot themselves.' But once convinced of the veracity of Bend Or's charges he sent a private request to Beauchamp to resign all his official appointments. Bend Or, in the meantime, had gone so far, according to Evelyn Waugh's biographer, Christopher Sykes, as to invite his nieces, Beauchamp's four daughters, to give personal testimony against their own father – though this was a proposition which, Sykes says, they rejected with contempt.

It was at Bend Or's instigation that the Home Office issued a warrant in 1931 for the arrest of Beauchamp on homosexual charges carrying severe prison sentences, and Beauchamp, only just dissuaded from suicide by his son Hughie, went into exile in Australia. A few years later his wife Lettice died, heartbroken by the tragedy.

The 2nd Duke of Westminster's rationale of the vendetta which he waged with such fervour against the fellow aristocrat he liked to call his 'bugger-in-law' was always his concern for his sister. He was performing an act of mercy, he liked to argue, sparing her the pain she would have suffered from her husband's disgrace, and there can be no doubting the strength of his family loyalty and affection.

But such evidence as can now be assembled makes it clear that it had been Bend Or himself who originally made his brother-in-law's private proclivity into a public scandal. Lord Beauchamp's homosexuality was of concern to comparatively few people for most of his life. It was the Duke of Westminster who chose to make an issue of it in the late 1920s, and then his frequent, open and provocative insults stung his brother-in-law into bringing a legal action to defend his name.

The case was held in camera, and the Grosvenors have managed to keep its sordid and bitter family recriminations secret to this day, but it was the evidence that Bend Or dug up to provide sexual chapter and verse for his personal allegations that provided the basis for the subsequent Home Office warrant of 1931. The 2nd Duke of Westminster had a remorseless appetite for the hunt – and the death of his sister under the strain of events served only to intensify the rancour with which he hounded his quarry.

Lord Beauchamp heard of his wife's death at the end of July 1936 when he was in Venice, and he immediately made arrangements to return to England to be present at her funeral. But Bend Or had already been in touch with the Home Secretary, making it clear that he would not have the burial of his beloved sister desecrated by the odious presence of her husband. So when Lord Beauchamp arrived at Dover on a cross-channel steamer he had to be persuaded by his family to return to the Continent without setting foot on English soil, since he still risked immediate arrest. Lord Beauchamp died two years later.

The 2nd Duke of Westminster's extraordinary persecution of Lord Beauchamp has sometimes been explained in terms of an episode of sexual embarrassment that Bend Or may possibly have suffered in his youth. It has also been suggested that the Duke was envious of the high public dignities which Beauchamp had earned, especially the Garter. Bend Or was disqualified from such honours by the notoriety of his own private life – in 1920 he had had to resign the Lord Lieutenancy of Cheshire as a result of his first divorce and remarriage.

But the delusions of omnipotence with which Bend Or used blackmail to play the medieval tyrant, banishing miscreants from the realm, stemmed from more central problems, for he had been able to indulge his every whim ever since he could remember without any real personal cost or effort. It is given to few to test out the truths embodied in the myth of Midas, and in the case of Lord Beauchamp, Bend Or's character proved unequal to the strain of absolute wealth and the illusion of absolute power that went with it.

At his best Bend Or could enjoy his wealth with the innocence of a child. When the chauffeur with whom he had gone to war fell ill, the Duke immediately sent him to an expensive private hospital, and got most worried when his friends expressed surprise. 'Oh,' asked Bend Or, 'isn't it very good then?'

That was the amiable side to his character, and Winston Churchill, in his obituary tribute to Bend Or in July 1953, praised the generosity with which his old friend loved giving pleasure to others – though he forebore to mention that this generosity included buying Churchill's chips to the tune of several hundred pounds whenever the two men went gambling together at Monte Carlo.

It was, somehow, in devising gratification for other people that the 2nd Duke of Westminster could sidestep, for a moment at least, the dilemma of finding it so easy, yet so impossible, to gratify himself. Most people's economic circumstances sentence them to a life of learning to like what they have, but Bend Or's riches enabled him to have what he liked, without learning – or earning – and his life suggests that that apparently welcome fate can, in fact, prove the crueller tyranny.

Towards the end of her amusing, yet ultimately sad book *Grace and Favour*, Loelia Westminster describes how once, up in the wilds of Scotland, Bend Or learned that the lichen which grew on the rocks was used by the Highlanders as a dye. So he promptly scratched off a basketful, boiled it, strained it and used the resulting solution to dye an old white pullover, which came out orange brown – a colour called crotal. Bend Or was delighted, and for the next few days he dyed everything he could lay his hands on, so that all round the hunting lodge you could see nothing but crotal scarves, crotal cushions, crotal tablecloths and even crotal pocket handkerchiefs. His Grace the Duke of Westminster was, for the moment, a very happy man.

But suddenly the craze was over. Bend Or was bored again. As usual he found it impossible to stay in the same spot for more than a few days on end. So he told his third wife to get ready to set out once again on their travels – Eaton for the pheasants, Mimizan for the boar hunts, Monte Carlo for the gambling, London for the parties. Life with the Duke of Westminster, reflected his wife, was a never-ending quest for pleasure – 'the opium,' as she later wrote, 'to make us forget that we had not found happiness.'

Very rich, beautiful, high-born people
who live in palaces and have no troubles
– except what they make for themselves.

EVELYN WAUGH's definition of aristocrats,
to Lady Dorothy Lygon, 1944

X · 'CAN'T A FELLOW HAVE A BISCUIT WHEN HE WANTS ONE?'

WHEN Hitler came to Regensburg in 1936, he wished to crown his visit with a reception in Schloss St Emmeram. So his staff paid a call on Prince Albert von Thurn und Taxis, son of Sissi's sister Helen and grandfather of the present Prince Johannes.

'Hitler? Hitler?' inquired the Prince. 'I do not recollect seeing that name in my Visitors' Book.'

Aristocrats could call on aristocrats when they wished, but castle etiquette prescribed that lesser mortals should pay a preliminary visit and inscribe their name in the visitors' book at the gate. The Prince would then consider whether or not he wished to grant an audience.

The Führer declined to pay a preliminary visit. So Prince Albert von Thurn und Taxis declined, in turn, to receive him.

The German aristocracy played an important role in the early rise of the Nazi party, for there were noblemen prepared to go to any lengths to prevent the Bolshevik revolution spreading westwards. Aristocrats were involved in the murders of Eisner, Liebknecht and Rosa Luxemburg, and Hitler's National Socialists were supported in their early years by the conservative and right-wing clubs in which aristocrats played a leading part. The DAG, one association of German noblemen, gave the Nazis endorsement in 1932, and the two establishment politicians most responsible for Hitler's assumption of absolute power were both aristocrats – von Hindenburg and von Papen.

But there was always an element of disdain in this support for a low-born demagogue.

'No one can expect me to make conversation with this Austrian corporal,' complained von Hindenburg in 1932. Like the rest of the nobility he saw Hitler as a means to the preservation of the status quo. The assumption was that the Nazi leader could be manipulated by his social superiors, and that, being anti-Communist, he must therefore stand for a society in which the traditional propertied classes would be treated with esteem.

They had reckoned without Hitler's highly sensitive social antennae. He was well aware that he was being patronized. Nor had they taken account of his feelings, as a corporal, about the officer classes, and his conviction that the snobbery and rigidity of the largely aristocratic officer corps had been one reason for Germany's defeat in the First World War.

'The nobles dominate our corps of officers,' Prince Friedrich Karl of Prussia had complained in the previous century. 'They believe commissions are really meant for them alone and bourgeois are only admitted on sufferance.' When a report of 1909 regretted the poor education of young German officers, the Chief of the Military Cabinet replied that he did not mind 'so long as the supply of character keeps up', for there was no comparison in his opinion between the calibre of well-born German officers and that, say, of the French where 'so many captains and lieutenants have been promoted from the ranks'.

Hitler wanted to eradicate such attitudes from his new Reich. He mistrusted the old establishment, and he used the SS, the massively expanded development of his own personal bodyguard, to monitor the loyalty of the officer corps. From an early date it could be a disadvantage for an officer to have a 'von' in front of his name, and in 1941 the Führer proudly boasted of his removal of 'all privileges, classes, prejudices and so on' from the army. That, he argued, was the difference between his Reich and the Kaiser's. 'When all is said and done, that was a class state.'

The socialism in National Socialism was not entirely devoid of meaning. The SS, the Gestapo and the Nazi party were classless organizations, inasmuch as advancement depended on devotion to their own grisly objectives and methods, and the elite created by the Third Reich turned out to be a curiously faithful reflection of its founder: self-made, perverse and insecure.

By the end, Hitler had become actively anti-aristocratic, for as the war turned against him he began to look for scapegoats, and to the international conspiracy of Jews and Socialists, 'the Red International', he added 'the Blue International' – a subversive alliance of the blue-blooded: Churchill was a nobleman's grandson, Roosevelt came from America's top ten thousand and de Gaulle's aristocratic origins were evident from his name.

The bomb plot which narrowly failed to kill the Führer in July 1944 justified his worst suspicions. It was hatched by Count Claus von Stauffenberg, Count Fritz-Dietlof von der Schulenburg, Count Helmuth von Moltke and a clutch of other 'vons', and in retaliation all princely and most titled officers were cashiered, some being executed and many being sent to concentration camps. Schloss Wilflingen, von Stauffenberg's castle close to Schloss Taxis, was confiscated and turned into a prison worthy of the Middle Ages: members of noble families were held hostage there, their lives dependent on the good behaviour of their relatives. So the German aristocracy could be said to have ended the Second World War on the right side.

But that, of course, does not absolve the nobility from the help they gave Nazism in its early days. The gulf that opened between the Führer and the 'vons' was more a matter of Hitler turning out to be anti-aristocratic than the nobility being inherently anti-Nazi: 18 per cent of SS officers were of noble birth. Anti-semitism was a long-standing and proudly proclaimed characteristic of the German upper classes, and Nazi theories of a master race were a direct popular extension of the Teutonic nobility's obsession with its own blood purity. Nor does it seem likely that there would have been a bomb plot in July 1944 if Germany had still been winning the war.

Still, a number of German noble families earned their stripes by making clear their dislike of Hitler at a time when it was dangerous to do so, and among them were the Thurn und Taxis. The Gestapo took careful note of Prince Albert's little joke about his Visitors' Book, and when RAF bombing raids reached Regensburg it was a Thurn und Taxis residence that was selected as a decoy. One of the family castles outside the town was painted and lit to look from the air like the nearby armaments factory which was the RAF's real target, and the Prince's second son, Karl August, father of Prince Johannes, was arrested and imprisoned. Accused of referring to Hitler in derogatory terms and of listening to the BBC, he spent the rest of the war behind bars – though the Thurn und Taxis were by no means unanimous in their attitude towards the Führer: two members of the family participated actively in the war effort as members of the armed forces, for when it comes to survival, it seldom hurts to spread your bets.

Of all Europe's aristocrats only the Spanish were left unscathed by the Second World War. In Italy the Frescobaldi's castle at Nippozano, up the river from Florence and the centre of their Chianti production, was occupied and blown up by the Germans when they retreated. After the charges had gone off, it was discovered that one corner of the castle was left standing: the cellar in which the family stored their oldest and finest wines – so perhaps the engineer in charge of the mines had been not so much inefficient as a secret lover of the grape.

At Courances, the Ganays suffered two explosions. When the Germans who had been billeted there departed, they blew up their ammunition – to the detriment of all the windows in the chateau. Then, scarcely had they been repaired, than the Americans moved in and a careless GI set off their magazine. So the glaziers had to start all over again.

Out in the Western Desert, Gerald Grosvenor, a cousin of Bend Or and himself later to become the 4th Duke of Westminster, had a curious experience. Coming across a set of unidentifiable vehicle tracks in the sand, he grew anxious that Rommel might have some new secret weapon at his disposal. So he sent photographs of the tracks home to London for identification, to receive back the answer that there were no known German vehicle tyres of that pattern – but they did match up with the tyres of certain models of Rolls-Royce, manufacture *c.* 1914.

If the Second World War proved anything about the relative class structures of its protagonists, it seemed to show that Britain, class ridden and untechnocratic though it might be, enjoyed more social cohesion than did Germany. As in the First World War, the German military machine achieved impressive early victories that testified to the preparedness of its officer corps and to the efficiency of the bourgeois manufacturers who munitioned them. But there was no love in the alliance, and as the war progressed social divisions seemed to become more, not less noticeable.

Over the long haul the British upper classes, mercantile and landed, proved to have more staying power as a national elite. They stuck together and proved able to command popular support for their leadership through the darkest days. Even when the election of July 1945 swept away Churchill and voted in the Labour Party with a massive majority, the new Socialist leader Clement Attlee was a solicitor's son, from a moneyed patrician dynasty of the variety commemorated by Galsworthy in his *Forsyte Saga*, that exemplar of the Victorian upper-middle-class ethic, 'buttressed, chiselled, polished . . . till it was almost undistinguishable in manners, morals, speech, appearance, habit and soul from the nobility'.

Attlee's Socialist attitude towards the House of Lords was not to change or abolish the institution, but to create more Labour peers so that his party could have a louder voice there. One of his early elevations was Walter Citrine, a one-time electrician who, as general secretary of the Trades Union Congress, had led the General Strike of 1926 – and thus was created that uniquely British phenomenon, His Noble Lordship the Retired Trades Union Leader.

The half dozen years of austerity and levelling legislation presided over by Clement Attlee did not destroy inherited privilege in Britain, but it did make the enjoyment of it much harder work than it had ever been before. Increasingly severe rates of death duty lent death in the family an extra dimension of sadness, while the cost of maintaining Labour's new 'Welfare State' led to rates of taxation and national insurance contribution that sharply increased the cost of labour.

Servants became a luxury that fewer could afford, and this wreaked traumatic changes in the lives of noblemen who had grown used to attendants dealing with every detail of their lives – even down to placing paste upon the noble toothbrush: the Duke of Marlborough's rude shock at the reality of life without a valet was marked by a roar of dismay from his bathroom.

'What's the matter with my toothbrush? The damned thing won't foam any more!'

The 6th Duke of Portland was equally incensed when informed that rising labour costs meant he would have to dispense with the services of his second pastry chef.

'What!' he exclaimed. 'Can't a fellow have a biscuit when he wants one?'

The wealth of the Grosvenor family insulated them from the more painful adjustments that other noblemen had to make in the years following the Second World War. But to maintain that wealth their London estates had to adapt to the changing styles in national life, and these changes were most necessary in the grand houses built on their land in Eaton Square. Today Eaton Square – not so much a square as two very long series of terraces and gardens running down either side of the King's Road from the back of Buckingham Palace – is the jewel of the Grosvenors' London properties and it commands some of the highest rents in the capital; a desirable three-or-four-bedroomed residence there in the 1980s requires outgoings of some £25,000 a year.

But at the end of the Second World War Eaton Square did not offer such an appealing return to its landlord. Some of its houses had been requisitioned for those made homeless in the Blitz, and the buildings were badly dilapidated. More seriously, the expense of living-in domestic servants meant an end to the grand style of life for which the five- and six-storey houses in the square had been designed. Upstairs, downstairs was no more (the

1970s television series of that name was set in Eaton Place) and its replacement by daily ladies, domestic 'help' and au pairs threatened the square, in its original form, with redundancy.

The Grosvenor empire proved equal to the challenge, for following the fall of Detmar Blow the 2nd Duke of Westminster had introduced more professional administrators into the running of the family estates, and in the late 1940s these new managers set about redeveloping Eaton Square with the expertise of so many latter-day Cubitts.

Instead of renewing tenancies as they fell in, they retook possession of any house whose lease had run its term, and when they had a group of vacant houses side by side, they sent in builders to break down the vertical walls that divided one building from the next. Then they had the interiors remodelled to create single-level, luxury apartments which stretched horizontally across the width of two or three of the old town houses. So although the exterior of Eaton Square today still looks very much as it did in the days of Thomas Cubitt, it has, in fact, become a vast complex of modern purpose-built flats stacked on top of each other and interlapping behind the original façade.

These restyled apartments have offered their landlord many more opportunities than ordinary houses would have done to increase rents at regular intervals, so the Grosvenor Estate has found itself well placed to cash in on the Americans, Iranians, Arabs and other wealthy foreigners whose successive invasions have marked London's long and enjoyable post-war decline. They have also given great flexibility to the Estate's unique portfolio of accommodation: Belgrave Square, the flagship of the original 1830s development, has proved an ideal twentieth-century location for embassies and the offices of worthy public institutions; Chester Square, originally planned as the third and most humble tier of Belgravia living, has been left with its relatively manageable houses side-by-side; while at the back of all these elegant addresses, the mews cottages of the 1830s have been turned into modern *pieds à terre*. So as the main houses and grand apartments of Belgravia are today taken over by the sultans and sheikhs who can afford the Duke of Westminster's rents, the English gentleman – who cannot – is happy to live in their back yards, occupying the mews that were once the lodgings of his forefathers' grooms, chauffeurs and horses.

The Duke of Westminster's largest single tenant is the Government of the United States of America, for the US Embassy stands in Grosvenor Square. Normally the American government refuses to allow anyone to be its landlord, since it insists that every American embassy, wherever it might be in the world, should stand on its own little piece of American soil – freehold. But with the Duke of Westminster, the US goverment found that it could not insist.

Grosvenor Square contained the residence of the American Ambassador from an early date, and after the Second World War the State Department started acquiring the leaseholds of the houses along one side of the square by approaching the individual lease-holders and buying them out. The plan was to knock down all these individual houses and to build one huge building that would dominate the western side of the square. By 1950 they had got half way to their ambition, even if it had proved expensive, for as soon as the individual leaseholders had worked out who was buying their leases, they took great pleasure in holding the American government to ransom.

But having secured some title to the land they wanted, the State Department still had to obtain the consent of the Grosvenor family to their plan, and it took some high-level arm twisting by Washington on Sir Anthony Eden himself, then Foreign Secretary, before they achieved their aim – or some of it, at least. Under heavy pressure from Whitehall and Downing Street, the Duke of Westminster reluctantly agreed to grant the US government a 999-year lease on the site in exchange for a substantial sum.

Only 999 years? Why not the freehold itself? demanded Lewis Douglas, the American ambassador at the time.

Well, replied the Duke of Westminster's representative, the freehold could possibly be arranged. He had spoken to the Duke, and His Grace was prepared to make an exception. He would grant a freehold in Grosvenor Square if the US government would agree in return to hand back to the Grosvenor family a plot of land which they had been granted in Florida in 1769. This land

Franz Josef, Prince of Liechtenstein since 1938

Her Serene Highness Gina, Princess of Liechtenstein

Gross national product: 12 per cent of Liechtenstein's treasury income is from stamps

Vaduz Castle, Liechtenstein. The royal bicycle shed

LEFT: *Youngest son, Franz Josef Wenzel, Prince of Liechtenstein, deer hunting*

PREVIOUS PAGE: *Vaduz Castle, foreground; background, most of the rest of Liechtenstein*

Next in line, Their Serene Highnesses Crown Prince
Hans-Adam and Princess Marie of Liechtenstein

had been taken from them during the War of Independence and they had never received any compensation for its loss.

How much land was this? asked Lewis Douglas.

About 12,000 acres, he was told.

And where might this land be? inquired the ambassador.

His Grace was not quite sure, came the answer, but he thought that today the place was called Miami.

So the Government of the United States decided to make do with a lease on the western side of Grosvenor Square, and they even consented to a clause in the contract whereby their embassy could be repossessed by the Grosvenor Estates if ever the US government should go bankrupt. The Grosvenor family realizes it is unrealistic to anticipate that bankruptcy in the immediate future, but they do look forward to getting their land back in the year 2955.

It was difficult for Prince Franz Josef of Liechtenstein to take a long-term view in the years after the Second World War. In 1945 the Soviet army crossed the Danube to capture Vienna, occupying everything in its wake – and that meant an extinction of aristocracy in eastern Europe as total as that accomplished in Russia by the Revolution of 1917. In a matter of months the Liechtensteins lost twenty-two castles and over 100,000 acres surrounding them.

All noble estates to the east of the Iron Curtain were confiscated by the Russians or by the Communist governments which they established in the countries that they conquered. Some noblemen chose to stand and fight, and they were slaughtered defending the thresholds of their ancestral homes. Most managed to salvage their lives and a small selection of their worldly goods from the catastrophe, though few went to the lengths of the Prince zu Dohna-Schlobitten who set off westwards with a caravan of 200 carts, 300 men and 4000 cattle.

The Liechtensteins' wagon train was made up of buses crammed with works of art – half a dozen Rubens, some Rembrandts, the odd Van Dyck and several hundred other paintings. These had all been hidden around Vienna on Nazi orders on the outbreak of war, and as the Red Army advanced, Prince Franz Josef, who had become head of the family and hence ruler of the

Principality in 1938, applied for permission to evacuate his treasures to Vaduz. He could only obtain a permit for a hundred paintings, unnamed, so his buses shuttled to and fro, using the same permit, until the entire collection was saved.

Others were less fortunate. Great dynasties like the Esterhazys, Schwarzenbergs and Andrassys, who had once ruled mini-kingdoms covering hundreds of thousands of acres, lost almost everything. Those who escaped death or arrest at the hands of the advancing Russians ended up refugees, pawning the family jewellery and struggling to stay alive in the world of the black market and Harry Lime.

'We lived the life of the jungle,' wrote Prince Constantine of Bavaria, describing these years, 'and the survivors of the flood had to obey the laws of the jungle if they were also to survive. . . . They had to eat or be eaten. The veneer of civilisation was gone. What had been hidden was now revealed. . . . Every banknote might well be forged, every oath a lie. Was the duchess a whore, the minister a gangster? It was all quite possible.'

Aristocracy does not stand up well to misfortune. It is a fair-weather way of life. Noblemen demonstrate a highly developed sense of class consciousness when they are on top, and from that position they can be zealous in defence of their privilege. But, downtrodden and oppressed, they do not seem to manifest the class solidarity that the working class would display in similar circumstances – though they have not, of course, had that much practice at survival in adversity. In the years since the Second World War one looks in vain amongst dispossessed aristocrats for the spirit displayed in the same period by the dispossessed Jews: there is no Zionism of nobility. The fallen noble accepts his defeat – it would be unsporting to do otherwise – and it is rare that any other more fortunate peer will make much effort to redeem him.

The Liechtensteins were exceptions to this. During the Second World War their castle overlooking Vaduz became an aristocratic refugee camp where relatives from the east could receive succour, and a couple of noblemen willing to pocket their pride opened souvenir shops down in the town which do very nicely out of coach parties to this day. But Prince Franz Josef was now left with little more than the Principality itself to his name,

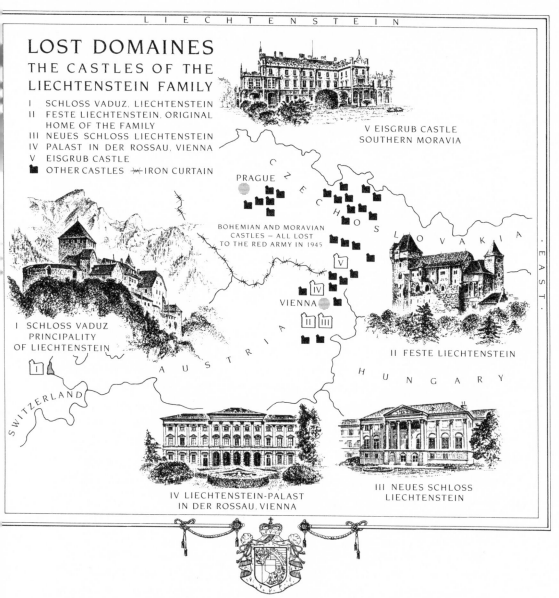

LIECHTENSTEIN

LOST DOMAINES
THE CASTLES OF THE LIECHTENSTEIN FAMILY

I SCHLOSS VADUZ, LIECHTENSTEIN
II FESTE LIECHTENSTEIN, ORIGINAL
     HOME OF THE FAMILY
III NEUES SCHLOSS LIECHTENSTEIN
IV PALAST IN DER ROSSAU, VIENNA
V EISGRUB CASTLE
▪ OTHER CASTLES ⟋⟍IRON CURTAIN

V EISGRUB CASTLE
SOUTHERN MORAVIA

PRAGUE

CZECHOSLOVAKIA

BOHEMIAN AND MORAVIAN
CASTLES – ALL LOST
TO THE RED ARMY IN 1945

VIENNA

I SCHLOSS VADUZ
PRINCIPALITY
OF LIECHTENSTEIN

SWITZERLAND

AUSTRIA

HUNGARY

· EAST ·

II FESTE LIECHTENSTEIN

IV LIECHTENSTEIN-PALAST
IN DER ROSSAU, VIENNA

III NEUES SCHLOSS
LIECHTENSTEIN

since the lands lost in the east represented 80 per cent of the family holdings.

The story of Liechtenstein's rise since the Second World War to an affluence unparalleled anywhere else in Europe is partly a consequence of the nimble manoeuvre that distanced the country from the Austrian economy in 1923, since the Principality has shared in the material success of the Swiss Confederation of which it is, in many respects, an extra canton. But the people and Prince of Liechtenstein have worked hard for their prosperity. They are now, statistically, Europe's most industrialized country, with 55 per cent of the working population in manufacturing; their forty-five-hour maximum legal working week is Europe's longest – and they have also developed an ingenious extra line of business: the Principality has taken advantage of its independent status to frame its own tax laws, and it can thus offer some of the world's most attractive facilities for tax avoidance.

The way to avoid tax Liechtenstein-style is to channel your affairs through a company incorporated in the principality, an 'anstalt'. The number of anstalts currently in operation is a secret – confidentiality is one of the services the Principality offers its clients – but no one disputes that the number of companies operating in Liechtenstein today comfortably exceeds the number of inhabitants (26,000 in 1983). Should you wish to set up an anstalt of your own, you can travel to Vaduz and receive expert advice there from the principality's fastest expanding bank, the Bank in Liechtenstein AG, whose assets currently total two billion Swiss francs – and which is 95 per cent owned by the princely family.

So in turning the disregarded annex to his family estates into the heartland of his present prosperity, Prince Franz Josef of Liechtenstein has proved that an aristocrat can not only survive the perils of life in the late twentieth century, he can also prosper. His principality may be a minnow amongst the sharks of international politics, but it is a clever minnow. Its existence is tolerated for the sake of the services it can render, and the Prince has managed to accomplish this by making a business out of tax, the very problem that has put so many of his fellow aristocrats out of business since the Second World War. A fellow can still have a biscuit nowadays if he wants one, but he has got to do a little extra work to get it.

Buying and selling is good and necessary;
it is very necessary and it may, possibly,
be very good; but it cannot be the noblest
work of man.

ANTHONY TROLLOPE,
Dr Thorne, 1858

All English noblemen, according to
themselves, are ruined.

NANCY MITFORD,
Noblesse Oblige, 1956

XI · HEIRS
& GRACES

WHEN Sir William Harcourt, Chancellor of the Exchequer, rose in the House of Commons on 16 April 1894 to announce the introduction of a new tax to be known as 'estate duty' his ambitions stretched little further than reorganizing the existing jumble of levies that had raised revenue from the death of the rich till that date.

The rate proposed for this new unified death tax was moderate – 1 per cent on estates worth from £100 to £500, rising to a maximum of 8 per cent on estates valued over £1 million – and the proposal encountered little serious opposition. It was passed by both the House of Lords and by the Liberal majority in the Commons with relative ease, and when, in the following year, the Conservatives took power under Lord Salisbury, they left the arrangement of death duties unchanged. No one in the aristocratic establishment seemed to appreciate the threat that they represented, and in 1902 Sir William Harcourt was even offered a peerage.

But Lady Bracknell, as usual, saw the point. 'What between the duties expected of one during one's lifetime and the duties exacted from one after one's death,' she declared in *The Importance of Being Earnest*, 'land has ceased to be either a profit or a pleasure. It gives one position, and prevents one from keeping it up. That's all that can be said about land.'

The legal advisers to Hugh Richard Arthur Grosvenor, 2nd Duke of Westminster, took the point as well. In order to safeguard the Grosvenor fortune from the duties that would be levied following the death of the Duke, they devised an ingenious trust for the benefit of his eldest, elder or only son.

But Bend Or could produce no son to make use of the trust. He fathered only one boy, who died in 1909, and the Duke had to go to law in the 1930s to win the right to transfer even a small proportion of his estate to his two daughters. So as he approached the watershed of three score years and ten in 1949, the colossal bill that would follow his death became the principal concern of his professional advisers.

Rates of estate duty had been increasing dramatically in the half century since Sir William Harcourt introduced the levy. Mr Attlee's post-war Labour government had been especially severe, and the failure of Bend Or's trust scheme in the absence of a son placed the immense wealth of the Grosvenors almost totally at the mercy of the Inland Revenue.

Nor was this the end of the problem. Bend Or's inability to produce his own direct male heir meant that the Westminster title, and the estates, would have to shift sideways through a succession of three or four elderly cousins, all grandsons of Hugh Lupus like Bend Or, and thus not significantly younger than he. So even if the Grosvenor estate survived the duty it would have to pay upon the death of Bend Or, it was bound to be caught within a relatively short time by three or four more crippling assessments in quick succession. After 1949 the maximum rate of personal death duty stood at 80 per cent. Repeated three or four times, even with the benefit of rapid succession relief, the compound levy would monstrously deplete the Grosvenor assets.

This devastating prospect was a classic illustration of the way in which a graduated inheritance tax could theoretically remove inherited aristocratic wealth and privilege – and the Grosvenors' response to the problem was a classic illustration of how inherited aristocratic wealth and privilege could still, in practice, gather round it the resources to shrug off the challenge.

The problem of the future, elderly Dukes of Westminster was quite easily dealt with, for in December 1951 Colonel Robert George Grosvenor – later destined briefly to be the 5th Duke – had a son Gerald, and when the news of the baby's arrival reached Bend Or there were celebrations at Eaton.

'How splendid,' said George Ridley, the Grosvenors' chief agent, 'that keeps the line going.'

'Come up tomorrow morning,' said the Duke, 'and we will see what washing we have got on the line.'

The upshot of the next morning's conference, and many more subsequent meetings with financial and legal experts, was an elaborate scheme which split the Grosvenor legacy into twenty parts and distributed them like shares among the five most immediate heirs. The baby Gerald was the largest single shareholder, for the ideal was that the bulk of the estate should pass directly to him on Bend Or's death, so that only one set of death duties was payable. But his father and the uncles who were scheduled to become dukes before him also had to be provided for – and the possibility also had to be considered that one of the uncles, though elderly, might still father a son.

The exact provisions of the scheme, like all the details of the Grosvenors' personal financial arrangements, are secret and are likely to remain so, but the observable mechanics by which Bend Or's wealth was transferred to his young second cousin Gerald worked with exemplary smoothness.

The first heir, Captain Robin Grosvenor, considerately died in 1953, just a few months before Bend Or, so he caused no trouble at all; his cousin William, known in the family as 'Mad Billy', was only interested in breeding exotic varieties of heavy-laying ducks in the garden of his bungalow near Eastbourne, and he spent the last ten years of his life more concerned with his feathered friends than with the fact that he was the 3rd Duke of

Westminster, let alone with the possibility of producing a fourth; he was succeeded in 1963 by his cousin Gerald Hugh, who was succeeded in turn by his brother Colonel Robert.

So when Colonel Robert's son Gerald became 6th Duke in 1979 at the age of twenty-seven, the twenty shares in the estate could be reassembled, in their totality, allowing only for the life interest in certain properties granted to sustain the various widowed or divorced Duchesses of Westminster – of which there were by that date a considerable number.

But the most ingenious system of transferred shareholdings was pointless if no fortune existed in which to have shares. The primary problem was to minimize the death duties payable before the transfer scheme could come into operation, and it was to this end that the Grosvenors' chief agent, George Ridley, obtained Bend Or's approval in 1947 to recruit some specialist reinforcement for the great battle that was due to be fought after Bend Or's death.

Ridley had worked for the Grosvenors since he started sweeping leaves as an assistant forester on the Eaton estate at the age of seventeen, and, through successive promotions, he had carried the devotion of a family retainer up into the realms of high finance. The aristocratic willingness to entrust total care of their children and their fortunes to the humbly born is not as paradoxical as it seems. Detmar Blow, an exotic import to the Grosvenor organization, had swindled it as he might have swindled any other employer.

But family retainers, whatever their other shortcomings, are loyal. They derive something of their masters' satisfaction from serving a cause greater than the here and now. They see themselves as part of the family, setting their endeavours in the same time-defeating family context which stretches back into the past and forward into the future. They defend the family interests as if they were their own, and it was in this spirit that George Ridley prepared to do battle to save the Grosvenor inheritance from the hands of the Inland Revenue in 1947.

He started by engaging legal consultants to supplement the work of the family solicitors Boodle Hatfield who actually lived in the headquarters offices of the estate at Davies Street. They had taken care of the family's legal work ever since an Edward Boodle witnessed a deed for the Grosvenors in 1757, and though the last Boodle to be a partner had died in 1931, nobody had ever dreamed of changing the company name.

Ridley did not enlighten Bend Or that the principal partner in the alert city firm of William Charles Crocker whom he co-opted to the campaign was a Jewish refugee from Nazi Germany. Everyone thought it was an enormous joke to hire Sir Bernard Blatch, who had just retired from being principal legal adviser to the Inland Revenue – and since goods and chattels would form a major part of the estate's valuation, Peter Wilson, the chairman of Sothebys, was also retained.

The fees paid to these advisers, together with a team of top-rank accountants, stockbrokers and surveyors, were the wonder of professional London as news of the Grosvenors' head-hunting leaked out. But the Estate was spending thousands to save millions.

The first and obvious decision was to sell all Bend Or's stocks and shares and to transfer that capital into land, for stocks and shares have a defined price on the day that a man dies. There can be no arguing about their value. But the real worth of a piece of land can be haggled over endlessly: short-term cash losses could be created by investing in sluggish farms and developments that would, on paper, be of relatively low value on the day of death – and, most important of all, there were the considerably reduced rates of death duty levied on agricultural land and on land given over to forestry.

So suddenly, in the late 1940s, obscure corners of the Gros-venors' estates found themselves benefiting from the cash released by the sale of Bend Or's stocks and shares. The Duke of Westmin-ster appeared overcome with a tree-planting urge, putting down thousands of acres to spruce, larch and pine with a mystifying disregard for the advice of government forestry experts, whose approval meant qualifications for government grants: whether he got the grants or not, the Duke went on planting out his forests.

In 1950 he bought nearly 6000 acres in Shropshire belonging to the Bridgewater family, and in 1951 he diversified into rural industry. The little port of Kinlochbervie, standing on Grosvenor land in the northwest corner of Scotland (acquired through the family's nineteenth-century connection with the Dukes of Sutherland) found itself the focus of an ambitious development plan. Grosvenor money was poured into this obscure village and its surrounding area to reopen the harbour, build a cold store and create a transport system whereby fish that were landed one evening could be marketed next morning in Aberdeen and Glasgow.

It was, on the face of it, a quixotic gesture, for on the day Bend Or died in July 1953 there was no way his estate could immediately recoup the millions of pounds he had invested in agricultural land, forests and developments like Kinlochbervie. The money sunk into the silted-up harbour there could even have been presented to the valuers of the Inland Revenue as a loss.

But by the mid-1960s the little port had become a thriving and very profitable concern which it was possible to sell off to a local syndicate. So the Grosvenor estate did not just minimize death duties and make a long-term investment which proved most remunerative. They also got the credit for reviving a rundown rural community and for handing it back as a going concern to the locals.

Rising property values provided an additional dividend for the death-duty strategy. Having benefited from the reliefs on agricultural land, the Bridgewater estate in Shropshire was resold in 1972 for £2 million – and one further irony was that, in getting out of stocks and shares to create investment projects of their own, the Grosvenors had put their fortune on a sounder basis. Even the government forestry experts changed their minds and decided, five years later, that 2500 of the acres put down to trees by Bend Or were a good idea after all – and paid out the grants retrospectively.

The valuing of goods and chattels was dealt with in a similarly adroit fashion. The family jewels, paintings, furniture and fittings – from chandeliers to silver cutlery, porcelain and crystal glassware – were worth millions of pounds and presented a sitting target for the valuers of the Inland Revenue. So Peter Wilson, the co-opted connoisseur from Sothebys, mounted a massive operation to prepare long inventories of every Grosvenor possession before Bend Or died. Everything down to the last corkscrew and salt shaker was valued so that, within days of Bend Or's death, the trustees of his will were able to present the tax inspectors with a mountain of documents to study.

The studying lasted years, for the size and the ramifications of the Grosvenor estate were so complex that the Inland Revenue had to set up a special department to deal with nothing else, and it was more than five years before they were ready to start discussing the estate's own valuation of its assets.

Normally you must pay interest if the payment of your taxes is delayed. But when the Inland Revenue included interest in its assessments on Bend Or's will the Grosvenor accountants indignantly rejected these additional charges. It was not their fault that the Revenue had taken so long to present their bill – they had made every relevant document available at the moment of Bend Or's death, when they had been ready to pay – and they could scarcely be penalized if the tax men took so long to consider their verdict. The sheer immensity of the Grosvenor estate and its possessions had been swung round from being a vulnerability: it turned out to be the trump that won the game.

It was 1969 before the Inland Revenue finally completed its negotiations with George Ridley, sixteen years after the death of Bend Or, and those years saw an inflation in Britain which reduced the value of the money by some 63 per cent. Real estate prices had increased especially rapidly in that period. So whereas the finally agreed tax bill of £19.1 million (free of the interest which would have doubled the amount payable) could only have been met in 1953 by massive sales of land and possessions, by 1969 the Grosvenors only had to divest themselves of a comparatively small portion of their assets. The bulk of their estates remained intact, and the extra borrowing they needed was easy to arrange on the security of their now vastly more valuable current holdings.

Some of these had appreciated in a truly spectacular fashion. Rubens's painting *The Adoration of the Magi*, valued in 1953 at £7500, was sold in 1959 for £275,000 to the Allnatt family who donated the painting to King's College, Cambridge, where it hangs today, and this provided a satisfying little twist in the tail of the great Grosvenor estate duty saga. Not only was the price an English record, it represented an increase of more than 3000 per cent on the valuation on which estate duty had been levied – and the tax inspectors not unnaturally demanded a revaluation.

So Peter Wilson (today Sir Peter Wilson) presented himself before the Special Commissioners of the Inland Revenue at Somerset House with a wheelbarrow full of documents to argue that 1953 was 1953, and that the Grosvenors could not be penalized for the extraordinary derangement of the art market that had happened since then.

But his crucial argument was the fact that at the same time as he had been valuing the Grosvenor pictures, Wilson had also been acting on behalf of the Leconfield family, who were settling a death duty bill of their own by handing over family pictures to the government. The government valuers had then been very strict, and had only allowed the Leconfields a few thousand pounds per picture – so they could hardly argue that similar Grosvenor pictures, valued at the same time, were worth a great deal more than that. The Inland Revenue were hoist with their own petard.

The entire exercise had been carried out within the law, and George Ridley rejects the idea that his twenty years of sustained ingenuity and negotiation were devoted to a purpose that was in any way immoral.

'There is a certain difference,' he says, 'between tax avoidance and reducing the incidence of tax. The Inland Revenue will tell you that it is incumbent upon you so to arrange your affairs as to pay the minimum amount of tax – and that is precisely what we did.'

There is also a certain difference between being a ducal retainer and being the duke himself. For a Grosvenor to have devoted the better part of his working life to battling with the Inland Revenue over the pounds shillings and pence of his own estate would have been so self-interested as to be demeaning. For George Ridley, the forester turned financier, fighting the same battle for twenty years was a matter of selflessness and devotion: by ducal retainers is ducal dignity preserved – not to mention the ducal fortune.

Nor was the will of Bend Or, the 2nd Duke, the only example of how well the Grosvenors were served by their advisers. On the death in 1967 of Colonel Gerald Hugh Grosvenor, who had been 4th Duke of Westminster for only four years, the trustees of his £4 million estate submitted that he had died of war wounds and should, thus, be exempted from death duties of any sort, and the trustees won.

Colonel Gerald Grosvenor was the veteran of Alamein who discovered Bend Or's Rolls-Royce tracks in the sands of the Western Desert. More than twenty years were to elapse between the date when he was struck by shrapnel and 1967, when he finally died from cancer and blood poisoning. But a succession of medical witnesses testified that the Duke would have lived longer still if it had not been for his wounds – he lived the last twenty-three years of his life in considerable pain as a result of them – and a succession of professional men accepted this claim, even though the resistance of the Inland Revenue led to a case in the High Court, which was decided in the Grosvenors' favour.

It was 'neither here nor there' declared Mr Justice May on 12 October 1978, whether the plaintiff was the Duke of Westminster or 'Private Smith'. The principle remained the same.

Day-to-day reality had not borne out the judge's legal theory. Since the late 1940s the widows of several hundred Private Smiths had been filling in forms and waiting in queues at the Ministry of Defence in order to receive the exemption claimed so successfully by the executors of the 4th Duke of Westminster, and they had not met with the same good fortune. Often struggling to survive on widows' pensions, they had not had the resources to combat the bureaucratic reluctance to grant relief from death duties on their husbands' estates, and when evidence of such Civil Service delay and obstruction was produced in court it provoked Mr Justice May to pronounce with some asperity upon the lethargy of the Ministry. His judgement in favour of the 4th Duke led to the final and rapid settlement of all these cases – which proved that there were still causes in which an aristocrat could help the humble and helpless by riding into battle, even if his sword was unsheathed primarily on his own account.

It is not known how much the Dukes of Westminster have

paid in death duties since the beginning of this century, but Bend Or's £19.1 million bill was certainly the largest single amount paid by anyone in Britain at any time – and, considering the style of the man, that was only right and proper.

Yet it is now more than thirty years since Bend Or died, and it is surprising, given the falling value of money, that no other inheritance levy on a noble estate has ever approached £19.1 million. The legal exceptions made for the inheritance of forestry land and for other special legacies have become more stringent, while capital transfer tax, introduced in 1975, has rendered the passing on of great wealth still more difficult to achieve.

So other George Ridleys have clearly been at work. The British aristocracy did not take death duties too seriously when Sir William Harcourt first introduced them in 1894 because they concluded – off the record – that anyone with a clever agent, accountant, or legal chappie could avoid the worst of the damage, and – off the record – such would appear to have been the case to date.

'I shall be the same shape in the bath.'

MR GEORGE THOMAS on his elevation
to the rank of viscount, July 1983

Sandra Harris, 'Today' interviewer: 'Tell
me, Miss Cartland, have class barriers
broken down?'

Miss Barbara Cartland: 'Of course they
have, or I wouldn't be sitting here talking
to someone like you.'

Quoted in *Class*
by JILLY COOPER, 1980

Mankind will not always consent to allow
a fat, elderly gentleman to fill the first
place, without insisting upon his doing
something to deserve it. I do not under-
take to say in what particular year hereditary distinctions will be abolished: but to
the philosopher . . . the ultimate fate of
such distinctions is already decided.

JOHN STUART MILL,
The Examiner, 1832

XII · A WORLD OF DIFFERENCE

THE Count Michel de Ganay, younger brother of the Marquis Jean Louis, did not really want a big wedding. His son Pierre was planning a civil marriage ceremony with his fiancée Patricia Haulpetit-Fourichon in June 1982. But it would be fun to bring all the family together a day or so later for a service in the local church, and to have some friends round for a few drinks afterwards. So invitations were sent out to one thousand.

Blond and bronzed from spending most of the year in Argentina, the Count Michel is one of the four younger Ganay brothers who share the occupancy of Fleury-en-Bière, the chateau just down the road from the principal family seat at Courances. The two chateaux have been associated since Cosmo Clausse built both of them in the sixteenth century, and Fleury with its lawns, wooded avenues and mirror lake (see jacket illustration) is the ideal spot for a summer evening's garden party. It would be prudent, the Count calculated, to anticipate that more than half the thousand guests invited would accept.

He was not too worried when he had to expand his catering plans for six hundred by one hundred, and then by a hundred again. But when his acceptance list passed the nine hundred mark the Count began to be mystified. Fleury might be a beautiful place, and the Ganays a popular family, but a one hundred per cent acceptance rate for a wedding reception was unheard of. Nor did the acceptances stop there. People rang up to say they had heard about the party and would be in the area that evening, might they drop in? So as the day of the party dawned, the kitchens of Fleury were chilling champagne and preparing canapés for twelve hundred.

By then the Count Michel had discovered why every wedding giver's nightmare had happened to him. Cut off in Argentina for much of the year from the harsh realities of life in Socialist France, he had not realized how rare an event a really good party had become. The *haut monde* was invitation-starved, and a trip down to Fleury on a summer's evening offered a rare chance of fun and smart company. More than that, it was safe, an opportunity to indulge some conspicuous consumption and display sheltered from the agents of Monsieur Laurent Fabius.

Laurent Fabius is to France's 'haves' as Anthony Wedgwood Benn is to their equivalents in England – only Fabius is worse. Not only does he have power, as Socialist Minister for the Budget he has direct responsibility for taxing the rich, and it is a task that he enters into with appetite and ingenuity. One of his ideas was to monitor the trade in luxury goods by making it compulsory for all transactions above a certain level to be executed by cheque. He hoped to keep track of big spenders through the computers of the nationalized banking system – until it was pointed out that this would infringe a cherished liberty of every Frenchman. Why should husbands have to explain to their wives every payment to Cartier or Boucheron that appeared on their bank statement?

Fleecing the noble rich, however, was another matter. The spirit of 1789 remains alive in France, and Fabius recruited task forces of agents to scan the pages of society magazines, start files on those giving and attending lavish parties, and even to obtain valuations on the clothes and jewellery that socialites were photographed wearing.

Until the advent of President Mitterand's Socialist regime a wealthy Frenchman could explain away his wife's diamond necklace as a family heirloom, of no relevance to income tax. But Mitterand's introduction of the wealth tax, administered with such zeal by Laurent Fabius, has changed all that. Just to possess, say, a million franc diamond choker can incur a levy of up to 15,000 francs a year – so the rich and aristocratic are France's new underground. Whenever they celebrate they celebrate discreetly.

It has put at least one society columnist out of business. Hélène de Turckheim, who used to chronicle the social world for the right-wing newspaper *Figaro*, felt she owed it to her society friends to stop writing about them.

'We didn't want to give the government sticks to beat our readers with,' she explained – and in the absence of the titled and chic, the season was scarcely worth writing about anyway.

'Nothing but culture and business promotions. The *nouveaux riches* used to throw themselves at the cameras to get in the paper. But now even they stay at home.'

So the Ganay wedding, convened down in the forest of Fontainebleau behind the solid walls and wide moat of a sixteenth-century castle, provides the French aristocracy with a rare opportunity to display their plumage in safety. The courtyard is lit with flares. The waiters stand to attention with champagne at every pillar. The Bentleys, Ferraris and Lamborghinis rumble over the courtyard to be watched over by attendants in the stable yard, and as the butler announces the guests at the foot of the main staircase, it is as if the old world has been recaptured:

'Son Altesse le Prince de Polignac, Monsieur le Comte de Vogüé, le Prince de Faucigny Lucinge. . . .'

A wedding is always a happy occasion, but at the Ganay wedding of June 1982 the celebrations were, somehow, especially heartfelt.

Prince Johannes von Thurn und Taxis has never concerned himself greatly about concealing his wealth.

'Why are you wearing that dinner jacket?' demanded a long-haired demonstrator on one occasion as the Prince strolled in handcut suit with red carnation, into a Munich society gathering.

'Because,' replied the Prince with the cherubic and apparently ingenuous smile in which he specializes, 'I am very rich.'

The boar hunts that Prince Johannes von Thurn und Taxis holds every December outside Regensburg are numbered among the grandest events of Bavaria's winter season, and they are staged in flamboyant style. The boar are driven through the forest by an army of beaters all dressed in long red and blue tabards, and at midday, as the beaters sit resting inside the inn which the hunt has taken over for lunch, they could be extras relaxing between takes of some celluloid epic set in the Middle Ages. Beer steins foam over onto the trestle tables as the beaters eat, and leaning by the door are their weapons – heavy metal-headed pikes which are the height of a man.

Down the corridor the gamekeepers wear a different uniform. Their green tufted hats hang above their green loden capes on a neat row of hooks beside the entrance to their dining room, which is rather more genteel than the beaters' taproom where wenches ladle soup from steaming tureens. The keepers are all waited on individually at their little cabin-class tables, and their dogs line up obediently against the wall.

The aristocrats themselves eat in the top-class saloon, the hunters warming themselves with schnapps after their morning in the woods while they venture some languid boasting to the ladies who have been chauffeured from the town in a fleet of long black Mercedes. There are three princes, three princesses and a healthy selection of dukes, margraves and assorted nobility who have travelled from as far afield as Belgium and Liechtenstein. There is only one untitled name on the guest list, and that is double-barrelled.

A tractor draws up in the courtyard and the beaters load themselves into its trailer, their jokes and laughter forming steam in the air. The gamekeepers drive ahead of them in their Audis and Opels, ready to deploy their little regiment across the woods, and twenty minutes later the hunters themselves saunter out into the cold, their black rifles slung over their shoulders. These are the steely-eyed knights of the afternoon's combat, and their damsels act out their own part as they kiss them farewell.

Out in the forest the theatre comes closer to reality as the master of the hunt explains the rules of where to fire and when, for these hunting rifles fire tumble-shells that can kill at a mile's distance: the shells roll in the air and they land with such impact that, even if they strike an arm or a leg, the shock can kill their quarry – man or pig.

There is hoar frost on the trees which is melting slightly and dripping down onto the hunters' hats. Distantly, from over the hill, comes the sound of the beaters who are whistling and tapping as they move through the trees, and a horn is blown with a distinctive call. Beside the hunters one of the gamekeepers lifts his horn to his lips to answer.

It is the signal for the marksmen to go into battle, and they spread out, a dozen of them, abreast in the woods. They start moving forward carefully, stepping over brush and fallen branches, looking occasionally to either side of them, but mainly looking ahead, into the mist from which the boars will emerge at any moment.

The sound of the beaters grows louder. There are rustlings in the undergrowth, branches crackling, creatures approaching, big hump-backed black shapes shouldering their way past bushes and ferns, the glint of small angry eyes. The rifles start firing.

At half-past five, after schnapps, tea and cakes, the hunters muster again to offer their salute to the fallen. It is now after dark, so the car park is lit by flickering torches. For the last hour brightly painted bulldozers and dump trucks have been carting the carcases out of the woods for the butcher to cut them open and castrate them, and now they lie in rows, seventy-five dark bristly pigs with long snouts, laid out side by side for the final salute.

According to the pagan mythology of the German forests, all creatures have souls, so hunting the boar is like a duel between warriors: the victor must do homage to the slain; he must send him out of this world with a courteous salute, and he should mark this by placing a sprig of fir in the animal's mouth as one last piece of fodder for his journey to the gods.

That is the theory. The practice seems less poetic, as dump trucks shovel up the bodies and lay out Valhalla in a pall of diesel fumes.

At 5.45 p.m. the aristocrats appear to complete the ritual. The gamekeepers blow rounds of horn salutes to the different categories of adversary vanquished, one tune for the ordinary boars, a more elaborate fanfare for the dozen tusked monsters who lie in the front rank, and the men who shot these beasts step forward for their accolade, a sprig of pine branch dipped in the dead boar's blood. The sprigs are tucked under the huntsmen's hatbands, and they walk off proudly out of the torchlight to their limousines – ennobled, says tradition, by the blood of the fighters they have slain. The engines of the dump trucks cough into life and the carcases are carted away.

Boar is not on the menu for dinner at Schloss St Emmeram. The dish of honour is venison, the produce of another afternoon's endeavours. Nearly forty people line either side of the great table below the tapestry of the Countess Alexandrine in the state dining room, the women in evening dress topped off with jewels the size of hazelnuts, the men in dinner suits whose jackets are dark green.

They are seated in strict order of precedence, beginning with Prince Franz Josef of Liechtenstein, the guest of honour, on one side of the Princess Gloria von Thurn und Taxis and Duke Max in Bavaria on the other. They are also served in order of precedence by footmen in the blue livery of tailcoat, knee breeches, silk stockings and silver-buckled shoes created a century ago by the would-be Empress Helen. This is the half gala uniform of the Thurn und Taxis servants; for full gala – weddings, christenings and funerals – they wear their powdered wigs as well.

The servants indicate the end of dinner by placing a gold-rimmed plate in front of each diner, and since there is no food on the plate the guest can study the castle or church that is painted upon it – another courtly item devised by the etiquette-conscious Helen. She commissioned the gold service to illustrate the possessions of the Thurn und Taxis in her day, each plate depicting a different family estate – which meant there were enough plates for forty settings.

The double doors at the far end of the room are thrown open, and the ladies take their gentlemen's arms to saunter beneath chandeliers and panelled ceilings. They go down several hundred yards of marbled corridors to the family bowling alley, built of oak, a long polished parquet ball run, where the skittles' footman waits in the distant darkness. As the guests bowl balls to knock the skittles down he runs forward to set them up again, a task he performs with apparent enthusiasm from 10 p.m. until after midnight.

Down the panelled walls of the alley are painted in gold the names of the princes who have sent the skittles flying with particular distinction in the last hundred years. But there seems little danger of these feats being emulated this evening. Prince Franz Josef of Liechtenstein smashes a ceiling light on his second throw, and Prince Johannes von Thurn und Taxis does not even venture a sally. He circulates among the less sporting members of the party who stay sitting in the adjoining salons where the footmen pour brandy and where antique clockwork birds in gilt cages chirp and trill and whistle.

Prince Johannes is sometimes looked down upon in the rarefied world of European aristocracy as being just a trifle less than genteel. It seems bordering on the vulgar to possess quite so much wealth, and almost offensive to spend it with such ostentation and relish. But few invitations to shoot at Schloss St Emmeram are actually refused, for there are not that many chances to shoot boar these days, and visiting the castle at Regensburg does offer one a glimpse of how one's ancestors lived.

'How on earth does he still afford it?' marvels one Belgian prince, struggling to conceal his envy – and failing.

The Belgian might find the Thurn und Taxis wealth less difficult to live with if he looked at Prince Johannes less as an old-fashioned aristocrat whose lifestyle has survived by some freak into the present day, than as a new-fashioned businessman who has chosen very deliberately to spend his profits on keeping up the aristocratic way of life that is his family legacy. Prince Johannes certainly could not live as he does if he spent all his time boar shooting.

He has been manager of the family business assets since 1951, and their current state of health is largely the result of the skill with which he has handled them. The Thurn und Taxis did not forfeit quite as much as the Liechtensteins did to the people's government of Eastern Europe between 1919 and 1945, but the loss of 200,000 acres and half a dozen castles made a heavy enough dent in the family fortune, and Prince Johannes decided that more of the ancestral portfolio should be invested in industry. He settled on Pforzheim, a rundown town between Karlsruhe and Stuttgart where the work force specialized in craft work with jewellery and precious metals.

Prince Johannes knew something about the industrial uses of precious metal. Ordinary metals are too corrosion-prone for long-term, high-voltage electrical contacts. Only gold, silver and more exotic metals like palladium are proof against degeneration over an extended period of time. The trick of making such components is to bond the minimum necessary quantity of precious metal into a secure mount of ceramics, plastic or some other inexpensive non-conductor, so the Prince decided to put his money into Doduco, a company specializing in this work, recycling the precious waste from Pforzheim's jewellery industries into electrical equipment.

He purchased Doduco in the 1950s and provided the investment to recruit a skilled work force from the more traditional declining workshops of Pforzheim, so that Doduco today is an enterprise established as a world leader in its specialized field. With a factory in America and profitable contracts in Japan and the Far East, the company has ridden on the wave of microelectronics and its future seems assured as a supplier of components for computer technology.

So is the Prince any different from any other clever businessman? He himself believes that he is, for he feels that the aristocratic view of life makes for solid long-term decisions which are better balanced than those based solely on the conventional profit motive.

'It is like buying good wine. I have just invested in some Burgundies, wine that would be good to drink when I am eighty or ninety and since, according to the insurance companies, West German life expectancy is 76.8 years, I may never actually drink the wine. But that does not stop me making the investment, because the important thing to me is that the family should benefit.'

Similar thoughts must be going through the mind of Doña Victoria Eugenia, Duchess of Medinaceli, as she sits down at the council table of the town of Ubeda, north of Granada with the local mayor and corporation.

This is the first democratic council to administer Ubeda for more than half a century. It was voted into power in the elections that followed the death of General Franco, and the mayor is a Socialist. He has offered to take the local castle of Ubeda, one of the hundred or so ruins that the Duchess owns, off the hands of the Medinaceli, and, proudly signing the deeds of transfer with the Duchess, he clearly feels that he has secured a bargain, since the Duchess will only retain one small corner of the building for her private use, a tower marked red upon the plans. The rest of the edifice, a rambling Hollywood dream of a castle in Spain, will be given over to the public, a magnificent and historic extension to the amenities of Ubeda and a monument to the vision of its first democratically elected mayor.

Yet the Duchess of Medinaceli is not surrendering the freehold of her castle to the locals. She is only granting them a lease, and in one hundred years the castle should, by law, revert to some future generation of her clan; a whole century may seem more than enough to the democrats of Ubeda, but the scion of a noble house which has taken six centuries to attain its present eminence naturally inclines towards a longer term view.

The question is, of course, whether Spanish law will still allow the Duchess's descendant to take back the castle of Ubeda in the year 2082. After a hundred years of enjoying the building and providing the money to maintain it as a community asset, the town may not be inclined to hand its castle back, and if the case went to court, who could be sure that the absentee landlord would win? Some future duke or duchess might hold the legal title, but find it impossible to enforce.

Landlord power has been eroded all over Europe in the last quarter of a century as lawmakers reflect the increasingly popular basis of political authority – the majority can do no wrong. So although a landlord's title to his property should, in theory, be as strong as that of any ordinary householder who has legally acquired and paid for his property, in practice new laws of lease-hold reform are establishing a contrary principle – that the land-owner should be compelled to surrender his freehold if his tenant so wishes. Political feeling appears to be moving in favour of this assumption.

As an interested party, the 6th Duke of Westminster is fighting this trend which developed from Britain's Rent Acts – which were fatal blows in themselves to many landlords. In 1982 the Grosvenor Estate took the British government to the Euro-pean Court of Human Rights to dispute the Leasehold Reform Act which gives tenants the power, in certain circumstances, compulsorily to purchase their own homes, for the Duke believes that the rich have as much human right to their property as the poor – and he has now won the first stage of his legal campaign.

But whether he will, in the long term, win the whole war, is doubtful. Aristocrats succeeded in forcing kings to surrender feudally held land in the Middle Ages by exercising squatters' rights remorselessly across the years, and today they are vulner-able to the same process. It is difficult to foresee householders in central London still paying rents in a century's time to an aristocrat – and when it comes to the Medinaceli's long lease on their castle in southern Spain, the mayor of Ubeda may yet have the last laugh.

Successful aristocrats like Prince Johannes von Thurn und Taxis are exceptions in the age of the common man. It may be a source of wonder that so many of the titled and noble defy gravity and still succeed today in hanging on to their wealth and special influence to the degree that they do. But while displaying remark-able staying power in the late twentieth century, aristocracy can in no sense be described as a growth industry. It shows no sign of the rather surprising rejuvenation enjoyed by representative monarchy, and while Spain has welcomed back her King and evidently sees a role for him, there is no evidence of popular concern outside the gossip columns for the Duchess of Medinaceli.

If you mention the name Medinaceli to most ordinary Spaniards nowadays it is not the family they will first think of, but a brooding, dark-skinned image of Christ which stands above the high altar of an Augustinian church in the middle of Madrid. The statue was recaptured from the Moors and brought back to Spain by a seventeenth-century Duke of Medinaceli who had the carving, which is curiously swarthy, costumed in a purple robe and erected in the chapel behind his palace.

The shrine soon became a place of pilgrimage. It seemed miraculous that the Christ of Medinaceli should have survived the indignities of Moorish capture, which had included being dragged through Moroccan streets and being hurled into a pit with lions. Cures and blessings mysteriously descended on those who worshipped it. The pious travelled from all over Spain, crawling the last hundred yards of the way to plant a kiss upon the statue's feet, and the Dukes of Medinaceli had copies of the image made and placed in the chapels on their estates across Spain so that their retainers might derive some benefit from the replica of the replica.

Friday is the day especially dedicated to veneration of the image, and every Friday in Madrid nowadays, the Calle de Medinaceli, Medinaceli Street, starts filling up soon after dawn. Candle sellers mingle on the pavement with beggars and gypsies offering good luck charms. Taxis wait there, knowing that they can get custom. And the faithful, as they enter the church, kneel down and stay that way, murmuring to themselves and gesturing God's semaphore as they shuffle forward on their knees, a half-height procession that sways eerily down the darkened aisles towards the purple clothed figure which dominates the church.

Religion in Spain can still operate the subconscious switch that throws the human mentality into the deferential mode – and so can monarchy. But aristocracy does not. Worshippers coming out into the street, exalted by their contact with the Christ of Medinaceli, cannot explain what Medinaceli means. Some know that it is the name of a noble dynasty, but they assume that the family must be long dead, and when informed that there is still a Duchess of Medinaceli, their interest is not stirred.

So she lives in Seville, in the Casa de Pilatos? Eyes glaze over. If anyone bothers to visualize the Duchess, it is as caretaker of some corner of what the brochures like to call Spain's national heritage. The Dukes of Medinaceli have become less important than the artefacts they created.

If anyone exemplifies the modern aristocrat as vanishing species it is Doña Victoria Eugenia, Duchess of Medinaceli. Aristocrats have been in decline ever since there were aristocrats, and her happy years of playing bridge while the great revenue-producing heart of her inheritance has been lost, is in a grand tradition of wasting glory: the Medinaceli dynamic has hibernated for hundreds of years, exhausting the reserves of fat built up by its energetic founding fathers, until today there is little left.

But whereas, in the past, new recruits to the aristocracy have presented themselves to assume noble dignity and to take over the lands of those who had proved incompetent at maintaining their patrimony, there is no one today willing or able to be called to the colours. If financial embarrassment had come to them in the seventeenth or eighteenth century, the Dukes of Medinaceli would have sold off their palace beside Medinaceli Street, Madrid, to some up-and-coming magnate who was searching for a palace of his own in the capital.

But in the twentieth century there are no such individual noble buyers. When the Dukes of Medinaceli sold off their Madrid palace it was to a property development company. So while their chapel still survives today, thanks to its dark-skinned idol in the purple robes, the palace itself has been demolished, and in its place, on Medinaceli Street, there now stands a hotel called The Palace – and also a flourishing 'Salle de Bingo'.

The Frescobaldi well remember the best party they ever gave. It was in 1672. They invited all their friends to the great hall at Monte Castello and, since it was a warm evening, everybody took their clothes off. The orgy has gone down in history as 'The Angels' Ball' because, when taxed with his wickedness, one member of the clan retorted that angels do not wear any clothes, so he did not see why he should either.

But this argument did not impress the Pope. He demanded that the head of the family should walk to Rome to explain his conduct – a promenade of 150 miles – and when he arrived the Pontiff told him to walk back again and then to bestow, on his arrival, endowments upon no less than forty Florentine churches. Angels never found fun so expensive.

Nowadays parties at the Frescobaldi's palazzo on the Via Santo Spirito are a little less exuberant. But the guest lists have not changed very much in three hundred years. The *magnati* who wine and dine with the Frescobaldi today were wining and dining with them in the seventeenth century – and in the thirteenth century as well for that matter. The Antinori, the Pucci, the Capponi and half a dozen other ancient feudal families still flourish in Florence and in the hills around. There is no other aristocracy in Europe whose personnel has remained so little altered over such a long period of time.

This is partly because the patrician families of Florence were never exclusively rural aristocrats. The town was always the focus of their lives. So while their estates in the hills gave them security and continuity, the town gave them vigour and human contact, a permanent antidote to stagnation. They might retire into the country to escape the consequences of bankruptcy, political mis-adventure, or the plague. But it was social and business success in town that ultimately mattered.

City culture is more volatile, more eccentric, more open to ethnic and intellectual innovation than the rural way of life. It is more fun. And this is what originally drew aristocrats to court, to the centre of government. But while the tension between town and country could make for vulnerability – as it did among the nobility of pre-revolutionary France – in Florence it has served over the centuries to create resilience and integration. Nearly 40 per cent of the electorate in Florence today vote Communist. But the Frescobaldi and other *magnati* families remain honoured guests at important civic functions.

'They are part of our history,' explains Franco Camarlinghi, one of the Communist party bosses. 'We recognize what they have done for this city in the past, and we respect the usefulness of what they are still doing today.'

The Frescobaldi earn points with the Socialist establishment of Tuscany because of their readiness to stay on their estates and invest in them, unlike aristocrats further south who have sold out to multinational offshore corporations, the modern absentee landlords who can put a whole town out of work if the local factory is not fulfilling its quotas.

The Frescobaldi survive and prosper in the 1980s because, while staying true to the authentic landed and local roots of aristocracy, they have not got stuck in the passive rent-collecting aristocratic tradition. They remain half merchants, half country gentlemen as they were in the Middle Ages, and if today the Marquis Dino demonstrates the family appetite for culture and politics, the mercantile tradition is upheld by his younger brothers Vittorio, Leonardo and Ferdinando.

This trio of junior marquises run the family wine business. They took over estates which, in the 1960s, were still run on the old semi-feudal system of produce being divided between landlord and tenant, and they have transformed them into some of the most modern and efficient vineyards anywhere in Europe. Their production today exceeds five million bottles a year. Few Italian wines are granted comparison with those of the French chateaux, but the Frescobaldi's red Nipozzano and the white wine from their estate at Pomino are now acknowledged to be in that class. Leonardo Frescobaldi is the Marquis-in-charge of foreign sales; Ferdinando supervises the home market, and Vittorio is the company president.

The brothers also keep a few pigs on the side. It is not that they are worried about the wine business, but if eight centuries teaches you anything it is that it does no harm to diversify – even into the slaughterhouse business. A Common Market concession to West Germany allows the sale of East German pigs inside the European Economic Community, and since there is no means of telling, when a pig presents itself at the border, whether it has come from East Germany, Hungary, Poland or any point east, Communist pigs have flooded into West Germany and thence onto the north Italian pork market, where they have severely undercut the profits of the local farmers.

But the Frescobaldi's response to the problem has not been to get out of the pig business. They have, rather, extended their slaughterhouse work force and facilities so that they can now take their own rake-off from the competition.

The shop stewards representing the Frescobaldi workers have

Victoria Eugenia, Duchess of Medinaceli and Duchess of five other titles, fourteen times a Marquise, sixteen times a Countess, four times a Viscountess and eleven times a Grandee of Spain. 'Mimi' to her friends

Family history. Ignacio, Duke of Segorbe,
youngest son and protector of the family archives (left)

*East meets West: A gilded Moorish dome above the
main staircase of the Casa de Pilatos, Seville,
and, left, a Venus reclining beneath a trophy of arms
brought to Seville from Sicily*

PREVIOUS PAGE: *Casa de Pilatos, the main courtyard*

*Luis, Duke of Santisteban del Puerto, eldest son,
and heir to the Dukedom of Medinaceli*

their quarrels with their noble bosses, who indulge the Italian employer's bad habit of delaying wage payments from time to time. But they seem to feel none the less that aristocrats Frescobaldi-style are a luxury that Italian society can still afford.

The sentiment is reciprocated. In the course of his travels investigating wine production elsewhere in the world, the Marquis Vittorio Frescobaldi was offered an investment with promising profit potential in the vineyards of President Pinoche's Chile. He declined.

'It was too much right wing,' he says, 'and Latin America is not so quiet. I have nothing to share with the mentality of the Communists in our country. But they are our people.'

Prince Franz Josef II was seldom more embarrassed than when he went to Bulgaria. From 1936–80 he represented Liechtenstein on the International Olympic Committee, and in that capacity he travelled all over the world with his wife the Princess Gina.

It was a point of pride on the Olympic Committee that titles should count for nothing. Seniority was decided strictly by length of service on the committee itself, so when protocol required that the members arrange themselves in some graduated order, they were often headed by a Mexican gentleman, whose term of service went back into the distant past, while the titled committee members – among them the Grand Duke of Luxembourg and His Serene Highness the Prince of Liechtenstein – happily fell into place behind him.

This arrangement functioned perfectly until the Olympic Committee travelled to Bulgaria in 1973. A charabanc was waiting to take them to their hotel, and the Liechtensteins and Luxembourgs were queueing patiently for it when they felt their elbows being grasped. Before they could protest they found themselves being whisked away in opulent black limousines towards the country, their destination a palatial dacha on a private estate where servants waited at every door.

It was the country residence of an important party functionary, who evidently lived in some style. When the Liechtensteins and Luxembourgs came down to dinner they discovered the dining room occupied by two magnificently ornamented long tables, with just two places set at each. The butler had presumed that the Grand Duke and the reigning Prince would wish to eat at separate tables, and he was quite surprised that they should be unwilling to consume their dinner solemnly sitting back to back.

But next day the aristocrats discovered how far Socialist equality can go. The Bulgarian President gave a reception in the committee's honour, and as the Liechtensteins arrived, they were shown to their seats at a raised table together with the Grand Duke of Luxembourg, the Bulgarian President himself, and certain other titled Olympians. It was only as they sat down on the dais that Prince Franz Josef and his wife noticed that all the non-aristocratic committee members were still standing – and that was how the party proceeded, the plebeians standing, balancing their glasses and plates as best they could, while the aristocrats ate in comfort on high, ranged either side of the Bulgarian President.

'He wasn't just doing it to be polite,' says Princess Gina. 'Status and special treatment is what those people live for.'

That is the sort of story a modern aristocrat loves to tell. It is so comforting to catch one's enemies indulging in the sins of social distinction, and to secure proof that aristocratic rank and title are not so much causes of mankind's snobbery as local aspects of its many-faceted reflections.

The pursuit of equality has been one of the great religions of the twentieth century, and like all religions it has generated more than its fair share of hypocrisy. Half the world has been over-turned on the strength of Marx's promise that the eradication of aristocratic and bourgeois elites would lead to the collective sharing of privilege. Yet whereas today in western Europe's busiest streets special lanes are reserved for the passage of public buses, in eastern Europe the equivalent reservations are conse-crated to the limousines of the party elite: special segregated holi-days, secret luxury shops, private medical treatment, personal servants and reserved seats at the Bolshoi – the elaborate cocoon of preferential treatment that the Soviet establishment has woven for itself may have some way to go before it becomes hereditary, yet it is anything but egalitarian.

It is certainly difficult to imagine a Communist head of state celebrating his birthday in quite the style that Prince Franz Josef II chooses. His birthday is in the middle of August, coinciding with the Catholic feast of the Assumption, and it is celebrated as Liechtenstein's national day – an industrious society thus squeezing two holidays into one. There is a procession through the streets of Vaduz, and on the previous night, the Prince goes with his family to some other village in the principality.

Trestle tables and benches are set out in the village square. A sausage stand and beer tent are erected. The local band clears a space for itself beside a makeshift dance floor, and the Prince and Princess start off the proceedings. They dance with each other first, and then in a bewildering chain of excuse-mes, they move on from villager to villager. Princess Gina tries to take time for a rest, but one of the village elders grasps her hand and insists she continue dancing, gripping her firmly round the waist and whirling her through the steps of a foxtrot followed by a nimble quick step. When the Princess does finally succeed in regaining her seat, there is more than one firm black footmark smudging the white patent leather of her shoes.

A hundred years ago the Prince and Princess of Liechtenstein would have sniffed at the notion that they might go dancing in the streets with their Alpine subjects. Such a suggestion would have been most distasteful to them, not to say so unlikely as to strike them as quite mad. In those days the Liechtenstein family thought they were being quite gracious enough if they condescended to visit their principality on a hunting trip – and if compelled to have dealings with the hoi polloi they would have insisted, at the least, on a dais.

So, even if egalitarianism has yet to triumph in Europe's communist countries nominally dedicated to its cause, it can claim some progress in those societies where social distinctions remain. The great shock that the twentieth century has administered to aristocracy has made those who have survived it more vulnerable and natural people, on the whole – less offhand and more approachable than their ancestors. The world of difference has taught modern aristocrats the price of arrogance, and to judge from Prince Franz Josef and his wife as they dance in the street

211

beside the beer tent, they have also discovered that getting closer to their fellow human beings can really make life quite fun.

The Ruritanian rapport between prince and people in the little country of Liechtenstein has elements of that ancient affection between lord and peasant which was the ideal on the feudal estate. But its essence is more modern – that twentieth-century blend of intimacy and deference which characterizes the bonds between Elizabeth II and the people of Britain – for Prince Franz Josef II has turned himself from an aristocrat into a constitutional head of state, and as such he has benefited greatly from the paradoxical revival that representative monarchy has enjoyed in the age of the common man.

Gerald Grosvenor, 6th Duke of Westminster, has no such advantage. He is just an aristocrat. Denied the option of rising above the law, he has to find ways to steer his inherited wealth through it and round it, and he also has to earn the respect that is accorded more and more grudgingly these days to inherited status that is not royal.

Gerald Grosvenor has done that by reviving the traditional role played by the squires of Eaton – he is Chester's own lord of the manor. Bend Or had no time for the locals. But his youthful cousin-once-removed has thrown himself into provincial life with all the vigour of a keen new prefect trying to rouse the house spirit. His diary is filled months ahead with the 200 or more local functions he attends every year, and the evening of Tuesday, 7 September 1982 finds him in a dusty church hall with the members of the local junior five-a-side soccer team.

The hall belongs to the Eaton estate and is leased to the youth club for £1 a year. Five little boys are standing nervously to attention in the middle of the room as their parents peek proudly from behind a door, and, with his hands behind his back, the thirty-year-old Duke strolls down the line in a dark chalk stripe suit trying to make them feel at ease. He presents them with new soccer jerseys provided by a local sports firm, delivers himself of a short speech and poses for the benefit of a cameraman from the local paper. Then the ceremony is over, and the little boys scamper off relieved, anxious to get their new jerseys dirty.

The Duke himself scampers off in his Aston Martin Lagonda, getting home in good time for dinner. He is not usually back so early. Most evenings find him surrounded by the cigar smoke and speeches of the local Rotarians or other worthies. If he is lucky he may be accompanied by his pretty young Duchess, but she is often out herself at charity functions, since she has a programme of local engagements of her own.

It seems an extraordinary way for the richest man in England to occupy his evenings. Does he do it from guilt? Is an hour at the boys' club the price he feels he has to pay to justify his privilege?

'Not at all. I believe in playing a positive role in my local community, and this is the role people seem to want me to play.'

But surely he would prefer an evening at Annabel's or a hop down to Monte Carlo?

'I could never join the jet set. I find that way of life brittle and superficial, quite lacking in satisfaction. This is what I enjoy.'

And he means it. The Duke of Westminster's official 'List of Commitments' makes impressive reading – six sheets of tightly typed paper listing his patronage, chairmanship or membership of 186 organizations from the Shetland Sheep Dog Club of North Wales via the local Glee Club to the Chester Plastic Modellers' Society. It takes in most of the major fund-raising associations for the deprived and the disabled, and the Duke and his wife have a weekly schedule of hospital visiting and foundation stone-laying that can stand comparison with that of their friends the Prince and Princess of Wales. Local journalists proudly refer to the Grosvenors as 'Chester's own royal family', and most local associations, offered the choice of the Lord Mayor or the Duke of Westminster at their annual dinner, would plump unhesitatingly for the Duke.

The tenants who have to pay his regular rent increases in Eaton and Chester Squares are less warmly disposed towards His Grace. The ducal mind suffers no confusion between public works and private wealth. But Gerald Grosvenor does dedicate a substantial portion of even his free time to worthy local activities. He spends at least one weekend a month with the Territorial Army, when he goes on map reading exercises, sleeping rough, for the best part of thirty-six hours as Captain Westminster in the Cheshire Squadron of the Queen's Own Yeomanry, and straight after his month's holiday shooting grouse at Abbeystead every year, he goes off for two weeks' full-time manoeuvres with the TA.

In preparing the local militia for battle, Gerald Grosvenor is, of course, going right back to the origins of aristocracy. In 1983 he is carrying out precisely the same function in Cheshire as the Norman Hugh Lupus and the founding fathers of the Gros Veneurs – though the enemy he is training to resist lies somewhat further away than the green and rock-strewn Welsh hills.

But Gerald Grosvenor is not that well informed on the history or philosophy of nobility. Few aristocrats are. They know all about the history of their own particular family and are full of ideas as to how its own individual prosperity can be maintained. Yet while outside observers lump them all together as members of 'the aristocracy' they themselves seem less conscious of their own class identity – or if they are conscious of it, they are not prepared to admit as much.

Insofar as he does theorize, Gerald Grosvenor believes that the future survival of aristocrats depends upon their usefulness to local communities as reminders of the past and upholders of traditional values, and that they no longer have much of a national role to play. In particular he feels that the House of Lords has outlived its usefulness.

'I fundamentally disagree with its present make-up. There is a need for some sort of Second Chamber, but there has to be an element of election involved, some genuine representation. It is no longer appropriate today for someone to have a full vote in Parliament merely by virtue of an accident of birth.'

The greatest opponents of revitalizing the British House of Lords, of course, have always been the members of the House of Commons. They have no interest at all in sponsoring a dynamic Second Chamber which could not help but diminish their present power, and it has suited them very well for the authority of the Lords to decline as it has done in the course of this century.

The 1963 Act whereby peers could disclaim their titles spelt out the political redundancy of the aristocrat. It was born of the radicalism of Mr Anthony Wedgwood Benn, unwilling to become Viscount Stansgate and end his career as a populist Labour MP. But it was a couple of Conservatives who exploited it most significantly within a matter of months. In the autumn of 1963 Viscount Hailsham and Lord Home both renounced their titles as the price of contention for the leadership of the Conservative Party, for though both men had been prominent in Harold Macmillan's Cabinet, nobody imagined that anyone could possibly run a government any longer while sitting in the House of Lords.

Macmillan's 1958 attempt to inject new life into the Second Chamber by awarding non-hereditary 'life' peerages, had had, if anything, the contrary effect. With a few notable – and usually female – exceptions, the majority of life peers were venerable chargers being put out to pasture, and worn-down trades union leaders hardly contributed to the radicalism of debate. The payment to the Lords of daily 'attendance allowances' inveigled the ancient and retired to the House, but made no difference to anyone who had something better to do with his day, and the place ended up more of an 'old folks' home' than ever. By the 1960s and 1970s the most obvious use for the Second House of Parliament was as an Aunt Sally for aspiring radicals who could be sure of warm applause for denouncing it at Labour Party conferences.

Harold Wilson, however, undermined the Lords in a more ingenious fashion. His honours list provoked controversy to rival those of Lloyd George, his most splendid ennoblement – Marcia Falkender aside – being that of his raincoat maker, Joseph Kagan. Kagan was convicted of theft in September 1980 and, having served eight months in prison, returned to the Second Chamber unabashed, to resume his seat as Baron Kagan, of Elland; his fellow peers could have debarred him, if they had wished, by a special Act of Parliament, but it seemed like too much trouble at the time.

'The only justification of the Lords is its irrationality,' Lord Campbell of Eskan explained to Anthony Sampson in 1982, endeavouring to elucidate the mysterious ways of their noble lordships. 'Once you try to make it rational you satisfy no one.'

The paradox sounded amusing, but it was scarcely a persuasive argument for the aristocracy playing a dynamic role in politics. In March 1982, after months of deliberation, Andrew Robert Buxton Cavendish PC, MC, 11th Duke of Devonshire, son of Duke Eddie the great salmon lure maker, and one of the great magnates of the realm, decided to abandon the Conservative Party, in one of whose governments he had once been a Minister of State, and to become a Social Democrat. Nobody took any notice.

In June 1983, the victorious Mrs Thatcher decided to perpetuate the fame of her Deputy Prime Minister and of the retiring Speaker of the Commons by creating two new hereditary titles. But neither the new Viscount Whitelaw nor the new Viscount Thomas possessed any male heirs. They might as well have been life peers. No British Prime Minister has created any other traditional, hereditary peerages since 1965, and though it is known that Elizabeth II personally considers her power to create hereditary nobility to be undiminished, she also believes that that prerogative can only be exercised if a Prime Minister should recommend it.

So it appears that the hereditary British peerage is slowly but remorselessly becoming extinct. Since 1961 the dukedom of Leeds has died out and, though living, the Duke of Portland has no heirs. There are nine fewer marquesses than there were twenty-two years ago, and forty-six fewer earls. At this rate the entire hereditary peerage of Great Britain, now some 800 strong, will have vanished in little more than 300 years.

It is already possible to foresee with surprising accuracy the fulfilment of John Stuart Mill's prediction of 1832 – the year of Britain's first modern parliamentary reform – and one can anticipate the public excitement as aristocratic numbers dwindle: bets will be laid on the favourites for longevity, and factors affecting fertility and mating capacity will doubtless be studied as keenly as they are today in the sagas of panda survival – though, unlike the panda, the British aristocrat does not need to mate with his own kind: any female will do.

The flaw in this scenario is the progressive reduction of infertility achieved by medical research in recent years, not to mention the possibility that parents may even be able to select the sex of their children in the not too distant future. Noblemen will find it as easy as anyone else to guarantee the succession of a male heir. So, never reluctant to harness the novelties of its contemporary world in the age-old cause of its own survival, aristocracy may well find its immortality guaranteed by science – in terms of blood and title, at least.

Blood and title alone, however, are not enough. Indeed, aristocracies who have relied too heavily on blood and caste for their survival have invariably perished. Aristocracy is a way of thinking and behaving, a cast of mind. It is a style of dressing and speaking, a whole code of social signals that convince you and your like that you are superior, and which somehow persuade your fellow human beings to give you deference. It is the ability to maintain your land and property against all threats in your own lifetime and, most important of all, it is the ability to raise your children so that they are committed to the same ambition – being willing, if necessary, to defer immediate gratification for the sake of preserving the material family heritage that is the enduring repository of family identity.

This has always been the challenge facing the aristocrat. He spends his life building and cherishing the family land and heir-looms, then hands them on to the next generation trusting that they will not waste it all on riotous living – and, give or take the odd rake and black sheep, the continuously renewed generations of European aristocracy have proved remarkably self-disciplined in preserving this tradition.

But today the most selfless dedication to the family heritage is not proof against the ravages of inheritance levies and wealth taxes. Does one sell the Meissen to pay the wealth tax on the Louis Quinze desk, or vice versa? And what does it matter, when you will have to sell the survivor next year in any case to pay the tax on the Rembrandt? Spain and France already have wealth taxes. The Labour Party and the SDP promise one for Britain. They are positive inducements not to preserve a family heritage for its own sake, and that, of course, is their intention.

Hans-Adam, Crown Prince of Liechtenstein, has organized the family holdings into a trust which, he hopes, will last forever.

It has been established for the benefit of the family, but no family member will be allowed any participation in its running – a provision specifically designed to prevent one spendthrift generation from dissipating what its predecessors have built up.

But the noble house of Liechtenstein is in the fortunate position of living in its own tax haven. Elsewhere such trusts may keep the family assets out of the hands of family wastrels, but they are no longer proof against the attentions of the tax man, particularly where landed estates are concerned, for land is the largest and most obvious untaxed source of wealth in all the countries of Western Europe. With public spending levels effectively set by the ballot box, individuals who control large acreages of land must become increasingly vulnerable to taxation – and the most ingenious trust will not protect estates against this.

Capital transfer tax, the replacement of estate duty introduced by the British Labour government of 1975, provides the model towards which all other European tax machines are heading. Instead of taxing the transfer of family assets on death alone, it taxes their transfer during life as well, and it has special provisions for the discretionary trusts which had been able to sidestep previous measures. Under the provisions of CTT, the type of trust conventionally used by aristocrats to maintain their assets intact, irrespective of the death of individual family members, will now have to pay tax at regular intervals just in order to continue. The Conservative government which took power in 1979 put off the evil day by delaying the first assessment, but the tax remains, and under current regulations, effectively applied, CTT is thought capable, by most experts, of reducing the largest landholdings to pocket-sized estates inside two generations.

Two generations will take the Dukes of Westminster comfortably into the next century. Gerald Grosvenor is planning his taxation affairs to the year 2045, and the finest brains in the Grosvenor Estate offices are working in the tradition of George Ridley to ensure that whatever the forecast consequences of CTT it will not wreak ultimate havoc with the Grosvenor fortune at least.

But in the last twenty years the Grosvenor estate has lost the freehold of over one hundred of its properties to tenants under the provisions of the Leasehold Reform Act, and when he talks of the future, the Duke of Westminster does let slip that plans exist to shift him and his fortune offshore 'at the flick of a switch' if ever its preservation in Britain were to appear impossible.

The Grosvenor estates have systematically diversified since the war so that a progressively smaller proportion of their assets are in Britain, and their foreign investments, particularly in North America, are the fastest growing sector of their empire. Prince Johannes von Thurn und Taxis is diversifying in the same direction. The bulk of the modern Ganay fortune has always lain in Argentina. The Liechtensteins are effectively offshore by definition. Of the six families whose fluctuating fortunes have formed the theme of this book, only the Frescobaldi and Medinaceli eschew evasive action.

Europe's aristocracy was created by land. Its hold on the land survived the loss of its military functions and embraced the rise of the money economy. Its estates survived revolution and the early development of democracy. But now the systematic taxation of land is becoming a fundamental principle of European governments' revenue-raising policies, and the days of the great estates are numbered. Titles may survive the loss of land. Snobbery certainly will. But the essence of aristocracy as it has been known for the last thousand years will have gone.

Well, not quite the essence. Two thousand five hundred years ago Plato devoted himself to the study of inherited wealth and privilege. He wished to create a society in which all men were truly equal, in which no special status or advantage could be passed on from one generation to the next. And having considered every possible mechanical device which might accomplish this ideal end, the philosopher decided that there was only one truly effective way to prevent fathers working to build up their status and then hand it onwards to their sons – the family itself must be abolished.

BIBLIOGRAPHY

The following were consulted by the research assistants who are thanked by name in the acknowledgements:

GENERAL

ALMANACH DE GOTHA 1765–1944

ARNHEIM, M. T. W. *Aristocracy in Greek Society*. London: Thames & Hudson, 1977

ARNHEIM, M. T. W. *The Senatorial Aristocracy in the Later Roman Empire*. London: Oxford University Press, 1972

BARBER, RICHARD. *The Knight and Chivalry*. London: Boydell, 1974

BRANDON, RUTH. *The Dollar Princesses. The American Invasion of the European Aristocracy 1870–1914*. London: Weidenfeld & Nicolson, 1980

Burke's Royal Families of the World, Vol. I, Europe and Latin America. London: Burke's Publishing Co., 1977

BURY, J. B. *A History of Greece to the Death of Alexander the Great*. London: Macmillan, 2nd ed., 1920

DUBY, GEORGES. 'The Diffusion of Cultural Patterns in Feudal Society.' *Past and Present*, 39 (1968), pp. 3–10

European Communities. *Report on the Protection of the Architectural and Archaeological Heritage*. European Parliament Working Documents 1982–83. Docl-206182, 28 May 1982

FISHER, H. A. L. *A History of Europe*. London: Edward Arnold, repr. 1937

GREEN, V. H. H. *Medieval Civilization in Western Europe*. London: Edward Arnold, 1971

HAPPOLD, F. C. *Towards a New Aristocracy: A Contribution to Educational Planning*. London: Faber, 1943

HOMER. *The Odyssey* (new trans. by Walter Shendring). Oxford: Oxford University Press, repr. 1982

ISENBURG, PRINZ VON., new ed. BARON FREYTAG VON. *Europaische Stammtafel*. Hamburg: J. A. Stargardt, from 1973

JAHER, F. C. *The Urban Establishment*. London: University of Illinois Press, 1982

JOWETT, BENJAMIN (trans.). *Aristotle's Politics*. Oxford: Clarendon Press, repr. 1957

KOSPOTH, B. J. *Red Wins*. London: Macdonald, 1946

LOEWENSTEIN, PRINCE H. *Conquest of the Past*. London: Faber, 1938

LOUDA, JIRI and MICHAEL MACLAGAN. *Lines of Succession*. London: Weidenfeld & Nicolson, 1981

LUDOVICI, ANTHONY M. *A Defence of Aristocracy*. London: Constable, 1933

LUDOVICI, ANTHONY M. *The Quest of Human Quality. How to Rear Leaders*. London: Rider, 1952

MANN, THOMAS. *Royal Highness*. London: Penguin, repr. 1979

MONTAGU OF BEAULIEU, LORD. *More Equal Than Others*. London: Michael Joseph, 1970

MOORE, B. *Modern Aristocracy or The Bard's Reception. The Fragment of a Poem written in March 1830*. Geneva: Vignier, 1831

MORE, PAUL ELMER. *Aristocracy and Justice*. Shelburne Essays. Ninth Series. Boston & New York: Houghton Mifflin, 1915

MORTON, FREDERIC. *A Nervous Splendour. Vienna 1888/1889*. Boston: Little, Brown & Co, 1979

MOSCA. G. *The Ruling Class*. Edited and revised by A. Livingston. New York: McGraw-Hill, 1939

NAMIER, SIR LEWIS. *Vanished Supremacies. Essays on European History 1812–1918*. London: Hamish Hamilton, 1958

PETERSON, MERRILL D. *Thomas Jefferson and the New Nation*. London: Oxford University Press, 1979

POLIAKOV, LEON. *The Aryan Myth. A History of Racist and Nationalist Ideas in Europe*. New York: New American Library, 1974

POTOCKI, COUNT ALFRED. *Master of Lancut*. London: W. H. Allen, 1959

RUVIGNY & RAINEVAL, MARQUIS OF. *Titled Nobility of Europe*. London: Harrison, 1914, repr. Burke's Publishing Co., 1980

SINCLAIR, ANDREW. *The Last of the Best. The Aristocracy of Europe in the Twentieth Century*. London: Weidenfeld & Nicolson, 1969

TOLSTOY, NIKOLAI. *Victims of Yalta*. London: Hodder & Stoughton, 1977

TOLSTOY, NIKOLAI. *Stalin's Secret War*. London: Jonathan Cape, 1981

TUCHMAN, BARBARA. *The Proud Tower*. London: Papermac, 1980

WANDRUSZKA, ADAM. *The House of Hapsburg. Six Hundred Years of a European Dynasty*. London: Sidgwick & Jackson, 1964

WILLS, GARRY. *Inventing America. Jefferson's Declaration of Independence*. London: Athlone Press, 1980

ENGLAND

ABSHAGEN, KARL HEINZ. *Kings, Lords and Gentlemen. Influence and Power of the English Upper Classes*. London: Heinemann, 1939

AMORY, MARK (ed.) *The Letters of Evelyn Waugh*. London: Penguin, 1982

The Aristocracy and the People. A Letter to the Right Honourable Earl of Wilton on the Duties and Influence of the Aristocracy. Manchester: Joseph Pratt, 1830

ASPINALL, A. and E. ANTHONY SMITH. (eds.). *English Historical Documents*, Vol. 11. London: Eyre & Spottiswoode, 1959

BALSAN, CONSUELO VANDERBILT. *The Glitter and the Gold*. New York: Harper & Row, 1952

BARR, ANN and PETER YORK. *The Sloane Ranger Handbook*. London: Ebury Press, 1982

BARROW, ANDREW. *Gossip 1920–1970*. London: Hamish Hamilton, 1978

BENCE-JONES, MARK and HUGH MONTGOMERY-MASSINGBERD. *The British Aristocracy*. London: Constable 1979

BIRD, W. H. B. 'The Grosvenor Myth,' *The Ancestor*, I (April 1902). London: Constable, 1902. pp. 166–188

BIRD, W. H. B. 'Lostock and the Grosvenors,' *The Ancestor*, II (July 1902). London: Constable, 1902. pp. 148–155

BONHAM CARTER, MARK (ed.) *Margot Asquith, Autobiography.* London: Eyre & Spottiswoode, 1962

BUCKLE, RICHARD. *U and Non-U Revisited.* London: Debrett's Peerage, 1978

CADOGAN, THE HON. SIR EDWARD. *Before the Deluge. Memories and Reflections 1880–1914.* John Murray, 1961

CANNADINE, DAVID. *Lords and Landlords. The Aristocracy of the Towns 1774–1967.* Leicester University Press, 1980

CHARLES-ROUX, EDMONDE. *Chanel.* London: Jonathan Cape, 1976

COOPER, DIANA. *The Rainbow Comes and Goes.* London: Rupert Hart-Davis, 1958

COOPER, JILLY. *Class.* London: Corgi Books, repr. 1981

COWLES, VIRGINIA, *The Astors.* London: Weidenfeld & Nicolson, 1979

DAHRENDORF, RALF. *On Britain.* London: BBC Publications, 1982

THE DUCHESS OF DEVONSHIRE. *The House. A Portrait of Chatsworth.* London: Macmillan, 1982

DUFF, DAVID. *Alexandra. Princess and Queen.* London: Collins, 1980

EVERITT, ALLAN. 'Social Mobility in Modern England,' *Past and Present*, 33 (April 1966) pp. 56–73

FANE, LADY AUGUSTA. *Chit-Chat.* London: Thornton Butterworth, 1926

GATHORNE-HARDY, JONATHAN. *The Rise and Fall of the British Nanny.* London: Hodder & Stoughton, 1972

GATTY, CHARLES, T. *Mary Davies and the Manor of Ebury.* 2 vols. London: Cassell, 1921

G.E.C. (G.E. COKAYNE) et al. *The Complete Peerage*, 14 vols. London: St Catherine Press, 1910–59

GIROUARD, MARK. *The Victorian Country House.* New Haven: Yale University Press, rev. ed., 1979

GIROUARD, MARK. *Life in the English Country House.* London: Penguin, 1980

HAINES, JOE. *The Politics of Power.* London: Jonathan Cape, 1977

HAMILTON, LORD ERNEST. *Old Days and New.* London: Hodder & Stoughton, 1929

HARRISON, MICHAEL. *Lord of London. A Biography of the 2nd Duke of Westminster.* London: W. H. Allen, 1966

HARVEY, A. D. *Britain in the Early Nineteenth Century.* London: Batsford, 1978

HOME, LORD. *Border Reflections.* London: Collins, 1979

HUXLEY, GERVAS. *Lady Elizabeth and the Grosvenors: Life in a Whig Family 1822–1839.* London: Oxford University Press, 1965

HUXLEY, GERVAS. *Victorian Duke. The Life of Hugh Lupus Grosvenor, 1st Duke of Westminster.* London: Oxford University Press, 1967

KELSO, RUTH. *The Doctrine of the English Gentleman in the Sixteenth Century.* Urbana: University of Illinois Press, 1929

LANDER, J. R. *Crown and Nobility 1450–1509.* London: Edward Arnold, 1976

LEES-MILNE, JAMES. *The Country House.* London: Oxford University Press, 1982

LOWNDES, MRS. BELLOC. *A Passing World.* London: Macmillan, 1948

MARLBOROUGH, LAURA, DUCHESS OF. *Laughter from a Cloud.* London: Weidenfeld & Nicolson, 1980

MASTERS, BRIAN. *The Dukes. The Origins, Enoblement and History of Twenty-Six Families.* London: Blond & Briggs, 1975

MINGAY, G. E. *English Landed Society in the Eighteenth Century.* London: Routledge & Kegan Paul, 1963

MINGAY, G. E. *The Gentry. The Rise and Fall of a Ruling Class.* London: Longman, 1956

MITFORD, JESSICA. *A Fine Old Conflict*. London: Michael Joseph, 1977

MOSLEY, NICHOLAS. *Rules of the Game. Sir Oswald and Lady Cynthia Mosley 1896–1933*. London: Secker & Warburg, 1982

NELSON, MICHAEL. *Nobs and Snobs*. London: Gordon & Cremonesi, 1976

NICOLSON, NIGEL. *Mary Curzon*. London: Weidenfeld & Nicolson, 1977

PERROTT, ROY. *The Aristocrats*. London: Weidenfeld & Nicolson, 1968

PONSONBY, ARTHUR. *The Decline of Aristocracy*. London: Fisher Unwin, 1912

POWELL, J. ENOCH and KEITH WALLIS. *The House of Lords in the Middle Ages*. London: Weidenfeld & Nicolson, 1968

PRYCE-JONES, DAVID. *Unity Mitford. A Quest*. London: Weidenfeld & Nicolson, 1976

ROSS, ALAN S. C., NANCY MITFORD, EVELYN WAUGH, 'STRIX', CHRISTOPHER SYKES and JOHN BETJEMAN. *Noblesse Oblige*. London: Hamish Hamilton, 1956

SAMPSON, A. *Anatomy of Britain*. London: Hodder & Stoughton, 1962

SAMPSON, A. *The Changing Anatomy of Britain*. London: Hodder & Stoughton, 1982

SHEPPARD, F. H. W. (ed.) *Survey of London*, Vol. XXXVI. *The Parish of St Paul Covent Garden*. London: The Athlone Press for the Greater London Council, 1970

SITWELL, OSBERT. *Laughter in the Next Room*. London: Macmillan, 1949

STEWART-BROWN, R. *The Scrope and Grosvenor Controversy 1385–1391*. Liverpool: Historic Society of Lancashire and Cheshire, 1939

STONE, LAWRENCE. *The Crisis of the Aristocracy 1558–1641*. Oxford: Clarendon Press, 1975

STUART, DENIS. *Dear Duchess. Milicent, Duchess of Sutherland, 1867–1955*. London: Victor Gollancz, 1982

SUTHERLAND, FIFTH DUKE OF. *Looking Back*. London: Odhams, 1957

SUTHERLAND, DOUGLAS. *The English Gentleman*. London: Debrett's Peerage, 1978

SUTHERLAND, DOUGLAS. *The English Gentleman's Wife*. London: Debrett's Peerage, 1979

SYKES, CHRISTOPHER. *Evelyn Waugh*. London: Penguin, 1977

SYKES, CHRISTOPHER SIMON. *Black Sheep*. London: Chatto & Windus, 1982

THOMPSON, F. M. L. *English Landed Society in the Nineteenth Century*. London: Routledge & Kegan Paul, 1963

THOMPSON, F. M. L. 'The Social Distribution of Landed Property in England Since the Sixteenth Century,' *Economic History Review* (Second Series), Vol. XIX:3 (1966), pp. 505–17

USLICK, W. LEE. 'Changing Ideals of Aristocracy in England,' *Modern Philology*, Vol. XXX (November 1932) pp. 147–66

VICKERS, HUGH and CAROLINE MCCULLOUGH. *Great Country House Disasters*. London: Arthur Barker, 1982

WAGNER, ANTHONY. *English Genealogy*. Oxford: Clarendon Press, 2nd ed., 1972

WAGNER, ANTHONY and J. C. SAINTY. *The Origin of the Introduction of Peers in the House of Lords*. Oxford: Society of Antiquaries of London, 1967

WESTMINSTER, LOELIA, DUCHESS OF. *Grace and Favour*. London: Weidenfeld & Nicolson, 1961

WIENER, M. J. *English Culture and Decline of the Industrial Spirit*. London: Cambridge University Press, 1981

WILKINSON, RUPERT. *The Prefects. British Leadership and the Public School Tradition. A Comparative Study in the Making of Our Rulers*. London: Oxford University Press, 1964

WINCHESTER, SIMON. *Their Noble Lordships. The Hereditary Peerage Today*. London: Faber & Faber, 1981

Private papers

ELINOR GLYN. Memoirs written in 1915. The original manuscript owned by Lady Alexandra Metcalfe, daughter of Marquess Curzon of Kedleston

The private diaries of Baroness Ravensdale in possession of her nephew Nicholas, Baron Ravensdale

ITALY

ACQUAVIVA, S. S. and SANTUCCIO, M. *Social Structure in Italy: Crisis of a System*. London: Martin Robertson, 1976

ACTON, HAROLD. *The Pazzi Conspiracy. The Plot against the Medici*. London: Thames and Hudson, 1979

ADEMOLLO, A. *Marietta de'Ricci ovvero Firenze al tempo dell'Assedio*. 2nd ed. with corrections and additions by Luigi Passerini. Florence: 1845

ALBIZZI, FAMIGLIA. *Dizionario biographico degli Italiani*. Rome: 1960

AMMIRATO, S. *Dell'Istorie Fiorentine*. Florence: 1600

ARETINO, LEONARDO BRUNI. *Istoria Fiorentina*. D. Acciajuoli (ed.), Florence: 1861

ARMSTRONG, E. *Lorenzo de'Medici and Florence in the Fifteenth Century*. 1896

BANDELLO, MATTEO. *Novelle*, Lucca: 1554

BARON, HANS. 'The Social Background of Political Liberty in the Early Italian Renaissance,' *Comparative Studies in Society and History*, Vol. 2, 1959

BARZINI, LUIGI. *From Caesar to the Mafia*, New York: Bantam Books, 1972

BECKER, M. B. *Florence in Transition*. Vol. I. The Decline of the Commune. Baltimore: 1967

BELLORMI, T. and HOAD, E. (trans.) *A Visit to the Holy Places of Egypt, Sinai, Palestine and Syria in 1384 by Frescobaldi, Gucci and Sigoli*. Studium Biblicum Franciscanum No. 6. Jerusalem: 1948

BERNER, SAMUEL. 'The Florentine Patriciate in the Transition from Republic to Principato, 1530–1609,' *Studies in Medieval and Renaissance History*, Vol. IX (ed. Howard L. Adelson). Lincoln: University of Nebraska Press, 1972. pp. 3–15

BLACKMER, DONALD L. M. and TARROW, SIDNEY (eds.). *Communism in Italy and France*. Princeton NJ & London: Princeton University Press, 1975

BORI, M. 'Atti di un Capitano del commune e del popolo di San Gimignano, Berto Frescobaldi (4 gennaio – 4 maggio 1341) *Miscellanea storica della Valdelsa*, Vol. XIV. 1906

BORSOOK, EVE. *The Companion Guide to Florence*. London: Collins, 1979

BRUCKER, G. A. *Florentine Politics and Society 1343–1378*. Princeton: 1962

BRUCKER, G. A. *Renaissance Florence*, New York: 1969

CAGGESE, R. *Firenze dalla decadenza di Roma al risorgimento d'Italia* 3 Vols. Florence: 1912–21

CAMBI, GIOVANNI. Istorie di Giovanni Cambi. *Delizie degli eruditi toscani*, ed. Ildefonso di San Luigi, Vol. 20

CAMUGLIANO,. G, NICCOLINI DI. *The Chronicles of a Florentine Family, 1200–1470*. London: 1933

CANASTRINI, G. *Della Milizia italiana dal secolo XIII al XVI*. Florence: 1861

CELLINI, BENVENUTO. *The Life of Benvenuto Cellini Written By Himself*. Trans. Anne MacDonell, 2 Vols. London: J. M. Dent, 1903

COMPAGNI, DINO. *The Chronicle of Dino Compagni*. Trans. E. Benecke and F. Howell. London: 1906 ed.

DAVIDSOHN, R. *Forschungen zur Älteren Geschichte von Florenz.* 4 Vols. Berlin: 1896–1908

DAVIDSOHN, R. *Storia di Firenze.* Trans. and ed. E. Sestan. 8 Vols. Florence, 1960–69

DE ROOVER, RAYMOND. *The Rise and Decline of the Medici Bank, 1387–1494.* Camb. Mass.: 1963

Diario d'anonimo fiorentino dall'anno 1358 al 1389 in *Cronache dei secoli xiii e xiv.* Ed. A. Gherardi. Florence: 1876

EHRENBERG, RICHARD. *Das Zeitalter der Fugger: Geldkapital und Creditverkehr im 16 Jahrhundert.* 2 Vols. Jena: 1896

EINSTEIN, LEWIS. *The Italian Renaissance in England.* New York: 1907

EUBEL, C. (ed.) and others. *Hierarchia Catholica Medii Recentioris Aevi*

FIUMI, E. 'Fioritura e decadenza dell'economia fiorentina,' *Archivio Storico Italiano*, Vols. 115–117 (1957–9)

FRESCOBALDI, FAMILY. *Enciclopedia Italiana*

FRESCOBALDI, GEROLAMO, U. *Enciclopedia Italiana*

FRYDE, E. B. 'Public Credit with Special Reference to North-Western Europe,' *Cambridge Economic History of Europe*, Vol. III (1963)

FRYDE, NATALIE. *The Tyranny and Fall of Edward II, 1321–1326.* London: Cambridge University Press, 1979

GHERARDI, A. (ed.) *Le Consulte della Repubblica Fiorentina dall'anno 1280 all'anno 1298*, 2 Vols. Florence: 1896–8

GILLIODTS-VAN SEVEREN, L. *Cartulaire de l'ancienne Estaple de Bruges.* 4 Vols. Bruges: 1904–6

GINORI LISCI, L. *I Palazzi di Firenze nella storia e nell'arte.* 2 Vols. Florence: 1972

GOLDTHWAITE, RICHARD A. *The Florentine Palace as Domestic Architecture, American Historical Review*, Vol. 77 (4) October 1972, pp. 997–1012

GRAS, N. S. B. *The Early English Customs System.* Camb. Mass.: 1918

GRUNZWEIG, A. *Correspondance de la filiale de Bruges des Medici.* Brussels: 1931

GUTKIND, C. S. *Cosimo de'Medici, Pater Patriae, 1389–1464.* Oxford: 1938

HARTWIG, O. *Quellen und Forschungen zur ältesten Geschichte der Stadt Florenz.* 2 Vols. Marburg: 1875–80

HIBBERT, CHRISTOPHER. *Rise and Fall of the House of the Medici.* London: Allen Lane, 1974

ILDEFONSO DI SAN LUIGI (ed.) *Delizie degli eruditi toscani.* 24 Vols. Florence: 1770–1789

JOHNSON, C. 'The Frescobaldi: an Italian financial house in the fourteenth century.' Trans. *St Albans Arch. and Archaeol. Soc.* new series. Vol. I. 1901–2

JONES, P. J. 'Florentine Families and Florentine Diaries in the Fourteenth Century.' *Papers of the British School at Rome*, XXIV (1956)

JOURDAIN, E. *Les origines de la domination angevine en Italie.* Paris: 1909

KAEUPER, R. W. *Bankers to the Crown; The Riccardi of Lucca and Edward I.* Princeton: 1973

KAEUPER, R. W. 'The Frescobaldi of Florence and the English Crown,' *Studies in Medieval and Renaissance History*, Vol. X. Lincoln, USA: 1973

LANDUCCI, LUCA, *Diario fiorentino dal 1450 al 1516*, ed. I. del Badia. Florence: 1883

LATINI, BRUNO. 'Cronica dello pseudo-Brunetto Latini,' *Quellen und Forschungen*, ed. O. Hartwig. Vol. II, pp. 232 seqq.

LESTOCQUOY, L. *Aux origines de la Bourgeoisie: Les villes de Flandres et d'Italie sous le gouvernement des patriciens (xi–xv siècles).* Paris: 1952

Libro d'oro della Nobiltà Italiano. Collegio Araldico, Rome.

LITTA, P. *Famiglie Celebri Italiane.* 11 Vols. Milan: 1819–1902

LODDI, S. M. *Notizie della vita del Padre Lorenzo Agostino de'Frescobaldi dell'Ordine de'Predicatori.* Florence: 1716

LOPEZ, R. 'The Trade of Medieval Europe: the South,' *Cambridge Economic History of Europe*, II. Cambridge: 1952

LOPEZ, R. and RAYMOND, I. *Medieval Trade in the Mediterranean World*. New York: 1955

LYELL, L. and WATNEY, F. D. (eds.) *The Acts of Court of the Mercers Company 1453–1527*. Cambridge: 1936

MACHABEY, A. *Gerolamo Frescobaldi Ferrarensis (1583–1643)*. Paris: 1952

MACHIAVELLI, N. *The History of Florence from the Earliest Times to the Death of Lorenzo the Magnificent*. Bohn ed. 1847

MALESPINI, RICORDANO. *Storia fiorentina di Ricordano Malespini dell'edificazione di Firenze fino al 1282*. 3 Vols. Livorno: 1830 edn.

MALLETT, M. E. *The Florentine Galleys in the Fifteenth Century*. Oxford: 1967

MARTINES, L. (ed.) *Violence and Civil Disorder in Italian Cities, 1200–1500*. California: University of California Press, 1972

MASI, G. (ed.) *Statuti delle colonie fiorentine all'estero (secc. xv–xvi)*. Milan: 1941

MCKISACK, MAY. *The Fourteenth Century, 1307–1399*. (Oxford History of England). Oxford: Clarendon Press, 1959

MITCHELL, R. J. *The Spring Voyage: A Jerusalem Pilgrimage in 1458*. London: 1964

MOMMSEN, T. E. (ed). *Petrarch's Testament*. Ed. and trans. T. E. Mommsen. New York: 1957

MONTANELLI, I. *Dante e il suo secolo*. Milan: 1964

MORELLI, GIOVANNI DI JACOPO. 'Ricordi fatti in Firenze per Giovanni di Jacopo Morelli,' *Delizie*. Vol. 19. Florence: 1785

MORELLI, LIONARDO. 'Cronaca di Lionardo di Lorenzo Morelli,' *Delizie*, Vol. 19. Florence: 1785

MORTON, H. V. *A Traveller in Italy*. London: Methuen, 1982

OTTOKAR, NICOLA. *Il Comune di Firenze alla fine del Dugento*. Florence: 1926

PAATZ, W. and E. *Die Kirchen von Florenz*. 6 Vols. Frankfurt on Maine: 1940–54

PAOLI, C. *Della Signoria di Gualtieri, Duca d'Atene in Firenze*. Florence: 1862

PAOLI, C. (ed.) *Il Libro di Montaperti (an. MCCLX)*. Florence: 1889

PEGOLOTTI, FRANCESCO BALDUCCI. *La Pratica della Mercatura*. Ed. A. Evans. Camb. Mass.: 1936

PERRENS, F. T. *Histoire de Florence depuis ses origines jusqu'à la domination des Medicis*. 6 Vols. Paris: 1877–83

PERUZZI, S. *Storia del commercio e dei banchieri di Firenze*. Florence: 1868

PLESNER, J. *L'émigration de la campagne à la ville libre de Florence au xiii siècle*. Copenhagen: 1934

POWICKE, M. *King Henry III and the Lord Edward*. 2 Vols. Oxford University Press, 1947

PUCCI, ANTONIO. 'Delle Poesie di Antonio Pucci,' *Delizie*. Vol. 5. 1774

RENOUARD, Y. 'I Frescobaldi in Guyenne 1307–1312.' *Archivio Storico Italiano*, Vol. 122. 1964

REPETTI, E. *Dizionario geografico, fisico, storico della Toscana*. 6 Vols. Florence: 1833–46

RHODES, W. E. 'The Italian Bankers in England and their Loans to the English Crown,' *Historical Essays* by Members of the Owens College, Manchester, ed. T. F. Tout and J. Tait. London: 1902

RUBINSTEIN, N. 'La lotta contro i magnati a Firenze: La prima legge sul 'Sodamento' e la pace del Card. Latino,' *Archivio Storico Italiano*, Vol. 93. 1935

SALVEMINI, G. *Magnati e popolani in Firenze dal 1280 al 1295* and *La dignità cavalleresca nel Comune di Firenze*. Ed. E. Sestan. Florence: 1960

SALVIATI, IACOPO. 'Cronaca di Iacopo Salviati,' *Delizie*. Vol. 18. 1784

SANPAOLESI, P. 'San Piero Scheraggio,' *Rivista d'Arte*, anno XV. 1933

SAPORI, A. *La Compagnia dei Frescobaldi in Inghilterra*. Biblioteca Storia Toscana IX. Florence: 1947

SAPORI, A. *Merchants and Companies in Ancient Florence*. Florence (n.d.)

SAPORI, A. *Studi di Storia economica (secoli xiii – xiv – xv)*. 2 Vols. Florence: 1956

SCARAMELLA, G. *Firenze allo Scoppio del Tumulto dei Ciompi*. Pisa: 1914

SCHEVILL, F. *Medieval and Renaissance Florence*. Vol. I. Medieval Florence. 1963 edn.

SETON-WATSON, CHRISTOPHER. *Italy from Liberalism to Fascism*. London: Methuen, 1967

STEFANI, MARCHIONNE DI COPPO. 'Istoria Fiorentina di Marchionne di Coppo Stefani,' *Delizie*. Vol. 8 seqq.

TARROW, SIDNEY G. *Peasant Communism in Southern Italy*. New Haven & London: Yale University Press, 1967

TERLIZZI, SERGIO. *Documenti delle relazioni tra Carlo I d'Angio e la Toscana*. Florence: 1950

VELLUTI, D. *La Cronica domestica di Messer Donato Velluti*. Ed. I. del Lungo and G. Volpe. Florence: 1914

VILLANI, GIOVANNI etc. *Croniche di Giovanni, Matteo e Filippo Villani*. 2 Vols. Trieste: 1857–8

VILLANI, GIOVANNI. *Villani's Chronicle. Being selections from the first nine books of the Croniche Fiorentine of Giovanni Villani*. Trans. R. E. Selfe; ed. P. H. Wicksteed. London: 1906

VILLARI, PASQUALE. *The First Two Centuries of Florentine History*. Trans. L. Villari. London: 1908 edn. (A translation of *I primi due secoli della storia di Firenze*). 2 Vols. Florence: 1893–4

WALEY, D. 'The Army of the Florentine Republic from the Twelfth to the Fourteenth Century,' *Florentine Studies: Politics and Society in Renaissance Florence*, ed. N. Rubinstein. London: 1968

WOLF, STUART. *A History of Italy 1700–1860. The Social Constraints of Political Change*. London: 1979

YVER, G. *Le commerce et les marchands dans l'Italie méridionale au xiiie et au xive siècles*. Paris: 1903

Florence. *Archivio di Stato*. Passerini Mss. No. 47 – Genealogical notes on the Frescobaldi. Rosselli, Sepoltuario fiorentino 1657 Mss. 624–625. Carte Sebregondi; famiglia Frescobaldi.

GERMANY

ALMQUIST, PAULA. *Eine Klasse für sich. Adel in Deutschland*. Hamburg: Stern/Gruner+Jahr AG & Co., 1979

DER GROSSE PLOETZ. Freiburg – Würzburg: Ploetz, 1980

BAVARIA, PRINCE CONSTANTINE OF. *After the Flood*. London: Weidenfeld & Nicolson, 1954

BORN KARL ERICH: *Von der Reichgründung bis zum Ersten Weltkrieg*. Gebhardt – Handbuch der Deutschen Geschichte, Vol. 16. Stuttgart: Klett, 1970

BULLOCK, ALAN. *Hitler. A Study in Tyranny*. London: Pelican, repr. 1981

CRAIG, GORDON A. *Germany, 1866–1945*. Oxford: Clarendon Press, 1978

CRAIG, GORDON A. *The Germans*. New York: Putnam, 1982

DEMETER, KARL. *The German Officer-Corps in Society and State, 1650–1945*. London: Weidenfeld & Nicolson, 1965

ENGELMANN, BERNT and WALLRAFF GÜNTER. *Ihr da oben – wir da unten.* Köln: Kiepenheurer & Witsch, 1973

FUHS, MICHAEL. *Herrschaftsformen der früher Neuzeit.* Freiburg – Würzburg: Ploetz, 1978

Genealogisches Handbuch des Adels, Fürstliche Häuser. Hamburg: C. A. Starke

Genealogisches Handbuch des Adels, Grafliche Hauser. Hamburg: C. A. Starke

Genealogisches Handbuch des Adels, Freiherrliche Hauser. Hamburg: C. A. Starke

KOHN-BRAMSTEDT, ERNST. *Aristocracy and the Middle-Classes in Germany.* London: P. S. King, 1937

LEIGH-FERMOR, PATRICK. *A Time of Gifts.* London: Penguin, repr. 1980

LEYSER, K. 'The German Aristocracy from the Ninth to the Early Twelfth Century. A Historical and Cultural Sketch,' *Past and Present*, 41 (1968), pp. 25–53

PIENDL, MAX. *Das Fürstliche Haus Thurn und Taxis.* Max Piendl. Regensburg: Pustet, 1980

Studienbuch Geschichte. Eds: von Reinhard, Elze und Konrad Repgen. Stuttgart: Klett-Cotta, 1983

TREUE, WILHELM. *Wirtschaft, Gesellschaft und Technik von 16. bis zum 18. Jahrhundert.* Gebhardt – Handbuch der deutschen Geschichte, Vol. 12, Stuttgart: Klett, 1970

WINTER, INGELORE. *Der Adel. Ein deutsches Gruppenportrait.* Vienna: Molden, 1981

WYDENBRUCK, NORA. *The Letters of Rainer Maria Rilke and Princess Marie von Thurn und Taxis.* London: Hogarth Press, 1958

WYDENBRUCK, NORA (trans.). *Memoirs of a Princess.* London: Hogarth Press, 1959

Articles from:

Frankfurter Allgemeine Zeitung, Frankfurt. *Spiegel Magazine*, Hamburg. *Stern Magazine*, Hamburg. *Abendzeitung*, Munich. *Süddeutsche Zeitung*, Munich. *Quick Magazine*, Munich. *Kölner Tagesanzeiger*, Cologne.

SPAIN

BRAUDEL, FERNAND. *The Mediterranean and the Mediterranean World in The Age of Philip II.* 2 Vols. London: Fontana/Collins, 4th impression, 1981

BRENAN, GERALD. *The Spanish Labyrinth.* Cambridge: 1950

BONE, GERTRUDE. *Days in Old Spain.* London: Macmillan, 1938

CARR, RAYMOND. *Spain 1808–1975.* 2nd. edn, Oxford: Oxford University Press, 1982

CASTRO, AMÉRIGO, *The Spaniards. An Introduction to Their History.* Berkeley: 1971

Diccionario de Historia de España. Ed. Germán Bleiberg, 3 Vols., Madrid: 1968

Elenco de Grandezas y Titulos Nobiliarios Españoles. Madrid: Hidalguia

Enciclopedia Universal Ilustrada, Europeo-Americana, Espasa-Calpe S.A., Madrid

Figueroa y Melgar, *Estudio histórico sobre algunas familias españolas.* Madrid. 1967

FORD, RICHARD, *A Handbook for Travellers in Spain.* London: 1845, Centaur Press repr.: 1966

FRAGA IRIBARNE, M. *General Introduction to Spanish Law.* Madrid: 1967

GANDIA, ENRIQUE DE. *Del origen de los nombres y apellidos y de la ciencia genealogico.* Buenos Aires: 1930

História de España, Ed. R. Menéndez Pidal, Vol. XVII (*La España de los Reyes Católicos*). Madrid: 1969

Historia de España. Ed. Pericot García, Luis, 3rd. edn, Barcelona: 1967

JACKSON-STOPS, GERVASE. 'Casa de Pilatos, Seville; *Country Life,* 17 and 24 June 1982

JACOB, WILLIAM. *Travels in Spain*. London: 1811

KAMEN, HENRY. *The Spanish Inquisition*. London: Weidenfeld & Nicolson, 1965

MADOZ, PASQUAL. *Diccionario geografico estadistico histórico de España y sus posesiones en ultramar*. Vol. XI. Madrid: 1850

MORENO Y MÓRRISON, ROBERTO. *Guía nobilaría de España 1945–47* Madrid: 1947

MORRIS, JAN. *Spain*. London: Penguin Books, 1979

MUÑOZ Y RIVERO. *Los codices y documentos epañoles de los siglos, V al XII*. Madrid: 1919

PONZ, ANTONIO. *Viaje por España*. Madrid: 1947

READ, JAN. *The Moors in Spain and Portugal*. London: Faber, 1974

READ, JAN. *The Catalans,* London: Faber, 1978

TABOADA ROCA, MANUEL (Conde de Borrajeiros). *Los titulos nobilarios y sus regulación legislativa en España*. Madrid: 1960

THOMAS, HUGH. *The Spanish Civil War*. London: Eyre, 1961

TOWNSEND, JOSEPH. *A Journey through Spain in the Years 1786–7*. 3 Vols. London: 1792

ZABALA Y LERA PÍO. *España bajo los Borbones*. 4th edn, Barcelona: 1942

FRANCE

DE BARTHÉLEMY, ANATOLE. *De l'Aristocratie au XIXe Siècle*. Paris: Auguste Aubry, 1859

BAUCHAL, CHARLES. *Nouveau Dictionnaire Biographique et Critique des Architectes Français*. Paris: Librairie Général de l'Architecture et des Travaux Publics, Daly Fils et Cie., 1887

BLUNT, ANTHONY. *Art and Architecture in France 1500 to 1700*. Baltimore: Penguin Books, 1951. 3rd edn

BRAUDEL, FERNAND and LABROUSSE, ERNEST (eds.) *Histoire Economique et Sociale de la France*. Tome I: *De 1450 à 1660 – L'Etat et la Ville*. Pierre Chaunu et Richard Gascon. Paris: Presses Universitaires de France, 1977

BROQUELET, A. *Nos Châteaux*. Paris: Librairie Garnier Frères, 1924

CARRÉ, HENRI. *La Noblesse de France et l'Opinion Publique au XVIIIe Siècle*. Paris: Honoré Champion, 1920

COBBAN, ALFRED. 'The Survival of the Nobility during the French Revolution,' *Past and Present*, 39 (1968), pp. 169–171

DENT, JULIAN. *Crisis in Finance: Crown, Financiers and Society in Seventeenth Century France*. New York: St Martin's Press, 1973

DUNLOP, IAN. *The Companion Guide to the Ile de France*. London: Collins, 1979

DURANT, WILL and ARIEL. *The Age of Louis XIV*. (Part VIII of *The Story of Civilization*). New York: Simon and Schuster, 1963

FOSTER, ROBERT. 'The Survival of the Nobility during the French Revolution,' *Past and Present*, 37 (1967), pp. 71–86

GANAY, ERNEST DE. *Châteaux & Manoirs de France: Ile-de-France*. 5 Vols. Paris: Vincent, Fréal et Cie., 1938

GOODWIN, A. (ed.). *The American and French Revolutions*. (New Cambridge Modern History, Vol. VIII) Cambridge: Cambridge University Press, 1968

DE GRAMONT, SANCHE. *Epitaph for Kings*. London: Hamish Hamilton, 1967

DE GRAMONT, SANCHE. *The French: Portrait of a People*. New York: Putnam, 1969

GRANIER DE CASSAGNAC, A. *Histoire des Classes Nobles et des Classes Anoblies*. 2 Vols. Paris: H. L. Delloye, 1840

HARDING, ROBERT R. *Anatomy of a Power Elite: The Provincial Governors of Early Modern France*. New Haven and London: Yale University Press, 1978

DE LA CHENAYE-DESBOIS ET BADIER. *Dictionnaire de la Noblesse*. 3rd edn, rev. 19 Vol. Paris: Schlesinger frères, 1863. Repr. Nedeln, Liechtenstein: Kraus Reprint, 1969

LANCE, ADOLPHE. *Dictionnaire des Architectes Français*. 2 Vols. Paris: Veuve A. Morel et Cie., 1872

LIVELY, JOHN F. *The Social and Political Thought of Alexis de Tocqueville*. Oxford: Clarendon Press, 1962

LOOMIS, STANLEY. *A Crime of Passion*. Philadelphia and New York: J. B. Lippincott, Co., 1967

NOURISSIER, FRANÇOIS. *The French*. London: Hutchinson, 1971

ORWELL, GEORGE. *Down and Out in Paris and London*. London: Penguin, repr. 1982

PRÉVOST, M., and D'AMAT, ROMAN (ed.). *Dictionnaire de Biographie Française*. Vol. 8. Paris: Librairie Letouzey et Ané, 1959

The Royalty, Peerage and Aristocracy of the World. 90th edn. London: Annuaire de France, 1966

RUSSELL, LORD JOHN. *The Causes of the French Revolution*. London: Longman Rees, Orme, Brown, Green & Longman, 1832

SANDRAS, [GATIEN] COURTILZ DE. *Mémoires de Monsieur d'Artagnan*. Ed. Gilbert Sigaux. Paris: Mercure de France, 1965

DE SEREVILLE, E. and DE SAINT SIMON. *Dictionnnaire de la Noblesse Française et Supplément* (La Société Française au XX Siècle) Paris: Editions Contrepoint

SÉVIGNÉ, MADAME DE. *Correspondance*, ed. and annotated by Roger Duchêne. 2 Vols. Paris: Gallimard (Pléiade), 1972–8

DE TOCQUEVILLE, ALEXIS. *Oeuvres Complètes*. Vol. 2. *L'ancien Régime et La Révolution*. (intro. G. Lefèbvre) Paris: Gaillard, 1967

TUCHMAN, BARBARA. *A Distant Mirror*. London: Penguin, 1979

WEINER, MARGERY. *The French Exiles, 1789–1815*. London: John Murray, 1960

WILLIAMS, H. NOËL. *Henri II: His Court and Times*. London: Methuen, 1910

ZELDIN, THEODORE. *France, 1848–1945*. 5 Vols. London: Oxford University Press, 1980

LIECHTENSTEIN

BAUMSTARK, REINHOLD. *Masterpieces from the Collection of the Princes of Liechtenstein*. New York: Hudson Hills Press, 1981

GREENE, BARBARA. *Liechtenstein. Valley of Peace*. Vaduz: Liechtenstein-Verlag, 1967

JANSEN, NORBERT. *Francis Joseph II*. Vaduz: Press and Information Office, 1978

KRANZ, WALTER. *The Principality of Liechtenstein. A Documentary Handbook*. Vaduz: Press & Information Office, 5th revised ed., January 1981

SCHLAPP, MANFRED. *This is Liechtenstein*. Stuttgart: Seewald, 1980

WILHELM, GUSTAV. *Stammtafel des Fürstlichen Hauses von und zu Liechtenstein*. Vaduz: Druck Oskar Oehri AG, 1976

SOURCE NOTES

For details of all books and articles cited see Bibliography, p. 221.

CHAPTER I: SIX OF 'THE BEST'

This chapter is largely based on personal experience while at the homes of the six families who form the subject of this book. In a series of research and filming visits, which took place between April and December 1982, an average of three weeks was spent with each family on three or more separate occasions.

p. 16   *£400 million:* estimates of Grosvenor assets have ranged as high as £1000 million, but the present Duke of Westminster says that this is 'ridiculously high'. The Grosvenor Estate refuse to disclose any figures about their holdings, and point out, correctly, that it is very difficult to value properties leased out at so many varying rates and terms. It is also true, of course, that in the hypothetical event of the entire estate being put on the market, the total price realized would be considerably lower than the sum of its individual properties as now valued at current market rates. So the figure of £400 million has been arrived at by calculation from the £19.1 million death duty assessed at 1953 values on the estate of the 2nd Duke, Bend Or (see Chapter XI).

p. 17   *Herbert Asquith:* Cannadine, p. 21.

p. 17   *8 per cent:* there are sixty-three hereditary peers owning houses open to the public as listed in the directory *Historic Houses Castles and Gardens in Great Britain and Ireland, 1982.* (There are approximately 800 peers entitled to sit in the House of Lords.)

p. 18   *Ciampino Airport:* Barzini, p. 99.

p. 21   *England's most titled family:* The members of the Howard family currently holding hereditary titles are the Duke of Norfolk, the Earl of Carlisle, the Earl of Effingham, the Earl of Suffolk and Berkshire, Lord Howard of Penrith and Lady Herries. Lord Howard of Henderskelfe – George Howard, former Director General of the BBC – is a life peer. All can trace their descent from Sir William Howard (d.1308).

p. 22   *the 10th Duke Eddie:* The Duchess of Devonshire, chapter 1.

p. 22   *the length of Piccadilly:* Mosley, p. 2.

p. 22   *lady novelists on tiger-skin rugs:* Elinor Glyn, unpublished ms.

p. 22   *baskets of old bread:* Mosley, p. 16.

p. 23   *the Locker-Lampsons:* Sitwell, Appendix.

p. 36   *ruling class:* for the elaboration of this theme see Mosca.

CHAPTER II: NOBLE MEN

Marc Bloch's *Feudal Society* (London: Routledge, 1961) is an invaluable guide to the early Middle Ages.

p. 42 *men are like fish of the sea:* Bloch, p. 3.

p. 42 *priest-kings:* for more details see *The Long-haired Kings* by J. M. Wallace-Hadrill (London, Methuen, 1962), particularly the final chapters.

p. 45 *Hugh of Kevelioc:* the story as given here is the version commonly told by the Grosvenor family, but it is not supported by the available historical evidence. There certainly was a Hugh Lupus, and Orderic Vitalis describes him as follows:

> This man with the help of many cruel barons shed much Welsh blood. He was not so much lavish as prodigal. His retinue was more like an army than a household, and in giving and receiving he kept no account. Each day he devastated the land and preferred falconers and huntsmen to the cultivators of the soil and ministers of heaven. He was so much a slave to the gluttony of his belly that, weighed down by his fat, he could hardly move. From harlots he had many children of both sexes, who almost all came to an unfortunate end.

So this Earl of Chester was undoubtedly a fat huntsman, and he also had a tenant, who held eighteen manors of his, called Gilbert le Veneur.

However, the present-day Grosvenors descend from neither of these characters. Their line comes from a Robert of Budworth who, a century after the Conquest, was granted land by Hugh Kevelioc, who was Earl of Chester 1153–81. This Hugh, whom Welsh purists call Hugh of Gyffylliog, was the great-grandson of Hugh Lupus's sister.

The legend that Hugh Lupus was the Gros Veneur from whom the present-day family are descended probably arose from confusion over the two Earls of Chester, both called Hugh, and an understandable wish to trace the family descent right back to the Conquest. Still, having a direct line going back unbroken to the late 1100s is nothing to be ashamed of. Full genealogical details of the legend and the actual historical evidence are to be found in the article by W. H. B. Bird, 'The Grosvenor Myth', in *The Ancestor*, Vol. 1 for April 1902. A suggestion that Hugh Lupus was a nephew of William the Conqueror has been more recently disproved by the great authority on Norman history, the late Professor David C. Douglas.

I am grateful to Patrick Montague-Smith for his help with all these genealogical complexities.

p. 46 *Charles the Bald:* V. H. H. Green, p. 42.

p. 47 *Libri Memoriales:* K. Leyser, p. 25.

p. 48 *commemorating Geoffrey of Anjou: Royal Heraldry of England*, Heraldry Today, p. 14.

CHAPTER III: MONEY COUNTS

This account of the early history of the Frescobaldi family is based entirely upon the original research of Dr Alwyn Ruddock in the family archives and in London (see Bibliography: Italy). She was assisted in Florence by Dr Gino Corti. The section on chivalry draws heavily on Richard Barber's excellent *The Knight and Chivalry* and Barbara Tuchman's *A Distant Mirror*.

p. 60 *Odysseus and the Phaeacians:* Homer, VIII, 1–294.

p. 62 *the standing of a knight:* Barber, p. 29.

p. 63 *the Bend Or dispute:* W. H. B. Bird, 'The Grosvenor Myth'.

CHAPTER IV: BLUE BLOOD

I am grateful for the help of Ignacio, Duke of Segorbe, for his help in elucidating the early history of his family, and to Jan Read and Maite Manjon for the background material on the general history of the period. The Casa de Pilatos is well described by Gervase Jackson-Stops in his articles for *Country Life* on 17 and 24 June 1982.

CHAPTER V: CORRECT ADDRESS

The family historian of the Thurn und Taxis is Dr Max Piendl (see Bibliography), and I am grateful for the painstaking help he has given to my researcher George Weiss. A good summary in English of the family history, its dynastic tapestries and art treasures is Angelika von Schuckmann's article translated by Angus Malcolm in *Apollo* magazine for October 1967.

CHAPTER VI: STATELY HOMES

The role of the English country house has been definitively explained by Mark Girouard. I am grateful to the Ganay family for their notes and documentation on the early history of Courances. David Cannadine's *Lords and Landlords* is an excellent account of aristocratic investment in town development. I am grateful to Dr Gustav Wilhelm for his help with the early history of the Liechtenstein family, and to Aldina Nutt who translated at our meeting.

p. 93 *new sources of revenue:* Lawrence Stone's chapter 'The Inflation of Honours', *The Crisis of the Aristocracy, 1558–1641,* pp. 65–128 covers this and many other aspects of the sale of titles.

p. 94 *'belted earls':* see Wagner and Sainty for full details.

p. 96 *Mary Davies:* Charles T. Gatty's two-volume study deals fully with Mary Davies, the Manor of Ebury and the early history of the Grosvenor family.

p. 103 *405,000 florins:* I am grateful to Dr Reinhold Baumstark for showing me the original title deeds to the Principality.

CHAPTER VII: REVOLUTION

Francis Sheppard's article in *History Today* for November 1978, 'The Grosvenor Estate, 1677–1977' (pp. 726–733) is an excellent summary of the development of Belgravia, as well as of the earlier development of Mayfair.

p. 106 'Lord Finchley' by Hilaire Belloc is reproduced from *Complete Verse*, by kind permission of Gerald Duckworth & Co. Ltd.

p. 107 *William Pitt the Younger:* for letters and speeches on the House of Lords at this period, and Pitt's attitude towards it in particular, see Aspinall and Smith, *English Historical Documents, 1783–1832,* pp. 203–216.

p. 108 *the general election of 1754:* these figures come from Professor John Cannon's 1982 Raleigh lecture, 'The Isthmus Repaired' to be published shortly.

p. 110 *le Grand Nicolay:* the details of Courances during the Revolution come from notes in the possession of the Ganay family.

p. 112 *the proverbial nobleman of Beauce:* this and the other details of peasant 'noblemen' come from Alfred Cobban's *The Social Interpretation of the French Revolution* (Cambridge University Press, 1964, p. 29).

p. 114 *one coat of whitewash:* ibid., pp. 81–82.

p. 120 *a matter of regret:* Aspinall and Smith, p. 204.

CHAPTER VIII: NOBLESSE OBLIGE

The Urban Establishment by Frederic Jaher is a masterly survey of the plutocracies of five American cities from colonial times to the present day. The material on the dollar princesses is largely based on Ruth Brandon's book of the same name. I am grateful to André Maillard for pointing out the relevance of Thomas Mann's *'Königliche Hoheit'*. Wiener's study of *English Culture and the Decline of the Industrial Spirit* contains excellent material on the relations between middle class and aristocracy in the Victorian era. The account of Hugh Lupus, 1st Duke of Westminster, is based almost exclusively upon Gervas Huxley's biography, *Victorian Duke.*

p. 123 *1860 Censuses:* Jaher, p. 713.

p. 125 *Titled Americans:* Brandon, p. 3.

p. 125 *a mayor and corporation:* Consuelo Vanderbilt's book *The Glitter and the Gold* (London, Heinemann, 1953) is probably the best of the memoirs written by the dollar princesses. Her reception at Woodstock is described on page 59.

p. 126 *Comte Boni de Castellane:* Zeldin, pp. 41–2.

p. 127 *assaulted and raped:* I am grateful to informants at Courances, outside the Ganay family, for this information about the departure of the Nicolays from France.

p. 134 *to keep the middle classes in order:* I am grateful to Alan Brien for this particular piece of research work.

p. 143 *he never mentioned the shooting:* Lord Ernest Hamilton's memoir *Old Days and New,* chapter 11, contains 'some thoughts of Eaton Hall', a most amusing account of aristocracy at the turn of the century.

CHAPTER IX: FLASH GOLDEN

George Ridley generously placed at my disposal the material gathered for his own memoir on his beloved Bend Or, and the account of Bend Or going to war is largely based on this. I am grateful to Ian Curteis, and to other off-the-record sources, for help in shedding light on the less creditable side of the character of the 2nd Duke of Westminster.

p. 150 *burning his own bloody coal:* 5th Duke of Sutherland, p. 35.

p. 152 *war was a glorious affair:* cited in Sinclair, p. 50. Sinclair's chapter 'The Great Death, 1914–18' forms the basis of these paragraphs on the First World War, though he is incorrect in stating that the death of a father and his heir resulted in double death duties which 'finished the estate' (p. 103); in fact, such an event ensured total exemption on the second death.

p. 153 *we must learn to do things for ourselves:* Bence-Jones and Montgomery-Massingberd, p. 198.

p. 154 *'England is Changing Hands':* cited in Winchester, p. 275–6.

p. 155 *20 per cent of them:* I am grateful to Robert Allgauer for his help in elucidating the impact of land reform programmes upon the Liechtensteins' private estates.

p. 158 *he had, indeed, purchased his peerage:* I am grateful to Philip Knightley for his help with details concerning the Vestey family.

p. 159   *£2000 a year:* Whitaker's Almanack, 1901.

p. 165   *Beauchamp's four daughters:* Sykes, *Evelyn Waugh*, p. 165. I am grateful to Peter Blackaby for drawing my attention to this.

CHAPTER X: 'CAN'T A FELLOW HAVE A BISCUIT WHEN HE WANTS ONE?'

I am grateful to Fritz von der Schulenburg for his comments on Hitler and the German aristocracy, and to George Weiss for his documentation.

p. 170   *'The nobles dominate our corps of officers':* Prince Friedrich Karl's essay on the spirit of the Prussian officer is reproduced in Appendix 1 of Demeter, p. 257.

p. 174   *'a biscuit when he wants one?':* Bence-Jones and Montgomery-Massingberd, p. 190.

p. 176   *granted in Florida in 1769:* the deed by which George III granted this land to the Grosvenors is in the offices of the Grosvenor Estate in Davies Street.

p. 177   *200 carts, 300 men and 4000 cattle:* Sinclair, p. 134.

p. 178   *'the life of the jungle':* ibid., p. 136.

CHAPTER XI: HEIRS & GRACES

Some of the details of the Grosvenor Estate's activities since the Second World War are given by Douglas Sutherland in *The Landowners* (London, Anthony Blond, 1968), but most of this chapter is based on off-the-record information.

CHAPTER XII: A WORLD OF DIFFERENCE

Most of this chapter was written on the same basis of personal observation as Chapter I. I am grateful to Nicholas Fraser for allowing me to see his article 'Poor Rich France' and to Patrick Montague-Smith for details of recent extinctions in British noble lines.

ACKNOWLEDGEMENTS

I have always found it helpful in checking the accuracy of a book to send a draft copy of the manuscript, prior to publication, to those who form its subject, and in the case of *Aristocrats,* this provoked interesting reactions: the Germans threatened to sue; the Liechtensteins conducted negotiations through their private secretary; the Spaniards conducted negotiations through *my* secretary; the Ganays corrected my French; the Frescobaldi invited me for a holiday in Florence and the Duke of Westminister invited me out to lunch.

As a result of our discussions the accuracy of the facts in the manuscript have now been agreed upon – even if there remain some major differences as to interpretation and emphasis – and my first thanks must be to the six families who were such gracious hosts while the book and television series were being prepared in 1982, and who have gone to such trouble to provide me with documentation of their family histories.

Television is a team enterprise, and this book would not have been possible without the support, effort and expertise of the BBC. The idea stemmed from a suggestion of Adam Clapham, then an executive producer of Documentary Features, together with the head of that department, Will Wyatt. I could have had no gentler initiator into the pleasures and frustrations of documentary film-making than John Bird, who supervised the whole series in addition to directing two programmes himself, and I must also thank the other producers who made the series such a polished presentation – Jeremy Bennett, Ruth Jackson and Anne Paul, together with the film editors Alan Lygo, Jim Latham and Charles Davies and the rest of the *Aristocrats* team: Charmian Compton, Graham Frake, Hilary Holland, Louise Tilling, Geoffrey Tookey and Nigel Walters. Jane Monahan carried out research for the Spanish programme.

I have had to lean even more heavily than usual upon research assistance in trying to tie together such geographically wide-ranging subjects, and I am greatly indebted to the thoroughness and diligence of Kristina Dahl, Maite Manjon and her husband Jan Read, Victoria Mather, Anne Morrison, Catharine Reynolds and George Weiss. Dr Graham Martin briefed me most knowledgeably on Liechtenstein, and Dr Alwyn Ruddock laboured long and hard on the early history of the Frescobaldi family: her information on the part played by the Frescobaldi firm of London in the trade between England and Italy comes from her book, in preparation, on *The Earliest English Ships and Merchants in the Mediterranean Trade 1380–1558.*

Professor John Cannon kindly supplied me with the manuscript of his Raleigh lecture to the British Academy – 'The Isthmus Repaired: The Resurgence of the English Aristocracy 1660–1760'. Professor William Brock pushed me firmly towards some most illuminating and original research on the structure of elites in American society. Professor Michael Arnheim was most stimulating on the subject of aristocracy as a whole, and I am most grateful to him for drawing my attention to the story of Odysseus and the Phaeacians.

Loelia, Lady Lindsay, kindly granted me permission to quote from her book *Grace and Favour* and generously added much additional information and material, some of which will be appearing in her new book *Cocktails and Laughter,* to be published this autumn.

An avenue of research which, in the event, led nowhere so far as this book is concerned, was into the motives of those peers who have felt moved to renounce their titles since 1963 for the sake of personal conviction rather than political ambition; but Professor G. C. Archibald, FRSC, Dr Larry Collier, MB, Ch.B, DPH, MRCGP, Sir Hugh Fraser, Bt, Trevor Lewis JP, Victor Montagu, Christopher Reith, Dr Alan Sanderson and Arthur Silkin were kind enough to correspond with me on this subject, in some cases at considerable length. My thanks to Wilfred Massiah for his thoughts on the 'aristocracies' that have developed in certain British colonies since independence.

Anton Felton, Gerald Grant and John Millward read the manuscript and gave me the benefit of their special expertise. Michael Shea gave me vigorous and informed assistance in his own current speciality – and my most invaluable longstop and tireless source of knowledgeable consultation has been Patrick Montague-Smith whose unassuming mastery of the arcane details of title, precedence and descent has been a constant joy. My thanks to Phyllis McDougall for the index.

The beauty of this book is principally to the credit of its designer Christos Kondeatis, who seems to have done little else for the last year, and of Ric Gemmell, who worked meticulously to produce the photographs. Valerie Hudson has been a most painstaking copy editor, and I am grateful for the editorial advice of James Cochrane in this country and William Phillips in America. My agent John Cushman has been as supportive and constructive as ever.

I could not possibly have completed this book in the short time available between filming and script writing without the professional and devoted participation of Frances Ullman, and I shall find it difficult to replace the energy and efficiency with which Jacqueline Williams has supervised my research gathering.

I must thank my parents for the thoroughness with which they read the draft manuscript and subsequent proofs, and my wife Sandi for devising the original format of the book and typography for the series; both of which were subsequently developed by others. When writing *The Kingdom* I had to thank her for consenting to travel with me to Arabia. Now I have to thank her for consenting to stay at home while I went off for the best part of a year touring some of Europe's more beautiful castles and palaces in the company of a film crew — BBC practice decreeing that loved ones disturb the team spirit.

My son Sasha and daughter Scarlett suffered my absences with their usual good humour, helping me to unpack and repack on my brief appearances at home – though it was left to the cat to express the basic family feeling at my behaviour by jumping inside my suitcase and peeing in it.

It is my London agent Michael Shaw who first coordinated this book and television series, and he has borne the brunt of it ever since. With his unfailing capacity to see the brighter side of the worst disasters he has been the most solid and unperturbable source of intelligent support and encouragement, and 10 per cent cannot sufficiently express my gratitude. This book is dedicated to him.

ROBERT LACEY
June 1983

INDEX

Alba, Duchess of, 31
Alfonso X, King of Castile, 68
Alfonso de la Cerda, 'el Desheredado', 68
Almanach de Gotha, grades German nobility, 84
Alps, the, courier routes, 79, 80
Americans, business dynasties, 124; marriage into aristocracy, 124–5; grade European nobility, 124; directory of eligible bachelors, 125
Anti-semitism, German upper classes, 171
Arabs, 68, 72, 175
Argentina, 158, 195, 196, 219; Bemberg business empire, 126, 128
aristocrats, aristocracies, 23, 33, 94, 134, 207; ability to survive, 16, 17, 19, 21, 28, 30, 167–8, 173–4, 204, 207, 216–17, 219; concern with past and future, 21–2, 78–9, 202–203; contempt for trade, 26, 60, 83, 101; male primogeniture, 31, 47; meaningless without land ownership, 31, 46, 65, 67, 113, 158, 204, 219; European ruling class, 36–7; military origins, 41, 62, 65, 83; order of precedence, 41–2, 83–4; and *nobilitas*, 42; formal components, 46–7; modern ethos, 48, 133–4, 212, 214; officer/gentleman concept, 61, 134–5; social signals, 65, 217; blue blood concept, 66, 67, 217; and the arts, 78; and religion, 79; country-house ethos, 90, 92–3, 134–5; property developers, 98–101, 206; 18th-century creations, 107–8; go-between king and people, 112; replaced by plutocrats, 123–4, 159; marriage to 'dollar princesses', 125–6; threatened by universal suffrage, 132, 133, 158; directorships, 133; a concept of behaviour, 133–4, 217–18; destruction in First World War, 152–4, 157, 158; impact of death duties, 154, 185, 217; extinction in Eastern Europe, 158, 177–8; as a national elite, 173, 216–17; reaction to misfortune, 177–8; family retainers, 186; treatment under Socialism, 210–11
Arno, River, 53
Arnold, Matthew, 135, 139

arts, the, Gothic revival, 134
Ashburton, Alexander Baring, Baron, 21
Asquith, Herbert, Lord, 17
Asquith (née Tennant), Margot, 7, 153
Astor family, purchase of Cliveden, 141, and n.
Attlee, Clement (later Lord), 173; and estate duty, 174, 184
Austria, Austrians, 20, 27, 45, 103, 156–7; and Napoleonic wars, 114–15; bans titles, 157; high taxation, 157; Liechtenstein, severs links with, 157; Tyrol 80
Austria Hungary, 155

BBC television series, subjects covered, 18
Baden, 115
Bagehot, Walter, 135
banking, 54, 57
barbarians, and Western Europe, 40
Bardi, the, 57, 58
Baring dynasty, titled family, 21, 108
Baring, Johann, German immigrant, 21
battles: Adrianople, 40; Austerlitz, 114; Arezzo, 54; Aspern, 115; Crécy, 57, 150; Lechfeld, 45; Pistoia, 54; Wagram, 115; 'White Mountain', 102; Znaim, 115
Bavaria, 24, 25, 45, 80, 115, 129, 130, 198; Constantine Prince of, 178; Duke in, Max Emanuel, b. 1937, 200; Duke in, Maximilian Josef, 1808–88, 128
Beauce, nobleman of, 112–13
Beauchamp, William Lygon, 7th Earl of, cause célèbre, 164–6
Beauchamp (née Grosvenor), Lady, wife of above, 164–6
Bedford, John Robert Russell, 11th Duke of, *How to Run a Stately Home*, 33–4
Belgrave, manor, 95, 116
Bemberg (later Ganay), Marie Rose, 126, 128
Benn, Anthony Wedgwood, 196; Viscount Stansgate, renounces his title, 214
Bergamo, meeting place of courier routes, 79, 80
Berkeley of Stratton, Lord, property developer, 96–7

241